MW01234367

WE WILL NOT BE STOPPED

Evangelical Persecution, Catholicism and Zapatismo in Chiapas, Mexico.
by Arthur Bonner

With a foreword by Rev. Charles Van Engen, Professor of Biblical Theology of Mission School of World Mission, Fuller Theological Seminary, Pasadena, California.

Universal Publishers/UPUBLISH.COM 1999

Library of Congress Cataloging-in-Publication Data

Bonner, Arthur.
    We Will Not Be Stopped: Evangelical Persecution,
Catholicism, and Zapatismo in Chiapas, Mexico/by
Arthur Bonner
        p.   cm.
    Includes bibliographical references and index.
    ISBN 1-58112-864-9 (pbk.)
    1. Mayas—Missions—Mexico—Chiapas. 2. Mayas—
Government relations. 3. Mayas—Politics and government.
4. Catholic Church—Missions—Mexico—Chiapas.
5. Liberation theology—Mexico—Chiapas. 6. Ejército
Zapatista de Liberación Nacional (Mexico) 7. Chiapas
(Mexico)—History—Peasant Uprising, 1994–8. Church
and social problems—Catholic Church. 9. Catholic
Church and world politics. I. Title.
    F1435.3.M53B65 1999
    277.2'75082'08997415—dc21   98-54688
                                        CIP

Cover Design and Typesetting by
Terrence Nugent for Accutype Graphics, NY

DEDICATION

For Marianna Slocum who, fresh out of college, was called to the trackless mountains of Chiapas to bring the Bible—in their own languages—to indigenous people suffering centuries of neglect. A few were transformed, then others and then still more in a never-ending chain so that tens of thousands have new lives.

And for Miguel Gomez Hernandez, known as Kashlan. When the Word of God lifted his burden of guilt, he dedicated his new life to bringing the Bible to others. For that alone he was brutally martyred.

CONTENTS

Preface
Introduction 1
1 Evangelical Transformation 11
2 The Tzeltal and Chol Churches 18
3 The Beginnings of the Tzotzil Church 38
4 Passing on the Message 42
5 Caciques and Liberation Theology 47
6 The First Tzotzil Martyr 56
7 Pascuala's Story 60
8 How Evangelism Grows 65
9 The Growth of the Tzotzil Church 68
10 Pentecostal Churches 73
11 The Search for Justice 78
12 Organizing for Resistance 83
13 The Politics of Expulsion 88
14 The Relationship Between Evangelicals and Zapatistas 92
15 The Mitontic Expulsions 96
16 Punishment for Persecution 101
17 "We Will Not Be Stopped" 103
18 The Persecution Ends 111
19 Final Bloodshed and New Believers 118
20 "The Bible is the Best University" 123
21 Individual Choice 125
22 Seventh-Day Adventists 127
23 Growth and Prayer 129
24 Evangelism Made in Mexico 133
25 Catechists 135
26 The Diocese and the EZLN 139
27 Autonomy 161
Appendix I 167
Appendix II 169
Bibliography 172
Index 176
About the Author 182

FOREWORD
by Charles Van Engen

It was exactly 50 years ago that my parents, Rev. Garold and Ruth Van Engen, Reformed Church in America missionaries serving the National Presbyterian Church of Mexico, took me from Mexico City, where I had been born a few weeks earlier to San Cristobal de Las Casas in the mountains of central Chiapas. It became my home town where I grew up among a small group of "evangelical" Protestants, numbering at that time no more than a couple of hundred evangelicals in a town that in the 1950's numbered around 65,000 inhabitants.

San Cristobal historically is a place where the clash of cultures, the struggle for religious freedom, and the search for new identity amidst conflicting political and economic interests has been ongoing for centuries. The spontaneous and explosive growth of indigenous evangelical churches throughout the region, including in San Cristobal itself, has changed the face of the central highlands of Chiapas. During the last forty years, this small colonial town has also been the center of religious persecution, especially of (Protestant) evangelicals. The story of persecution and church growth is the heart of this book.

Bonner does his reporting not in terms of mission promotion, nor as an evangelical trying to prove a case. Rather, he maintains objectivity as a news correspondent, while showing sympathy, insight and understanding of the issues involved in the persecution and growth of evangelical churches in Chiapas. This book is not about persecution as such, but about evangelical growth stemming from the courage and faith of new Christians who stake their lives on the Bible's promises.

The book is a clear, readable and well documented account of the stories of real people, many of whom I have known personally. The persecution of evangelicals in the highlands of Chiapas has been going on for over forty years and the story has not been told. This story involves a number of Protestant denominations in the area: Presbyterians, Baptists, Nazarenes, Seventh-Day Adventists and Pentecostals. It is also intertwined with the mission work in the area by those denominations, along with Wycliffe Bible Translators/Summer Institute of Linguistics, Missionary Aviation Fellowship and others. The Reformed Church in America missionaries have cooperated with the Presbyterian churches of the area since 1925 and have been directly involved in the nurture, growth and development of the churches of the Mayan peoples among whom the most severe persecution has occurred. Yet clearly the growth of the indigenous churches happened because of the initiative, vision, courage and commitment of the indigenous Christians themselves. It has been a popular movement, guided more by the Holy Spirit than by any human agent.

As Bonner summarizes, the presence of evangelical believers and churches (and their persecution) is not a new phenomenon. Evangelical (mainly Presbyterian) churches in Chiapas date back to 1903 and 1904. The Reformed Church in America began to assist the Presbyterian churches there when John and Mabel Kempers arrived in 1925. By 1930 John Kempers and a Presbyterian pastor from Tabasco, Rev. Jose Coffin, had traveled by horseback throughout the entire region that is covered by this book. The historical background is important to show that both the growth of evangelicals and their persecution in the Diocese of San Cristobal are not isolated or recent phenomena in Chiapas—they are a long pattern of courage and grace in the midst of suffering at the hands of political and religious leaders of the region.

Reading Bonner's book transported me back to my own childhood. I know the story Bonner tells in this book is true because my family's story is intertwined with many of the events recorded here. I remember my father talking at home of his involvement along with Rev. Daniel Aguilar Ochoa in trying unsuccessfully to get the five men falsely accused of burning the church in Tumbala out of jail. My father helped build the first clinic in Corralito for Marianna Slocum and Florence Gerdel. Many Wycliffe Bible Translators like the Jacobs, the Weathers, Marion Cowan and others, were family friends and often were guests in our home. I was there when we had several hundred new Presbyterian believers camping out in our yard because they had been expelled in the early 1950's and 1960's from Chanal, Chilil, Chenalho or Oxchuc.

Years later, I was in the procession of people and cars when we buried the one whom Bonner has called "The First Tzotzil Martyr," Miguel "Kashlan" Gomez Hernandez. We processed right through the middle of San Cristobal to get from Nueva Esperanza (New Hope) to the cemetery on the other side of town. The procession closed down all activity in downtown San Cristobal for over two hours. We passed in front of the cathedral and Bishop Samuel Ruiz's offices, and alongside the town hall where thirteen years later, in January, 1994, the Zapatistas would be throwing all the furniture and files out of the windows. As we slowly inched our way down the street a couple of Spanish-speaking young men stood on the sidewalk and commented:

The one observed, "Look at all the cars and people in that funeral procession!"

The other responded with awe, "It must have been a priest, or bishop or cardinal or something to have that many people." Months later, I would be back at Nueva Esperanza to participate in the ordination of 24 Chamula elders and 24 Chamula deacons who would be led by Salvador Lopez Lopez, a graduate of the Tapachula seminary where my wife and I taught at the time.

Several times in the book Arthur Bonner mentions Rev. Daniel Aguilar Ochoa, who pastored the Divine Redeemer Presbyterian church in San Cristobal from the 1950's through the 1970's. "Don Daniel," as we called him, was my pastor and one of my models of church leadership. He was one of the earliest "Ladino" evangelical pastoral supporter of the growth of the indigenous churches, who encouraged, trained and empowered the leaders and church structures in the Ch'ol, Tzeltal (Corralito and Tenejapa) and Tzotzil (Chenalho) areas. Pastor Aguilar Ochoa was directly involved in the legal defense of those who suffered persecution during the 1950's and 1960's. He was also the director of the San Cristobal Bible School mentioned in the book, where he taught and discipled many of the earliest indigenous leaders and pastors of these movements. For thirty years, my father and mother were administrators and teachers in the same school in San Cristobal.

It is also important to place the book in the larger framework of similar research and study. First is the matter of faith in a Mayan context. Bonner is correct that much of what has for decades been trumpeted as uniquely Mayan is in fact a world-view that the Mayans of Chiapas share with many peoples of the world. The Chiapas context is one which in missiology we call "animist." It is a worldview that sees the physical world and the invisible world of the spirits as intimately interwoven. In such a context, faith is integral to all of life and biblical conversion means the full, holistic transformation of persons and all aspects of their lives in a given culture. But this does not necessarily imply the loss of their cultural, linguistic or social cohesion. To the contrary. The stories of conversion and faith that Bonner retells in this book demonstrate how interwoven this faith is in lives and communities of the indigenous peoples of Chiapas—and how their new faith in the promises of the Bible has transformed all of life for them. In doing so, cultural cohesion is pre-served. In a parallel context, Lamin Sanneh from Yale, for example, has demon-strated the same phenomenon going on in Africa. Bonner writes, "It is a misperception to see evangelical growth in Latin America as a movement of con-version from Catholicism. It is more accurately seen as an anti-shaman movement." (pg 13) Here the author demonstrates profound insight that is right on target.

In the Mayan way of life, religious faith, both personal and communal, is inte-gral to the interwoven fabric of the society, permeating all aspects of life. For many in Chiapas, this cohesion is disintegrating—but not for the evangelicals. The only major force that affirms indigenous cultural forms and fosters indigenous social cohesion in the various tribal groups in Chiapas is that offered by the growing indigenous evangelical churches. This book provides the reader with a careful reporting of first-hand accounts of persons who have been key actors in this search for new cohesion and life on the part of the indigenous peoples of Chiapas. The reader is allowed to look through a host of personal windows to see reality through the eyes of the indigenous peoples. We catch a glimpse of how the indigenous evan-gelicals themselves perceive how their biblical evangelical faith has provided the cultural, linguistic and social cohesion they seek.

This brings us to the second larger issue which this book addresses: evangeli-cal growth. The growth of the churches in Chiapas is an excellent illustration of a much larger phenomenon going on in Latin America. The face of religion in Latin America is in the midst of staggering transformation. During the 1970's and 1980's, while both Roman Catholic and Protestant advocates of Liberation Theology were trumpeting the "option for the poor," the poor of Latin America opted to become "evangélicos"—mostly Pentecostals. Only lately have social scientists paid atten-tion to the phenomenal proportions of this religions change.

The rate of conversion to a personal, born-again, Bible-based faith on the part of Latin Americans has no precedent in the history of the church. This largely ignored process is now receiving attention by Roman Catholics and Protestants alike, led by folks like David Martin, David Stoll, Virginia Garrard-Burnett, Phillip Berryman, Edward Cleary and others.

The third large topic under which this book falls is the matter of religious per-secution. Religious persecution is growing around the world. Of course, religious persecution does not only include the persecution of Christians by people of other faiths. There are instances around the globe of persecution of people of other faith by Christians. Yet the majority of cases around the globe have to do with people of other faiths or of no faith persecuting Christians specifically because of their faith in Jesus Christ. More Christians have died because of their faith in the Twentieth Century than in all the previous nineteen centuries combined. The saddest kind of persecution is that perpetrated by those who would call themselves "Christian" against others who also are Christians. This has been the case in Chiapas, and especially in the highlands. This is also true in much of Latin America, where evangelical churches are growing dramatically under conditions of severe persecution: physical, social, economic, political and religious.

So why are people willing to suffer in this way? In the case of Chiapas, Bonner clearly demonstrates that older, mostly narrow anthropological, social, economic, political or religious explanations are neither appropriate nor acceptable. Bonner allows the people to explain why they are willing to suffer: in a biblical faith that springs from a personal relationship with Jesus Christ they have found a way out of the fear, domination, oppression and addiction in which they formerly lived. And together in this faith they have found a way to affirm and empower their language, culture, worldview and social cohesion and autonomy.

Arthur Bonner is right on target when he says the ". . . indigenous evangelicals, who are a major part of the population of the Highlands and the selva, have achieved autonomy in their families, churches, communities and seminaries. They have created spiritual and social spaces where they speak their mother tongues and follow traditional communitarian patterns of social organization" (p. 164).

Churches and mission agencies will be very interested in reading this book because of its mission and church background. It is a case study of the growth of the church under conditions of persecution. But pastors and members of churches will also want to read this book because it tells the stories of people with whom their denomination or mission agency has been associated for many years. However, this book has a wider impact as well. It is an essential textbook which students of religion in society, researchers of religious change, students of the present reality in Latin America, and students of missiology need to read.

Whatever their background or motivation, I know the reader will enjoy this book—and lives will be impacted by the stories of people whose faces I have seen, whose lives have touched mine, and whose stories demonstrate the transformative power of a biblical faith in Jesus Christ.

October, 1998
Rev. Charles Van Engen, Ph.D.
Arthur F. Glasser Professor of Biblical Theology of Mission
School of World Mission
Fuller Theological Seminary
Pasadena, California

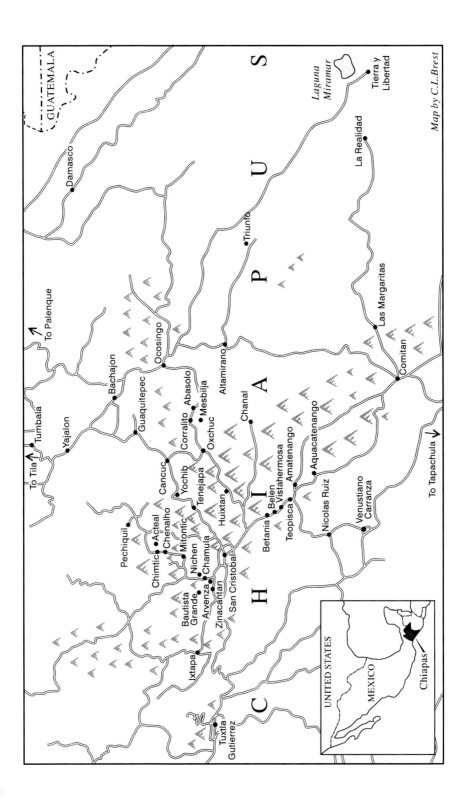

Map by C.L. Brest

INTRODUCTION

Evangelism is a history of Bible-inspired individuals. A major part of this book is the personal narration of those who felt themselves touched by the Holy Spirit and then, as apostles, evangelized others. It is a story of the planting of seeds and the flourishing of new congregations and churches. The book emphasizes practice as distinguished from theory—providing an empirical base for the study of evangelism. Focusing on individuals serves to diminish subjectivity and avoids trivializing religion as just another form of social movement.

Rosalva Aida Hernandez Castillo, in a critical review of books on Protestantism in Chiapas, cites some of the functionalist explanations given for evangelical growth: to "create a new community and better their economic resources;" "a crisis of world vision, brought by fertilizers and western medicine;" "a response to the situation of anomie;" "a search for power and authority;" and "the desire for prestige and social recognition" so that, in her words, "conversion appears to be merely a reflection of economic and political changes that affect indigenous communities."

She writes that she once reasoned along these lines but now "I have changed my mind. I reject the essentialist vision of ethnic identity, analyzing conversions to Protestantism as part of a wider historical project in the context of conflict and negotiation between the state and religious institutions."

She mentions "the silence of the voices of those who have been changed" and asks: "What is the living experience of the faith of the indigenous *Chiapanecos?* How can we speak of faith from the perspective of academic discourse and continue to see religious experience as a form of political struggle?"[1]

The primary purpose of this book is to end this silence. A secondary purpose is to balance academic and journalist accounts of contemporary indigenous life in Chiapas. While much has been written about the revolt of Subcommander Marcos and Zapatista efforts to establish autonomous indigenous communities, few are aware that a major percentage—perhaps a large majority (precise quantification is impossible)—of the indigenous population has achieved autonomous social space and needs no one to liberate them, least of all the hundreds of foreigners attracted to Chiapas by glowing cyberspace accounts of the "Revolt of the Indians" and the need for living shields to protect the human rights of armed and masked revolutionaries.

The indigenous Mexicans of Chiapas are suffering a double tragedy. First there were the expulsions of at least 15,000 evangelicals from the municipality of San Juan Chamula and other areas. Now, with the weakening of the ruling Institutional Revolutionary Party (PRI), there is an even more violent struggle between the PRI and its major challenger in south and central Mexico, the left-center Democratic Revolutionary Party (PRD) with the indigenous population being used as pawns trapped in the middle.

Dr Andre Aubrey, the director of archives for the San Cristobal diocese, describes this as:

> . . . an attack of history on communities irremediably dismantled and fractionalized within and without by diaspora, modernity and global-

1 (1992)

ization. This is not only a disintegration of individual identities but of collective identities as well. In the Indian culture, the *cargos* [responsibilities or offices] of civil society were balanced by a charismatic hierarchy called shamans, that is *curanderos* or healers. Now, among Protestants, even while you find a refusal to accept curanderos, many times there are healing ceremonies with prayers and the laying on of hands, but there is an important difference. Those converted to evangelist religions are not passive members of their churches. All of them are active members in their religious life; they are not objects. However, it should be kept in mind that the transition taking place among the Indians is not just a Protestant phenomenon. The catechist movement instituted by Bishop Ruiz here in Chiapas is also a modernizing process. Every member, as a living stone, is constructing his own church. I am speaking of a spiritual construction. The catechist movement is a movement of popular participation. The church is a part of a Catholic's community life. Often, what is referred to as a religious conflict is, in reality, a political battle between the exiting power structure and a new organization of civil society. The process of democratization and a new critical spirit recognizing the legitimacy of pluralism has entered through a religious channel.[2]

A religious norm shaped in this manner is autochthonous. This is what the "Indians" of Mexico did when they were forced to accept Catholicism. It was not a matter of "Gods Behind Altars," a continuing to worship ancestral deities. Within the first few generations, the names and attributes of the old deities were forgotten, but there was still a sacred geography of mountains and caves and shamans to ward off evil and cure ills.

The Swiss sociologist Jean-Pierre Bastian draws an analogy between this culturally created "traditional" Catholicism and the evangelical transformation:

> The sects [evangelicals] and traditional Catholicism have a point in common: both are religious expressions by the indigenous people themselves under the guidance of Indian leaders . . . As is the case with traditional Catholicism, the new religious groups have a body of Indian religious specialists as pastors and evangelists . . . When these religious societies are inserted into a national and international religious structure, it appears that their local and regional autonomy is maintained . . . At the same time, these religious movements accept and reinforce the ethnic identity of their faithful through translating, for the first time, religious documents in the ethnic languages. In the context of illiteracy, they encourage access to a sacred text. In an equal manner, these churches help develop small projects on a local scale . . . In contrast to traditional Catholicism, the sects offer the advantage of inculcating a relative modernity without being anchored to the ancestral ways. While the traditional religion maintained the community under the double tutelage of the caciques and the state, the new religious movements offer a glimpse of possible autonomy.[3]

2 Interview, Dec. 5, 1996. 3 (1996): 309-10.

Caciques, a title derived from the Caribbean culture encountered by the Spanish at the time of Columbus' initial voyages, represent an indigenous social structure that existed throughout Mesoamerica. Larger kingdoms or states were segmented into microstructures ruled by chiefs who extracted as much as possible from local labor and used this both to raise a military force to defend their tiny estates and to send gifts to ensure the friendship of the layer of authority above them. A social-scientist definition of Mexican *cacicazgo* is a patron-client relationship.[4]

Evangelical Growth

Paralleling Protestant growth throughout the Americas, there has been a massive increase in evangelicals throughout southeast Mexico. According to a 1989 survey conducted by Gilberto Gimenez for the Center for Anthropological Investigation of the Southeast (CIESAS), Protestants represent 45 percent of the population of Campeche, 40 percent of Chiapas and Tabasco, 35 percent of Oaxaca and 30 percent in Quintana Roo. The survey forecast that by the year 2000 half the population of the Southeast will be Protestant.[5]

The census of 1990 came up with a strikingly different finding. Out of the Chiapas population (over the age of five years), it showed 67.63 percent Catholic, 18.20 percent non-Catholic, 12.73 of no religion and 4.45 percent unspecified. Considering the proliferation of evangelical churches throughout Chiapas, the census results were obviously in error. And what does the 12.73 of no religion mean? Even pagans have a religion. As Rosalva Aida Hernandez Castillo commented: "The Gimenez book and articles by [Rudolfo] Casillas show [that] the government statistics have little credibility."

San Cristobal cathedral

4 Marcus and Zeitlin (1994). 5 (1988): 7.

If religion is judged by church buildings and church participation, evangelicals in Chiapas far outnumber Catholics. They worship in churches they have built, often with their own hands, out of their own meager incomes. Whole families flock to evangelical services and, when it is time for Sunday School, about a quarter of the seats are vacated by children ranging up to the age of 13 or 14, who troop outside or to another room.

Tourists are attracted to Chiapas by the colonial charm of San Cristobal de las Casas in *los Altos* (the Highlands), with its narrow streets, pastel-colored houses and brightly costumed indigenous women selling handicrafts on the streets. The traditional central plaza has a bandstand, tall trees and patches of flowers. The cathedral is on one side, government buildings are on another and colonnaded shops make up the remaining two sides.

The cathedral, the most spacious Catholic structure in San Cristobal, can seat about 600 worshipers and has standing room for perhaps another 200 in the wide side aisles but it is rarely fully occupied. I once attended a Christmas Eve mass—a peak of the religious calendar—and could easily find a place to stand near the center of the church. The rear five or six pews were completely vacant. Many of the benches were occupied by foreign tourists. Other Catholic churches, which are grouped mainly in the central historic zone, seldom have more than 100 or 200 worshipers.

The numerous evangelical churches are on side streets. Where I lived, six blocks from the central square, there was a small Baptist church a block and a half away in one direction and a Presbyterian church two blocks away in another direction. Just behind it, with an entrance through a narrow alley, there was a nondenominational church that had split away from the Presbyterian congregation. Such churches, within the traditional boundaries of San Cristobal, are mainly for the growing evangelical middle-class or Ladino population. A more concentrated evangelical presence is along the *Periférico Norte* (the northern ring road) where indigenous families, expelled from their lands because of their beliefs, have established refugee colonies.

At one point on the Ring Road, I counted four churches without moving my head. Two such refugee churches have long rows of benches and can accommodate upwards of 1,000 worshipers. When I attended one of these—a Pentecostal church—on a random Sunday, I estimated there were 850 worshipers.

Based on many weeks of walking or driving through all parts of San Cristobal, and being particularly alert to the presence of churches, it seems safe to estimate that evangelical churches outnumber Catholic churches in the city by about ten to one. The Ladino population, the core of Catholic support, is only three percent in the Highlands and *selva* (plains and jungle), which have been opened by roads only during the past 20 years. In these regions, there are relatively few Catholic churches so that evangelical churches outnumber Catholic churches by upwards of 20 to one.

The basis for this differential is as much economic as it is spiritual. Catholic churches depend on institutional planning and financing. Funds are scarce to build new churches or repair old ones. The only extensive repairs done to Catholic churches is carried out by the government, on the grounds that ancient churches are part of the nation's cultural heritage. But even if there were scores of new churches (and believers to fill their benches), who would staff them? For the entire diocese of San Cristobal, which includes almost half the geographic area of Chiapas, there are fewer than 100 priests and about 150 members of religious orders, (none of whom are indigenous, although the diocese has had a seminary for over 300 years).[6] There also were, according to a 1993 census, 208 Eucharistic Priests, that is, fully trained catechists who can perform all functions of a priest except administering the sacraments.[7]

Evangelical churches are built by the congregations that will use and staff them. Often, building a church is a matter of necessity. If there are roads, there is little public transport, and, even when there is, many indigenous families can not afford the fare. So, a church has to be within a community or no more than a moderate walking distance away.

Churches are social and spiritual spaces where indigenous evangelicals have reshaped their traditions. Many of those expelled from Highland municipalities were males enrolled in the ranked cargos to observe the fiestas of village saints. They progressively assumed more prestigious functions until they attained the status of elders (*principales*). Similarly, in evangelical churches, deacons are selected according to their abilities and probity and advance to the rank of elders and sometimes pastors.

In village society, curanderos prayed and chanted over the sick. A major reason for the growth of evangelism was that indigenous people became convinced that biblical curing was more effective than that of these shamans.

Evangelicals speak their mother tongues at home and in their churches, and women still wear their traditional elaborately embroidered blouses. However, evangelical and traditional societies are worlds apart in practice. Where getting drunk and having multiple wives were once the norm, evangelicals are ascetic and family-centered and Mexican *machismo* is a thing of the past.

Reliving Christian History

In Hebrews 13:8 there is the phrase, "Jesus Christ is the same yesterday and today and forever." As I traveled through Chiapas, it often seemed as if I was experiencing some of those yesterdays, beginning with the days of the Apostles. Men and women heard the Word and made it part of their daily lives according to their individual needs and circumstances.

December is the month of Our Lady of Guadalupe (the vision of the Virgin Mary believed to have appeared on a cloak of an Aztec convert named Juan Diego in December, 1531). In 1954, Pope Pius XII proclaimed Mary the "Queen of Heaven." As Mexico's national saint, the title is given to Our Lady of Guadalupe. One night in San Cristobal, I watched processions of the devout, including children in imaginary biblical costumes, passing through the streets and on up a hill to the church of Guadalupe. I later went to a Presbyterian church near the foot of the hill. The pastor took his text from Isaiah 2:8–9: "Their land is full of idols; they bow down to the work of their hands, to what their fingers have made. So man will be brought low and mankind humbled. Do not forgive them."

He went on to cite Jeremiah's denunciation of men whose wives had burned

6 Floyd (1997): 121-22. 7 See Chapter 24.

incense to other gods, specifically "The Queen of Heaven," a goddess whom Jeremiah denounces three times (44:17–19). The sermon ended with references to Paul, who almost caused a riot by preaching man-made gods are no gods at all to patrons of craftsmen who earned their living by making silver images and who proclaimed "Great is Diana of the Ephesians" (Acts 19:23–41).

However, to be precise, a question might be asked: Was the rioting in Ephesus touched off by Paul's preaching "religious" persecution? The question is relevant because it might also be asked if the attacks on evangelicals in Chiapas are, strictly speaking, religious persecution.

The evangelical community estimates more than 30,000 believers have been expelled from their homes and properties in San Juan Chamula. The Mexican National Commission for Human Rights puts the number at 15,000. Numbers in Mexico are always tricky. After the initial mass expulsions, the caciques used individual threats, saying evangelicals would be killed if they did not leave. No one could doubt the validity of such threats: if they left, seemingly of their own will, they could at least carry some of their possessions with them. Thus, voluntary departure was actually expulsion.

Refugee communities have sprouted on the outskirts of San Cristobal and along the Pan American Highway leading to Guatemala. Seeing these large colonies, and knowing that many others of the expelled were relocated or migrated far from San Cristobal, the figure of 15,000[8] seems reasonable. (See Appendix I for the acts of expulsion from Chamula.)

The Bibles they read every day warned evangelicals of the consequences of refusing to honor traditional norms. Christ said: "Be on your guard against men; they will hand you over to the local councils and scourge you in the local synagogues" (Matthew 10:17), and, "If they persecuted me, they will persecute you also" (John 15:20).

Nevertheless, evangelical communities grew because, along with the warnings, there were promises of protection and a better life. In sermons in the churches built by the expelled, I heard texts cited again and again. A favorite was Joshua 1:5, "I will never leave you or forsake you." Another is Isaiah 41:10, "Do not fear for I am with you . . . I will uphold you with my righteous right hand." Still another was Psalm 55:22, "Cast your cares on the Lord and he will sustain you. He will never let the righteous fall." More than any other, pastors read out the final words of the risen Christ: "I am with you always to the very end of the age" (Matthew 28:20).

Was this "religious" persecution or was it political persecution, in view of the obvious fact that the new evangelicals did not respect secular social norms?

It is the nature of *cacicazgo* that makes the Chiapas expulsions both political and religious. I discussed this with Dr Andres Fabregas Puig, the rector of the Autonomous University of Chiapas and one of the leading anthropologists of southeastern Mexico during an interview at his office in Tuxtla Gutierrez:[9]

> There is a legitimacy in the caciques. The Chamulans are people who have fought ever since colonial days to obtain respect from others. For example, there is a book published called *Auto del Pueblo de Chamula contra su Cura* (Act of the People of Chamula against its Priest), which is the story of a conflict that happened in the seven-

8 (1995): 48. 9 Jan. 15, 1996.

teenth century. If you read it, you find exactly the same as what is happening now. It is the same claim: "let us alone, leave us in peace." What I say is that one should understand the cultural basis of the cacicazgo and not only see it like a forced imposition. It is wrong that there are caciques, but caciqazgo is a phenomenon of Chamula society. It is a product of the history of the Chamulans.

Putting aside the violence of expulsions, I think the tendency to convert to Protestantism as a religious alternative is important in Chiapas. This is part of the many forces creating a new multicultural paradigm in Mexico. I think that what is going to happen is a similar process to what happened when the Spanish came to Mexico: a cultural process. The Indian communities are going to conform the evangelic message to their own culture and I think, as a result, a new way of looking at the world will be born. I think we are facing the birth of new cultural alternatives that will define the Indian world in the next century. The Indian cultures interpret the message according to their own culture and experience. Mexico, as many other countries, is heading toward multiculturalism.

Mexico is still a Catholic country but there is more than one line of Catholics. There are charismatic Catholics, traditional Catholics and Catholics who believe in an autonomous church reflecting Indian cultures as well as Apostolic Roman Catholics. All this is very important because it is the formation of new cultural realities. It is very important because it will bring changes in the existence of the people. We have to construct a more tolerant, flexible society. We should accept that other visions do not contradict the nation's progress. We have to accustom ourselves to live with people who think differently. All societies, all countries, are becoming multicultural. In a short time, 50 years or less, there will not be one country in the world that will not be multicultural.

Plan of the Book

Chapter 1 outlines the context of evangelical growth: Mayanist romanticism, poverty and the role of shamans in traditional curing. Chapter 2 traces the beginnings among the Tzeltals, the most numerous of the indigenous peoples of Chiapas. Marianna Slocum, the pioneering Summer Institute of Linguistics translator who spent seven years in remote mountain villages reached only by foot or mule back, devised a Tzeltal alphabet and written language and then searched for equivalent Tzeltal terms to express the Gospel message. At about the time that she completed her translation of the Gospel of Mark, Joy Ridderhoff, a former missionary in Honduras, developed a process for making Gospel recordings. Guided by Marianna and using Victrola "Talking Boxes," Tzeltal evangelists spread the message from community to community so that, within a few years, there were thousands of believers and dozens of churches and congregations. Chapters 3 and 4 trace the beginnings among the second largest indigenous group, the Tzotzils, who would later suffer the greatest persecution.

All this is one stream of the history that runs through the book. The other stream is the Roman Catholic Theology of Liberation with its belief in a God who intervenes in history in order to break down the structures of injustice. Samuel Ruiz, who was just 34 when he was named Bishop in Chiapas in 1960, enlisted the support of Jesuits and other orders to train catechists to teach the Bible and Roman Catholic practices, but also to conscienticize parishioners in the methods of political protest.

Chapter 5 chronicles the catechists' challenge to cacique traditionalists who dominated all aspects of life among Tzotzils of San Juan Chamula, employing both the cult of the saints and the clientelist largesse of the PRI, whose presidents have led Mexico without interruption since the party was founded in 1929. In the early 1970s, after catechists and their leaders twice attempted to have an opposition slate elected to the Chamula municipality, these reformed Catholic supporters, along with evangelicals, were loaded into trucks and dumped at the outskirts of San Cristobal. Later, the caciques evicted the entire Catholic apparatus and imported the bishop of a spurious Orthodox Church of San Pascualito to celebrate masses and administer baptisms.

Chapter 6 is the life and influence of Miguel "Kashlan" Gomez Hernandez, the leader of the Tzotzils. Before his conversion, he had worked on the coffee plantations of the Pacific coast and in Mexico City and had the reputation of a womanizer and heavy drinker. He became a believer when he met Ken Jacobs, another of the early SIL translators. Although the anger of the caciques was aimed specifically at the reformed Catholics, the mass expulsion swept up all those who appeared to challenge their leadership. Soon, since the evangelists did not dabble in politics, most were allowed to return to their homes, but not Miguel Kashlan. He found work as a translator in a hotel in San Cristobal, but he did not cease to evangelize. Among other things, he organized the first refugee settlement and church. In July 1981, he was seized, bundled into a car, tortured and hanged. Three days later, his coffin was carried in a procession through the main square of San Cristobal. An estimated 4,000 of the expelled followed it to the cemetery. He is now remembered as the first Tzotzil martyr.

Chapter 7 is the narration of a woman who was one of Kashlan's earliest believers. For her faith, she was shot, burned, and barely survived but, undaunted, went on, through prayer and faith, to become a successful business woman.

Chapters 8, 9 and 10 are testimonies of individual believers and narrations on the manner of church growth and the selection of deacons, elders and pastors to staff the ever expanding congregations and missions. These narrations, and others in later chapters, are vital to an understanding of evangelical growth. They document the process of individuation together with the assertion of a primary responsibility to God and family. They also clarify the relationship between a pastor and his congregation. Strong, authoritative leadership is essential to any displaced community, not to mention one faced with sweeping economic and social changes. A pastor is a source of certainty. The process of training and selection from within the community ensures that the pastor is firmly rooted in the mores of his congregation. Finally, as the history of Protestantism demonstrates, if a congregation does not like its pastor it can easily break away and build its own church.

Chapters 11, 12 and 13 are the narrations of the three principal leaders of the expelled. One is Abdias Tovilla Jaime, a pastor who, when the expulsions began, became a lawyer. He formed the State Committee for Evangelical Defense in Chiapas (CEDECH) to defend individuals and attempt to use the legal system to force the national and state governments to stop the expulsions. The second is Domingo Lopez Angel, who has been instrumental in finding new sources of income for those without homes or land. Many became vendors of vegetables or handicrafts. Others acquired taxis or trucks. He fought to get licenses for their vehicles and places in the markets for their goods, always against the fierce opposition of established Ladinos. The third is Esdras Alonso Gonzalez, who became a Pentecostal Nazarene after he was cured, through prayer, of a lung tumor. He was the leader of a large church in Oaxaca. When he heard of the work of Abdias Tovilla, he came to San Cristobal to help him.

Chapter 14 is the narration of two Presbyterian pastors in the municipality of Ocosingo, which was briefly occupied in the Zapatista uprising of January 1, 1994. One was forced to leave his home and lands to the Zapatistas in an area west of Ocosingo. They agree on the need for social and economic reforms but are opposed to violence to achieve these goals.

Chapters 15, 16 and 17 return to the theme of the expulsions. More than 230 men, women and children of the community of Mitontic were forced from their homes, marched for three hours, kept for three days in a sweltering warehouse without food or water and then put into trucks and sent to San Cristobal. The government, instead of forcing officials to restore their lands and homes, sent them far away to live among people whose language they do not understand.

In contrast, because of a split among politicians in the community of Amatenango, a group forced from their lands and homes was allowed to return and given help to rebuild. Those who approved the expulsions were heavily fined.

Such justice, however, was rare. Pentecostals from the nearby community of Aquacatenango were expelled three times. Each time, they received government support to return to their lands and rebuild their homes, but each time local authorities expelled them again. After the fourth expulsion, they received government help and returned again. Their pastor says: "We will not be stopped."

Evangelicals called for justice from 14 state governors and five national presidents, always without result. In 1993, out of sheer frustration, they began direct action. Chapter 18 is the history of an almost year-long occupation by a large group of the expelled of the compound of the Bureau of Indian Affairs in San Cristobal. The authorities' failure to respond to this occupation led to a seizure of a Chamula official, which precipitated a mass cacique attack on the compound and the use, by someone inside the compound, of an Uzi submachine gun to kill one of the assailants. Although the expelled had used guns before, this was the first use of such a modern weapon. It made the caciques aware that they could no longer expect to attack the evangelicals and escape unharmed.

Then, on New Year's Day, 1994, a former professor calling himself *Subcomandante* Marcos staged a brief seizure of San Cristobal and four smaller cities. This "Revolt of the Indians" drew international attention to the plight of indigenous peoples. The Mexican government was finally convinced it had to do something about the expulsions. Conciliation meetings were held with Chamulan leaders and a truce was declared.

Chapter 19 recounts a further clash in which six cacique attackers were killed, versus one evangelical defender killed. This convinced the caciques that the evangelicals, when attacked, would not simply await the "will of God" and they finally agreed to halt their attacks. Soon, evangelical life began again throughout Chamula.

The earlier chapters dealt mainly with the Presbyterian and Pentecostal churches. Chapters 20 through 24 are narrations to illustrate evangelical growth among other groups. The Mexican government generally discourages, through the withholding of visas, missionary efforts so that it is rare for new denominations to take root. Cusberto Perez was given a Bible by a traveling American missionary and, when he decided to commit himself, was accepted for a four-year course in a Baptist biblical school. After serving in the North, he returned to build a Baptist church in San Cristobal, where he was born

Another young man, Teodoro Vera Cortez, was 15 when he went to the United States "to look for my life but instead, I found sin and vices." With help, he became a Baptist, studied in a seminary and eventually came to Chiapas to find new believers from among the indigenous people and, with them, to build a Baptist church and school.

Seventh-Day Adventists have been in southern Mexico for more than 100 years. A regional official, Villaney Vazquez Alegria, says membership is expanding so sharply it has been necessary, for administrative purposes, to divide Chiapas into 58 districts, each with 20 to 40 congregations.

Pastor Jesus Castelazo Sanchez is a self-taught Pentecostal who was inspired to begin teaching the Bible in a saloon in central Mexico. He tells of coming to Tuxtla Gutierrez to turn a saloon and dance hall into a church. It expanded so greatly that he now has the *Templo Auditorio Cristiano*, which can seat 6,000. However, he now believes in small, neighborhood churches, especially for the indigenous population. He says he has 14 churches in Tuxtla and another 155 in the Highlands and the selva.

Rene Jimenez Guzman is the southern Chiapas administrator for the Nazarene church (the modern branch, which has grown away from its Pentecostal roots, as represented by Esdras Alonso Gonzalez). He believes the restriction on foreign missionary work was beneficial in that it encouraged the growth of churches that reflect Mexican culture. The Nazarenes have 105 congregations, 15 missions and more than 7,000 members in Chiapas.

Chapter 25 returns to the Catholic Church and its effort to develop communities guided by catechists. Bishop Ruiz had three main goals: the option for the poor, the training of catechists to evangelize indigenous peoples from within their own communities and the creation of something that approaches an indigenous autochthonous church. Msgr Felipe Toussaint Loera, the vicar general of the diocese, tells how catechists are chosen and outlines some of the principal obstacles to an autochthonous church, including teachings that the Church of Rome is the only true Church of Christ.

Chapter 26 relates the intertwined histories of Bishop Ruiz and Subcommander

Marcos. Catechists trained by the diocese played a major role in organizing groups clamoring for social and economic justice. Although there is no evidence that Ruiz's activism directly contributed to the rise of Marcos, the Zapatistas remain confined to the diocese of San Cristobal and are active nowhere else in Mexico. The government of Mexico dealt with the revolt by political negotiations while simultaneously organizing a war of low intensity, including paramilitary forces drawn from ranchers, small business owners and "individuals characterized by a high sense of patriotic duty." Then, just before Christmas, 1997, a paramilitary group massacred 45 villagers in the hamlet of Acteal.

The Zapatistas' foreign supporters are skilled in the techniques of the Internet. When news of the Acteal massacre spread through cyberspace, hundreds of foreigners descended on Chiapas to demonstrate support. They were promptly deported and a national debate began on the role of foreigners in Mexico's domestic affairs.

Chapter 27 deals with autonomy, the issue that led to the breaking off of peace negotiations. This is discussed by a foremost authority on indigenous affairs, Jacinto Arias Perez, an ethnologist and former Chiapas Secretary for Indigenous Affairs.

There are two appendices. The first details specific expulsions from 1966 to 1994. The second lists the extensive Internet Web sites created by Zapatista supporters and the nature of foreign support for their revolution.

An Editorial Note

A preliminary survey of Protestantism in Mexico, limited to Mexico City, Puebla, Cuernavaca and Oaxaca, was conducted in December, 1995 and January, 1996. Field research in Chiapas, including about 30 interviews and archival searches, was conducted in August and September, 1996 and from December, 1996 through February, 1997. The interviews were tape-recorded in Spanish and transcribed into English. For use in this book, questions were omitted, as well as material having no bearing on the topic discussed, but nothing was eliminated that would have altered the intent of the speaker.

1
EVANGELICAL TRANSFORMATION

Except for a handful of families within tightly restricted marriage circles, all Mexicans have ancestors who, if it were possible, might be traced to pre-Hispanic times. Mexicans are a distinctive blend of Hispanic and indigenous heritage. The Spanish conquerors fixated on race, with elaborate paintings to show *castas* (castes) according to the degree and type of ethnic mix. Eventually, the term Mestizo (mixed) was favored, but this seems to say that cultures are genetically coded. If a distinction has to be made, "Ladino" is a more accurate term, in that it points to social and cultural, rather than genetic, differences. A Ladino is someone who can be regarded contextually as not *Indio*, either because of his language, manners or color: that is, he is defined by what he does not have. Indio has been replaced in official and polite society by the euphemism *indígena* (indigenous). This, of course, is meaningless, since all Mexicans are indigenous but it seems the least objectionable way to refer to an ethnic difference.

The indigenous population is disappearing. They are simply being absorbed into the majority Ladino population. The national census of 1895 counted 20.5% of the population over the age of five as "Indian" (or 2.7 million out of a population of 13.3 million). A 1995 estimate put the indigenous population at 5.4 million out of 80.2 million above the age of five. Adding those children, the indigenous population is currently estimated at seven million, or about 7.5 percent of the population. They are concentrated in the states of Yucatan (44.2%), Oaxaca (39.1%), Quintana Roo (32.2%) and Chiapas (26.4%), with smaller pockets in Hidalgo, Campeche, Puebla, Guerrero, San Luis Potosi and Veracruz.

Chiapas, with a population of 3.2 million (1990 census), has about 830,000 indigenous people scattered among 20,000 hamlets of fewer than 500 inhabitants. The two largest groups, the Tzeltals and Tzotzils, live in the Highlands: like a crumbled paper of steepsided mountains. Chols live in the northeastern municipalities of Palenque, Salto de Agua, Tumbala, Tila and Sabanilla. Zoques, a rapidly disappearing ethnicity, are found on the lower lands at the northwestern border of the Highlands. Except for the UN-sponsored Montes Azules Biosphere Reserve, much of the Lacandon selva has been inundated by an estimated 200,000 Tzeltals, Tzotzils, Chols, Tojolabals and Guatemalan refugees, and the forests have been cleared for cattle ranches and small farms.

Linguistic labels applied to indigenous groups must be read with caution. They primarily serve academic and governmental convenience and mask the segmentation perceived by the peoples themselves. For instance, there are two major dialects of Tzeltal and five dialects of Tzotzil—as Bible translators found to their pain when they tried to produce a single Tzeltal or Tzotzil New Testament. Linda King writes: "Indians, whose ultimate loyalty lies with the community and its leaders, express their identity through language. Tzeltal Indians refer to themselves as Tzeltal speakers of a specific community; other Tzeltal-speaking communities are classified as foreign, although linguistic similarity is recognized."[1]

While ethnically divided, all are united by marginalization. About half of the indigenous people of Chiapas live below the official poverty line. Chiapas is 75,634 kilometers square, which is about 3.6 percent of the area of Mexico, yet it has the highest ratio of illiteracy. The major causes of death are intestinal and pulmonary infections and malnutrition, which are easily remedied, and deaths from tuberculosis are the highest in the country; yet there is only one doctor for every 1,500 inhabitants, most of whom practice in nonindigenous regions. Chiapas has three of the four highest dams of the country and exports electricity; however about one-third of the state's population lacks electricity. The population is growing at the rate of 4.5 percent a year. Since 60 percent live in rural areas and depend on farming for their livelihood, the shortage of land for family-size plots grows worse; yet 6,000 cattle-ranching families control about half the rural land.

---

1 (1994): 3, 5.

Romancing the Mayas

The indigenous people of Chiapas, indiscriminately labeled as "Mayas," have a special place among anthropologists. Robert Wasserstrom wrote: "Perhaps more than any other social group in recent memory, native peoples in highland Chiapas have been subjected to prolonged and continuous anthropological scrutiny." He counted "no less than 30 books and monographs" about them.[2] At least a dozen more have been written since he wrote.

Evon Vogt of Harvard set the goal posts. He proposed that the "civil-religious hierarchies" of pre-Spanish Mesoamerica survived the conquest and lived on under the thin disguise of Catholicism. In his view, such expressions as "God," "My Lord," "My Owner" and "My Patron," when used by the Tzotzils and Tzeltals, were not of Catholic origin, and that when they spoke of Christ they were really thinking of the Mayan sun god.[3] He also maintained that the cross venerated by the Tzotzils was not Christian but was a multipurpose boundary marker and a means of communication with the gods. In short, the Tzotzils and Tzeltals were living fossils, and by studying them, graduate students could unlock the secrets of the "Mayas."

It was modern mythmaking. As Alan Knight writes: "Empirical evidence points to the great gulf of historical experience and cultural transformation which separates twentieth century Mexican Indians from their supposed sixteenth century forbearers, and which consigns any notion of a collective psychological inheritance to the realm of metaphysics."[4]

An unfortunate corollary is that change, such as the adoption of new religious concepts, is decried as a corruption and a loss of culture. Anthropologists like Evon Vogt saw the cargo system of ranked civil and religious offices distributed through roles in saints' festivals as survivals of Mayan polity. Reality was far different. Eighteenth century cargos were a means by which parish churches defrayed priests' salaries and other expenses. When the church connection was dissolved, the cargo fiestas became the political instruments of local chiefs.

Sickness and Health

In projecting the mythology of pre-Columbian fossils on the tribes of Chiapas, anthropologists whitewashed reality. They wrote admiringly of people who worshiped the sun and moon, who lived in a cyclical time warp, who shaped their lives by dreams and followed the spiritual guidance of shaman wise men, obscuring the fact that these same people cowered before ghosts and evil spirits and sought the protection of curanderos similar to the witch doctors of Africa. It is a misperception to see evangelical growth in Latin America as a movement of conversion from Catholicism. It is more accurately seen as an anti-shaman movement.

For all except a privileged few, being Catholic signified little more than being baptized. The conquered people shaped Catholic images and teachings to their own needs, blending the worship of nature with the worship of saints. Highly-educated priests seldom mingled with their parishioners and saw the round of festivities honoring saints as crude but harmless expressions of primitive minds. There was no incentive for the indigenous people to take a deeper interest in Catholic services. Latin, of course, was unintelligible and priests had no interest in learning Tzotzil or Tzeltal, so their sermons, delivered in Spanish, were equally a mystery.

2 (1983): 1. **3** (1969): 366–68. **4** (1990): 95

The most comprehensive study of popular beliefs in Chiapas is Jacinto Arias' 1991 book *The Numinous World of the Mayas: Structure and Contemporary Changes*. Arias, a Harvard-educated Tzeltal "Pedrano" of San Pedro Chenalho, has served as the Chiapas Secretary for Indigenous Affairs, with offices in San Cristobal. What follows is a summary of some of his findings.

The Tzeltals and Tzotzils believed mountains, fountains, rocks, trees, pieces of land and caves were spirits and gave them specific names. They thought of the Catholic mass as a Ladino ceremony similar to those that they performed to placate the gods of sacred mountains and springs and who, if not honored, would bring calamities. They believed that the soul is separate from the body and could occupy another space and that "when a person sleeps, the soul leaves the body and visits strange places, mainly those that are not accessible during the day when the soul is confined to the body." Baptism was a symbolic act, "to give children souls . . . The idea is that the soul is near but not yet totally fixed in the body."

They also believed the world has two harmonious orders with a shaman (*j'ilol*), whose "eyes are open" so he can see the visible and invisible worlds, serving as guardian of the harmony. Sickness occurred when someone fractured this harmony. This could result from bragging, defying or abusing someone, any kind of dispute, justified or not, a failure to carry out an obligation, or a failure to respect or placate powerful invisible spirits including the saints, ancestors and the sun and moon. Sickness could also result from fright or bad wishes, such as envy. In addition, shamans could direct sickness at will, both causing and curing it. Sickness could come in different forms. The soul could become lost. Sickness was a partial process of death. The lapse between fault and final punishment allowed the shaman time to practice his techniques to determine the source of the danger. One way he could do this was through his dreams. The curing ceremony, called "giving or augmenting the hours of life," could make the soul return to the body.

The world over, gibberish, like the word "Alakazam," is part of popular magic. Among illiterate Spanish-speaking Mexicans, the Latin of Catholic priests was seen as an exorcism against the devil. Shamans in Chiapas learned a few Spanish words and mixed them with their incantations over monolingual Tzeltals and Tzotzils to give them greater force in confronting the devils that were causing a sickness. It seemed the shamans believed that devils were like humans and only understood Tzotzil and Tzeltal. Should a person die, the soul would continue to exist, but in another world somewhat like this world except, since there was no longer two worlds to be fractured, there would be no punishment. Punishment and recompense took place in this world, not in the other.

In one respect, a *médico brujo* (witch doctor) was like a Western doctor: better or worse (stronger or weaker) according to his experience and knowledge in prescribing available medicines. All shamans used chickens, eggs and *posh* (the indigenous almost 100 percent alcoholic drink), although the quantity of these ingredients varied greatly, depending more on the wealth of the patient than the perceived difficulty of the cure. The traditional perception of sickness was almost the reverse of the modern view. It was not seen from the viewpoint of its physical effect, but from an invisible cause that was perceptible only to a shaman. There was nothing particularly "Mayan" about all this. Similar beliefs were prevalent in Africa. A marked characteristic of tribal society is that "natural" misfortunes are ascribed to the evil wishes of witches or sorcerers, to the anger of spirits affronted by neglect of themselves or of a sufferer's obligations toward kin, to breaches of taboo and omission of rituals and to rightful cures by appropriate persons.[5]

Traditional Culture and Drunkenness

The Pedranos of Chenalho are Tzotzils. The more numerous Tzeltals live in the northern Highlands and the territory to the east that gradually descends to the Lacandon plains and the Guatemalan border. The earliest study of a Tzeltal community was conducted in 1961 in Tenejapa, 28 miles northeast of San Cristobal, by Andres Medina Hernandez, who presented it for a master's degree from the National Autonomous University of Mexico (UNAM).[6]

It was a clear-eyed view of reality by a Mexican, not the fuzzy mythology of foreign Mayanists. Medina wrote of "misery, disease, social and geographic isolation and the most ferocious exploitation." He found that 85 percent of the population spoke only Tzeltal and 88 percent were illiterate. Only eight percent were bilingual while seven percent, undoubtedly Ladinos, spoke only Spanish.

Forty-four of these Spanish-speaking heads of families controlled 16,000 acres of land while 1,121 Tzeltal heads of families controlled 10,600 acres. That is, Ladinos, who made up about four percent of a population of 125,000, had a bit more than 60 percent of the land, while the remaining 96 percent, who were Tzeltals, had 40 percent of the land. Because of the shortage of land, most Tzeltal men planted corn on their little *milpa* (plot), and then migrated to the Pacific coast coffee plantations for from three to six months, and returned to harvest the crop on their own land. Their seasonal migrations earned them the nickname *golondrinas* (swallows).

The Tzeltals of Tenejapa believed men had two souls with different characteristics, a normal soul and a forest animal, known as *lab*. They were born at the same time and lived parallel lives, including having the same sicknesses. The death of one meant the death of the other. Not everyone knew his animal, but they could guess. A child who died young must have had the lab of a bird. A rich and powerful man would have more than one lab, including that of a tiger. On death, a person's soul went to a resting place and later returned to repeat a cycle in the body of another person.

A persistent feature of all traditional societies is the way they segment into small units, making concerted action impossible. The municipality of Tenejapa was divided into 132 communities, each with its own name and sacred locations, with an *ojo* (often translated as "angel" but, more accurately a "spirit") hovering nearby, which had to be placated with day-long ceremonies. An indispensable ingredient of ceremonies was the powerful posh, along with a beer known as *chicha*. The Tenejapans made chicha in their homes from sugar cane juice and wheat bran. Posh was imported and was expensive.

The most important festival was Carnival, a 12-day celebration in the community center simultaneous with 10-day celebrations in each of the communities. Like the traditional carnivals of Europe, there was a great deal of dressing up, with men wearing Ladino clothing and trying to sound as if they could speak Spanish

---

5 Gluckman (1995): xxiii. 6 (1991, reprint).

and women wearing masks and men's hats. Carnival consisted of a series of marches within the community center and to several sacred spots, always accompanied by musicians playing a flute, drums and a rattle. In these marches, "they shout and talk in loud voices and grandly lift bottles of chicha to drink. A visit to all the sacred spots is long because neighbors invite the chief and his companions to drink chicha. Generally, they are offered a barrel of 20 liters. The group stays and dances in front of the house of the man who made the offer and can not leave until they consume all the beer, which means they are drunk during the entire festival."

In addition, a minor office holder had to donate food, a 20-liter barrel of chicha and a large bottle of posh. There were also annual three-day festivals for each of 11 images of saints that were cared for by six groups of *mayordomos*. These took place when the term of one set of mayordomos ended and the term of another set began. The surrender of offices opened in the church with offerings at the base of the saint to be honored. The former office holders then marched out to receive four bottles of posh and men and women began to dance to the tune of the musicians. They took clothing of the saint to a river to be washed by single women and daughters of the mayordomos while the incoming mayordomos sat watching and drinking posh and the musicians played endlessly. After that, they marched from house to house. When the food and drink were finished in one house, they went to another. The march was repeated on the second day and ended on the third day "*con grandes borracheras en las casas*" (with great drunken bouts in the houses). Being drunk was called a state of grace: "The state of grace allows the drunken individually to act in opposition to the norms of social conduct . . . When the mayordomos return to their houses they are met by their wives who recite the positions occupied by their husbands, but in the first person, making fun of the power and prestige of these important institutions. They sing in a drunken state, contrary to the code of humility and friendliness in which they act in other situations. Frequently during the fiestas, men and women beat each other and tear their clothes while they shout until some minor peacekeeper takes them to the *Ayuntamiento* [city center] where they are pacified by the municipal president. The next day they return to normal. They do not use arms. If there is a killing or serious dangerous wounds, it is called the work of a witch."

Friends and relatives would come down from the mountains to stay in a single house. They would shout and sing songs, and, in the darkness, there would be the writhing of bodies. The state of grace allowed all immorality.

Most Ladino land owners lived in San Cristobal or in Mexico City and did not even maintain houses in Tenejapa municipality. Of those who lived locally, "relations between the Ladinos and Indians were only what was necessary for market transactions . . . Both groups are said to be Catholics because they worship in the same church in the municipal center, but the Ladinos are in a completely different ecclesiastical structure, similar to the rest of the country, while the indigenous people maintain their autonomy at the community level, as can be seen in the fact that they have their own religious images completely different from those venerated by the Ladinos."

When, in 1949, a missionary of the Summer Institute of Linguistics established a base among Tzeltals in the adjacent municipality of Oxchuc, alarm bells sounded within the Catholic hierarchy in Mexico City. Two priests were sent to Tenejapa, the first resident priests since the beginning of the century. One conducted masses while the other carried out

> ... an intense proselytizing drive in the neighboring municipalities ... to counteract the work of Protestant missionaries ... The most effective action of the church was with the Ladino population and of them the most important were the rural school teachers. Masses were celebrated daily but they were attended exclusively by Ladinos. Baptisms, marriages and funerals were solicited only by Ladinos. The indifference of the church's activities toward the indigenous population could be seen in the interior of the church when there were religious ceremonies on one side, on the other there was the music, the happiness, the aguardiente and the cigarettes of the indigenous. They come and go without paying attention to what the Ladinos were doing. The priest tried, unsuccessfully, to change the indigenous ceremonies inside the church in ways that were considered "correct."

When indigenous persecution began, something happened that Medina had never seen before: "Ladino Protestants responded to the hostility and were obliged to appeal to the authorities in Tuxtla Gutierrez to ask for protection and to be allowed to live in peace. Nevertheless, the aggression took place frequently at the instigation of the priest until he was finally removed. It is interesting to note that the Ladino Protestants showed a friendly attitude and identification with the indigenous Protestants, a strange situation compared to what the Catholics did."

Creating a Separate Spiritual and Social Space

An insight into indigenous beliefs on sickness and curing is provided in a series of interviews conducted in March and April, 1992, by students of the Autonomous University of Chiapas (UNACH) under the direction of Carlos Fernandez Liria. They surveyed evangelicals who had been expelled, mostly from San Juan Chamula, and were living in two refugee colonies on the northern outskirts of San Cristobal. They gave three major sources of sickness: *espantos* (frights, terrors, ghosts), *brujos* (witches or witchcraft), and *envidia* (envy). One man spoke of the envy "that floats in the air" of a village. They believed sickness caused by frights was contagious. One woman said: "If at night something touches a house or an animal makes a sound or there is a blow of some kind to frighten someone it will not be long before someone in the house becomes sick. If the man is sick, the women will become sick and so will the children. I don't know why. Perhaps because there are devils in the house." When asked to elaborate on the source of sickness, she replied: "I became sick because my husband hit me the other day and when we began to fight the children also became sick because they were frightened (*se espantan*)".

A story was told of how, when a child fell sick, the curandero treated the mother, because her bad conduct was the cause. Another woman said her children were always sick because her husband abandoned her for another woman. Above all, people were afraid to be afraid. Fear was one of the worst calamities. It opened a door through which the soul could be separated from the body, wandering *por caminos desconocidos* (on unknown roads), never to return. A person then became comida *del ti'val* (food for a witch).

Over and over again, the expelled evangelicals told how they had found a separate place where they were, in effect, inoculated against sickness. *Costumbre* means more than "custom"in the sense of doing things in a certain way or wearing regional clothing. It also means a way of thinking and acting. One man said he no longer had *el costumbre* of being sick: "I don't get angry. I'm not envious and I'm not jealous of my wife. This is the good that I'm doing. My body feels better and I'm happy. Nothing molests me." Another man said: "We are always surrounded by devils, but in our hearts, if we always think of the Word of God, the devils can not enter our homes." Another said: "Witches still have power but with the Word of God they cannot win."

Since illness is the result of bad conduct, the best way to avoid illness was, as one man said, to "act toward your neighbors as true Brothers in Christ." A man was asked the difference in his life, before and after accepting the Gospel. He replied: "Before I was very sad. Now I have started to know my life. Before, I did not know where I was. It was as if I were lost."

When another was asked why he had accepted the Gospel, he replied: "I now know I was acting very bad before God. God did not want me to act that way. He does not want men to look for so many women and for women to look for so many men. I have five sons, and, because of my ignorance, they became sick, and we were always with doctors. I went to a pharmacy to buy medicine, but they were still sick. One day a boy came down with a very high fever. The doctor gave him an injection, but he was still sick. He was dying. I asked myself, 'Why is he dying?' I said, 'It is because I am acting bad and my wife is angry.' This is the reason for all this sickness. Now we have accepted the Word of God, and we are all well."

Many of those questioned said they were safe from sickness because they lived "with our Brothers" in an evangelical community. One said: "Here the sickness stops because we don't think of witches and witchcraft. We think directly of the Word of God."

Carlos Fernandez, summing up the interviews with residents in the colonies of the expelled, wrote of creating "a social space in which envy and witchcraft are no longer neighbors" and "a space, the family, in which the absence of sin does not permit the devils to live with humans."

The space is physical and spiritual—physically removed from the caciques who dominated their lives and spiritually removed from the witchcraft that caused their illnesses. A man spoke of the "family tranquility" that "immunizes" against sickness. He said "We are always surrounded by devils but, if in our hearts we always think of the Word of God, the devils can not enter our houses." As evangelicals, they are transformed real people, not living fossils.

2

THE TZELTAL AND CHOL CHURCHES

When John Paul II visited Mexico in January, 1979, (in his first visit abroad as pope), he warned of the inroads of non-Catholic "sects" and urged bishops and priests to fight back. The Catholic Church in Mexico was slow in following his lead. It was not until its 1986 annual meeting that the Mexican Episcopal Conference (CEM, after its Spanish initials) formed the Department of Faith in Regard to Sectarian Proselytism, headed by Flaviano Amatulli Valente. It was charged with producing pamphlets, books and video and audio cassettes to train priests, nuns and seminarians in how to evangelize the Catholic masses. One of these books had a series of questions and answers, including: "Protestantism with a label 'Made in the USA' is invading Latin America."

Historically, Made in the USA had some validity. Early Protestant missionaries were clearly American in language and social attitudes: the very qualities that made them attractive to Mexican Liberals eager to destabilize a conservative Catholic hierarchy. In 1860, President Benito Juarez issued a decree proclaiming religious freedom, and later expropriated Catholic properties. He said: "The Indians need a religion that obliges them to read and not to spend their savings on wax candles for the saints."

American missionaries were slow to enter the open door and, when they did, confined their efforts mostly to the northern border regions and the central plateau, avoiding the tropics and other areas with large indigenous populations. As Deborah Baldwin writes in her history of Mexican-born Protestants who aided the 1910–1920 Revolution, "Missionaries generally avoided the mosquito-ridden tropics, the poorest regions and the fanatically Catholic areas." In the process they also avoided those who spoke an indigenous language. By 1920, there were 200 mission stations, yet Protestants represented only two percent—principally the upper middle classes of the population.[1]

This began to change in the late 1930s with the arrival of the Wycliffe Bible Translators, better known as the Summer Institute of Linguistics. The WBT/SIL was founded by William Cameron Townsend, who had his early years as a missionary in Guatemala and who believed, as do millions of others, that the Bible must be translated into all languages.

One of the many reforms advocated by then-President Lazaro Cardenas was to establish schools and other institutions to assimilate indigenous peoples into the Mexican ethos, a process that came to be known as *Indigenismo.* His principal advisor was Moises Saenz, a graduate of the Presbyterian Theological Seminary in Coyoacan in Mexico City, with postgraduate studies at Washington and Jefferson College in Pennsylvania. Saenz, as head of rural education, invited Townsend to Mexico to establish schools for translators who would teach in bilingual schools that would wean indigenous people from their isolation.

Townsend never disguised that religion was his primary concern but, to sidestep the legal ban on foreign missionaries, he gave the Wycliffe Bible Translators the additional name of Summer Institute of Linguistics, implying its workers were scientists, not missionaries. Townsend said an organization with such a name would not "sound too pretentious" and "a suspicious country wouldn't consider it a threat." There was an added advantage: to American ears, it sounded non-denominational.[2]

The SIL translators/missionaries were never more than two individuals at any one place—generally a man and wife team but, at times, two women. Actual pros-

1 (1990): 178. 2 Hefley (1974): 96.

elytizing was limited. Their days and weeks were occupied with translating and distributing scriptural excerpts and later entire Bibles in the indigenous languages. They also served as guides, helping early believers to adjust to the wonders of the Spirit that soon engulfed them.

Once indigenous people had access to even portions of the Bible they reached out and took them: first, perhaps, in Spanish while working in the diaspora of coffee plantations of the Pacific Coast, then in their own languages. They did this in traditional fashion, beginning with a group discussion among family members and close friends. They also did this while preserving their own languages and customs. In a society that, ever since the Spanish conquest, had despised "Indios" as ignorant trash good only as a source of cheap labor, evangelicals formed communities where men and women could listen to preaching in their own language and join in song and prayer. They were still the poorest of the poor, but within the evangelical community they had friendship and dignity and could assume responsibilities and become community leaders.

The term Protestant was never used. They call themselves *evangélicos* (evangelicals), saying they are not protesting against anything or anyone but are bringing the *Evangelio* (Gospel) to those who, although nominally Christian, have never read or studied the *La Palabra de Dios* (the Word of God, that is, the Bible). They also call themselves Brother and Sister, creating a new identity and a new social space: building churches, electing deacons, elders and pastors and organizing seminaries—with congregations sprouting so fast that the equivalent of circuit-riding pastors are needed to keep up.

The Polemics

The SIL became the straw man amid an unusual convergence between Marxists who dominated the universities and the media, and who denounced religion as part of the oppressive superstructure of society, and a Catholic hierarchy that saw Protestants as a threat to their hegemony. At a November, 1980, conference of the Inter-American Indian Institute in Merida, Yucatan, delegates denounced the SIL for using a scientific name to conceal its religious agenda and a capitalist worldview that was alien to indigenous traditions.

This was, and still is, a frequent charge against evangelists: that they entice the poor away from the revolutionary struggle against systemic political evils. In May 1984, two Mexican social scientists wrote: "Today in Catholicism one finds a group of priests that, through biblical teachings, tries to elevate the level of conscience of those exploited in the countryside. In contrast, the Summer Linguistic Institute and a variety of religions (Adventists, Sabatistas, Presbyterians, Pentecostals, among others) in alliance with the State, have developed disruptive policies . . . like the construction of clinics and roads, leaving to one side the fundamental problem of campesinos: land. That is, defeating the campesinos by offering roads and clinics."[3]

The polemics were simply pulled out of the air, as David Stoll noted in an 1984 article in a Mexican scholarly journal:

> Far from only imposing its designs on the communities, the SIL has
> responded to their needs . . . The indigenous people frequently use

---

3 Ovalle Muñoz and Pedro de Jesus, "*Movimientos campesinos in the la zona tzeltal de Chiapas.*" Cited in Floyd (1997): 125–26.

---

them as a defense against others who are more oppressive. Its programs are more ambiguous than its opponents are capable of admitting. Religion limits some possibilities of political mobilization at the same time it opens ... new ways for the rise of autonomous forms of politics. In this sense, alienation and division can be considered as seeds of indigenous liberation ... Due to the open-ended character of missionary work and religious movements, neither evangelical missions nor their Indian converts are the puppets of U.S. imperialism as depicted in many of the polemics against the SIL.

Stoll titled his article, deliberately choosing words to frame the heated polemics, "Con qué Derecho Adoctrinan Ustedes a Nuestros Indígenas? (What Right Do You Have to Indoctrinate Our Indigenous People?).[4] Evangelicals responded, in effect, with a question of their own: "By what right do you claim indigenous people as your own?"

The Chols

Presbyterian missionaries were active among the Chols of northern Chiapas as early as the mid-1930s. Then, from 1943 to 1945, Garold and Ruth Von Engen were based in Yajalon to train Chol evangelists. In 1947, SIL translators John and Elaine Beekman arrived to begin work on a Chol Bible. Their translation of the New Testament was completed in 1960 and was dedicated in five different chapels.

One of the most frequent of the rumors spread against evangelicals was that they were plotting to burn down a Catholic church and its *santos* (saints). Burning candles before the saints was always a fire hazard. In February 1953, on a day dedicated to the Virgin of Candelaria, the Catholic church in Tumbala was ablaze with candles. They were left burning at night and the church burned down. Evangelical Chols were blamed and four men were arrested, tried, and served prison terms of almost five years.

But they were the last Chols to suffer and congregations and churches spread to the municipalities[5] of Salto de Agua, Palenque, Tila, Sabanilla, Yajalon and also among Chols who began to migrate to the then-empty Lacandon plains. A young Chol named Juan Trujillo Velasco slowly rose through the ranks to deacon and elder. After his congregation chose him as minister, he was sent for training to the Bible Institute in San Cristobal. In 1961, he was ordained as the first Chol Presbyterian pastor. When a separate Chol Presbytery was formed in 1974, Juan Trujillo was appointed as its first president.

During these years, work slowly progressed on other translations of the Bible into Chol. A complete Bible in the Tumbala dialect—both the New and Old Testaments—was translated by Evelyn Woodward Aulie and her husband Wilbur. It was published in 1970 by *La Biblioteca Mexicana del Hogar* (the Mexican Home Bible) with some additions to the Old Testament by the Mexican Bible Society. Other SIL members translated the New Testament in a third Chol dialect.

Ladino (Spanish-speaking) churches had taken root earlier. A Presbyterian church was established in Tuxtla Gutierrez, the state capital, in 1930. A Bible residential school to train Mexican pastors was added in 1931. In 1939 the Presbyterian

---

4 América Indígena, Vol. 46, 1984: 9–24. 5 Not to be confused with the term "municipal," in the sense of a town or city. A Mexican municipio is, roughly, the equivalent of an American county.

Divine Redeemer church was built on what is now National Army Street (*Ejército National*) in San Cristobal. The Bible School was soon transferred to San Cristobal and housed next to the church. The Ladino Presbyterian Prince of Peace Church was established in Yajalon in 1942. By this time, Mexican Presbyterians were a separate national church with only nominal ties with the Presbyterian Church in the United States. Actually, the link was through the Reformed Church of America, which had formed a partnership with the Presbyterians.

Beginnings of the Tzeltal Church

In 1938, a man named William Bentley attended the fifth session of Camp Wycliffe, the training center for would-be translators that Cameron Townsend had established in the Ozarks. Later that year, he traveled to Chiapas to live on a coffee plantation near Yajalon, a Chol-speaking region. It was not until 1941 that he was able to find a base among the Tzeltals. Miguel de Meza, a veteran of the Mexican Civil War, who had learned a little English and also a little of the Bible while fighting in the North, lived in the near-by community[6] of Bachajon. Bentley came to know of Meza and visited him in Bachajon, where he became popular playing an accordion and singing hymns. He was so well liked that Meza said he could set up a permanent mission in Bachajon.

A year earlier (in 1940), Marianna Slocum, fresh out of college, also attended Camp Wycliffe. She was assigned to work among the Chols along with another young woman, Evelyn Woodward. (Evelyn Woodward later married Wilbur Aulie and together they completed the Chol work.) Soon, Marianna and Bentley became engaged. Bentley rushed back to the Chol area to tell his fiancée the good news of the invitation to live in Bachajon. Before making the move, they returned to the United States for the wedding in Philadelphia. The preparations were almost complete when Bentley died of a heart attack in August 1941. Marianna called Townsend to tell him of Bentley's death and asked to be allowed to continue his work with the Tzeltals.[7]

She returned in November 1941. She was refused entry into the Bachajon Tzeltal area and settled instead at a German coffee ranch near Yajalon with SIL worker Ethel Wallis, to begin the arduous preliminary to actual translation—devising a written alphabet for a language that had previously been entirely oral. In an attempt to overcome this, Marianna took a biblical picture book and pasted Tzeltal captions over the English text. In 1944, after three years of working without a base among the Tzeltals, Marianna and Ethel moved to Yochib, in the municipality of Oxchuc. There they were able to get a six-month lease on a house built by the Mexican anthropologist Alfonso Villa Rojas for conducting field studies among the Tzeltals. The house was on a steep mountainside a few hundred yards from the main trail that extended from the low country communities such as Bachajon and Yajalon to the Highland municipalities. Many years later, Marianna recalled those first days:

> Professor Villa left us what little he had in the way of furniture. We
> slept in sleeping bags on folding army cots. Our washbasin sat on two
> wooden boxes that we turned outward for shelves. For light, we used

6 A collection of single-room, grass-roofed huts that might be scattered over as much as several square miles. The Chiapas word is *paraje* but that, in English, sounds like "parish," as if they were Catholic entities. Community seems to come closest to the actual situation—a grouping of peoples linked by marriage and tradition. 7 The following extensive quotations from Marianna Slocum are drawn from Slocum and Watkins (1988) and personal communications with Florence Gerdel. Other details are from Wallis (1959): 116-128.

Marianna working on translation at Corralito

a gasoline pressure lamp and a two-burner gasoline stove for cooking. When my only pen disappeared from the table right under the open window, we learned to keep our few precious belongings out of sight. The most important heritage willed to us by Villa was his friendship with the Indians. From the first day, the Oxchuc Indians, poorest of all the Tzeltals, made a path to our door. We gave them simple medicines for their many illnesses and we learned from them. Their dialect was different from that of the lowland Tzeltals, which I had been studying for the past three years.

"What is that?" I would ask, pointing to my informant's hair.

"*Stsotsiljol*" (A blanket for my head) would come the reply.

Laboriously, I repeated what I heard, trying to analyze the sounds into symbols, which could then be written down on index cards and filed. I immersed myself in learning the language, spoken in the context of the life of the Indians all around me. Whenever I heard a new word, I recorded it on a 3x5 card, and added it to the growing number of words in the dictionary I was compiling and used it in actual speech to store it in my memory.

It was a start, but there was still the problem of obtaining long-term permission to remain in Yochib. For Marianna, God provided the solution: "Nothing happens by 'chance' in God's plan. How many times I have seen a 'chance' encounter, a 'chance' meeting or a 'chance' conversation work out to the fulfillment of His overall plan for His people."

Yochib: building a house

This was long before the Pan American Highway was built. However, at the end of the trail from the North, there was a bus that struggled up a narrow dirt road to San Cristobal: "On one of my trips from Las Casas, I 'happened' to be riding on a bus filled with mestizos and an occasional Indian. Stops for flat tires were frequent. One time, when all the passengers disembarked for the driver to change a tire, I struck up a conversation with a mestizo who was obviously well educated. He turned out to be the [assistant] director of the Bureau of Indian Affairs for Chiapas and a true advocate for the Indians. His name was Don Manuel Castellanos."

Some time later, Castellanos learned of Marianna's problem and rode horseback to Yochib to plead her case with community authorities. After the customary consultations to arrive at a consensus, Marianna received permission to live in Villa's house for three more years. She settled down to work and found one hesitant convert, Martin Gomez Tsima, who came to Marianna to see if she could reduce the power that shamans had over him, "for perhaps this, more than the realization of Christ's forgiveness of his sins, drew him to the flannel-board stories."[8] As she later recalled:

Little by little, I was able to show him that God did not want him to live in fear for "perfect love casts out fear." I wanted to teach Martin to read, for then he would be able to learn from the Bible and not depend on oral teaching. For one who had never even held a book in his hands, learning to "see paper" was a time-consuming task. Between his reading lessons, Martin would forget what he had learned from the time before. The expression he used was, "I have lost it out of my heart."

It slowly dawned on me that if I could

Martin Tsima and family in Yochib

8 A light cotton flannel cloth fastened to a piece of wood or cardboard placed on a tripod. Another piece of flannel with a background drawn and painted on it (such as a lake or mountain) is placed on the board. A lesson is told by adding, one at a time, a figure of a person, animal, a group, or a book to illustrate the story. These drawings/figures are painted on paper with a strip of flannel pasted to the back. Since flannel sticks to flannel, adding the pieces as the story progresses keeps the focus and allows listeners to point out what they have learned by referring to a scene or figure. This could be used to illustrate elements of the Bible such as the Seven Days of Creation, the Birth of Christ, and the Crucifixion and Resurrection.

combine this expression with the Indian word for "sin," I would find a much-needed word for the Gospel of Mark I was translating. When Martin came for his next reading session, I tried the newly coined expression on him.

"Martin, when we believe on the Lord Jesus, God loses all of our sins out of His heart." His face lightened up instantly with comprehension.

"Is that what God does with our sins when we believe?" he asked. I had found the expression I needed for 'forgive.' As I worked more and more on the Tzeltal language, I realized that it was perfectly adequate to convey every spiritual idea.

Tenejapa: listening to victrola

Talking Boxes

At that time, a process was underway that would revolutionize the transmission of the Bible to indigenous people—the making of Gospel records. It served little purpose to translate the Bible if no one could read. Joy Ridderhoff had been a missionary in Honduras. When she returned home to Los Angeles in 1936, she remembered someone saying, on hearing a Gospel record in English, that he wished there were records in Spanish. She decided to take that one step further—to make records in indigenous languages. She taught herself how to do it, scrounged up equipment and, using her bedroom as a studio, made records of the Navajo Indians. In 1944, she and a companion, Ann Sherwood, drove to Mexico City with portable equipment in a large borrowed Buick and then borrowed a recording studio. They arranged with SIL translators to bring indigenous speakers to Mexico City.[9]

They also took their equipment to Tuxtla Gutierrez, where Marianna Slocum brought Juan and Carmen Ballinez from Yajalon to make recordings. Joy and Ann arrived in April and left 10 days later with records in six languages, including Tzeltal. They left their equipment in Mexico City as a permanent recording studio. In 1948, Marianna went there to record Psalm 115:3–8.

> Our God is in heaven, he does whatever pleases him.
> But their idols are silver and gold, made by the hands of men.
> They have mouths, but cannot speak; eyes, but they cannot see.
> They have ears, but cannot hear; noses, but they cannot smell.
> They have hands, but cannot feel; feet, but they cannot walk,
> Nor can they utter a sound with their throats.
> Those who make them will be like them and so will all who trust
>   in them.

Ethel Wallis left in 1944. After that, Marianna had a series of partners who came as part of their training experience. In January 1947, she was joined by a reg-

9 Thompson (1978): 48–58. (Since those pioneering years, Gospel Recordings has become a massive international Bible outreach, with recordings in almost 4,500 languages and dialects.)

istered nurse, Florence Gerdel, from California, who would become her lifelong partner. It was a twice-happy year for, also in 1947, Marianna's translation of the Gospel of Mark was published in an edition of 3,000 copies.

The spark that Marianna nurtured in the heart of her first believer, Martin Gomez Tsima, eventually lit an evangelical fire that would sweep the mountains of Chiapas, but he was a frail instrument to be so chosen: "Martin was the only believer for some time. When market day approached, we prayed constantly for strength for him to overcome the tremendous temptation for liquor urged on him by those who could not tolerate the fact that he no longer was one with them in riotous living. Martin came from a culture where drinking was part of life."

He was not a fluent reader. The Gospel recordings were his instruments. He took them everywhere, playing them for any who would listen, although he was not completely altruistic. Without Marianna or Florence knowing, he charged 10 centavos for every record that people listened to. Still, it took courage. The shaman of Yochib, Andres Kojt'om, often threatened his life and once Martin was slashed with a machete, leaving a long scar on his arm after Florence had sewed the wound.

One Sunday, he walked seven hours to the east to the village of Abasolo—also known as San Martin, after its patron saint—just across the border in the neighboring municipality of Ocosingo. It was the day of the annual fiesta. He knew the priest would be angry and was worried that he might destroy the Victrola and records if he found out about them, so Martin hid them in the woods just outside the entrance to the village. The square was full of music, processions and drunks. As he watched the festivities, Martin was recognized by two young cousins from the settlement of Corralito, Juan and Domingo Lopez Mucha. They asked him if he had brought the Victrola and he said no, but, when they asked again, he decided they were sincere and admitted he had hidden the Victrola near the trail. They invited him to their homes in Corralito, about an hour's walk away, and he accepted.

Juan was 22 and the sole support of his wife, two infant sons, his widowed mother

Early leaders at Corralito (left to right)
Francisco Nimail, Juan Mucha,
Tomas Kituk, Agustin Pe, Domingo Mucha

and her younger children, 14 in all. In addition, because his older brother, Mariano, was sickly, he contributed to that household too. Martin placed the Victrola carefully on the ground and played Marianna's recording of Psalm 115. (He never let anyone else carry the Victrola. Once the strap broke and it fell to the ground, which convinced Martin that the Devil was eager to destroy it.) The Muchas wanted to hear other records and then to hear them again. Martin was so carried away by their enthusiasm that, at first, he charged half price, five centavos, for each record and then nothing at all. He also told them of the two *gringas* who had taught him about God. When they asked if they could go to the house of the gringas for more information, Martin said they would be welcomed.

When one of the records ended with a hymn, Martin took out a worn hymnal and read the Tzeltal words. This was another revelation for the Muchas. They never knew that their language could be written on paper. The records were played until almost dawn, with Juan Mucha following the words with his fingers until he had memorized every hymn. When Martin said goodbye for the day-long walk back to Yochib, he left his copy of the hymnal and a final request that they not forget what they had heard.

The Muchas held offices in the gloomy seventeenth century church in Oxchuc, where the image of St Thomas—the patron saint—was on the altar and other saints lined the side aisles. One day, they made the four-hour walk to Oxchuc to test the words of Psalm 115. No longer blinded by the awe of tradition, they saw dust, broken fingers, peeling paint, torn garments and rats' nests and were convinced the Psalm was true. Juan Mucha wanted to go immediately to Yochib to find out more from the gringas, but his corn was ripening in the fields and he had to wait for the harvest. Then, with three other men from Corralito, Juan and his cousin walked to Oxchuc and then, for another two hours, to the house of Martin Tsima. Marianna recalled their visit:

> Martin said, "*me'tik* (a term of respect for a woman), these are the ones from Corralito whose hearts like God's Word. They have come to hear more." One of the men fished into his net bag and pulled out a well-thumbed hymn book, the one Martin had left with them months before.
>
> "Do you have more of these," he asked.
>
> I nodded. "Yes, we have a copy for each of you. Would you like to learn the hymns in Tzeltal?" I started to teach them the first hymn in the little book—they already knew it. Next page—they knew that one too. Every single hymn in that booklet they had memorized—at least the words, if not the tune. Amazed, I opened the Gospel of Mark in Tzeltal and started to read it to them.
>
> "I know how to read," volunteered Juan. "God willed it so that I would be able to read His Word." Reverently, he took the printed portion in his hands and read a few verses aloud. The words came painstakingly slowly because Juan was earnestly attempting to get every syllable perfect. We discovered he had also taught his older brother, Mariano, and his cousin Domingo, to read so they would be able to read God's Word for themselves. From the hundreds in Oxchuc who did not know one letter from another, the Lord sent us three who could read.

The visitors stayed with Marianna and Florence until nine at night, learning more about the Bible, and then left for Martin's house, where they remained several more hours discussing what they had learned and examining the Gospels, Bible stories and hymnals they had been given. They left but returned 10 days later amid a drenching downpour. This time, Juan Mucha brought eight men and boys, five women and three babies. They sat on the floor, listening and looking at the flannelboard pictures of the stories of the Creation, the Fall, the Flood and the three believers from the Book of Daniel delivered from the fiery furnace. The women took Marianna and Florence aside to listen as they repeated the words of the hymns to see if their pronunciation was correct. They could not read but they too had memorized every word in the hymn book. The group spent the night, the men and boys on the floor of the dispensary and the women and babies on the floor of Marianna and Florence's room. A house built for two now accommodated 19. The next day they started again. They listened to the Victrola records, memorized Scripture passages and joined in prayer.

Soon, five years had passed since Marianna had arrived at Yochib. The original three-year lease had been extended for two years, but now she was told she would have to leave. The land belonged to the shaman Andres Kojt'om and he wanted it back. Furthermore, the government school teacher in Yochib said he needed Villa's house for an addition to the school. Martin Tsima had some land and offered it to Marianna and Florence if they wished to build on it but Andres Kojt'om said he would put a curse on it.

They would have to leave Yochib, but to where? They would have the summer to decide. Florence was returning to Norman, Oklahoma, for a second course with SIL, and Marianna had enrolled at the University of Mexico for Mayan courses. In June, before leaving, they invited the new believers to San Cristobal for a few days of Bible study away from the demands of home and farm:

> Without any way of knowing how many would respond, we were over-joyed to find 24 eager students waiting for us at their first Bible con-ference. There were five from Yochib, 12 from Corralito and seven others. The evangelical church in Las Casas allowed us to use their building.
>
> "No saints," the Indian believers whispered to one another, peer-ing around the spacious, well-lit chapel. In place of the customary dust-covered images of the town church, a large open Bible was dis-played on the pulpit. Florence played the wheezing antiquated organ as the Indians crowded around to sing their much-loved hymns.
>
> On Saturday morning, we began with the Bible stories from the Book of Mark. The Feeding of the Five Thousand strengthened their hearts for the months to come when corn might be scarce. The accounts of Jesus healing the sick enabled Juan to pray for the heal-ing of Mariano, his brother. The words of the Lord through the storm, "Fear not, I am with you," were to provide encouragement for the days ahead when they would face opposition as the first believers of the area. That night, 20 of our Bible students slept side-by-side, using the whole length of the porch of the home where we were staying with fel-low missionaries. For their first Sunday service in a church, our Indian friends filled three or four rows of benches. Though the service was in Spanish and none of them understood a word of it, they sat very

still for the entire two hours. What they did understand was that they were among those of "like precious faith" and had been made welcome. Ordinarily, mestizos refused to mingle with Indians, calling them "dogs," but here, among the evangelicals, the mestizos called the Tzeltals "brethren."

Left on their own, Juan and Domingo Mucha continued as itinerant preachers. Marianna had given them a Victrola and a set of records, as well as her translation of the Gospel of Mark. Their most important convert was Francisco Gomez Sanchez who lived in Mesbilja, about two miles down a rocky side road to the south. He was in his early twenties and had worked on a coffee plantation on the Pacific coast, where he had picked up a little Spanish and had also met some Presbyterians, so he knew a little of the Bible. He became one of the most enthusiastic of the evangelical band. Marianna and Florence had left without knowing where they would live on their return. When the Corralito band decided to offer them a home, it was Francisco, with his knowledge of Spanish, who wrote the letter (via the church in San Cristobal) saying there were now 33 evangelical families (about 150 persons) who would welcome them.

When Marianna and Florence returned in October, 1949, Martin Tsima came to San Cristobal to conduct them to their new home in a caravan of six mules, two riding horses, two mule drivers and seven carriers:

> It was a two-day trail ride from Las Casas to Corralito. The closer we drew to our destination, the more believers came to meet us along the trail. Though some had never seen us, they greeted us as if they had known us all their lives. When we finally arrived at the little clearing, they led us to the little thatched hut, which we were to occupy until they could build us a home of our own. Anxiously, their eyes followed us as we investigated our new domain. The boards lashed in place with vines, two planks laid over forked sticks for beds, a large rustic chair that they had located and the dirt floor spread with fresh pine needles all revealed their love and eagerness to please. Juan led the group, at least seven of them, in a welcoming circle of singing. From wrinkled old men down to little tots, they all sang the hymns from memory.

Soon the menaces began. A letter was sent to Guillermo Sozaya, the director of the Bureau of Indigenous Affairs in San Cristobal, accusing the women and their followers of plotting to burn the Oxchuc Catholic Church and its saints. Furthermore, it was charged that they were really men in disguise, wearing rubber breasts to make them look like women and were sexually abusing Tzeltal girls. As if this was not enough, the letter said the disguised men were cannibals who kidnaped people, boiled them alive in large pots, and ate them.

One of those named as an accomplice was Francisco Gomez Sanchez and he was called to San Cristobal to reply to the charges. He said they were lies generated by the fact that evangelicals were increasing in numbers every day and that the Oxchuc caciques were angry because the believers no longer consumed alcohol, smoked tobacco or bought candles and incense to burn before the saints. He said that as believers in Christ, they respected other religions and the objects they adored, but were not obliged to have the same beliefs because there was freedom of religion in Mexico. Francisco Gomez was sent home with a warning not to offend other faiths. When he told others what had happened, his escape without harm was seen as evidence of God's protection, giving impetus to new conversions.

Typical early chapel

By 1950, there were so many believers they could no longer worship in their houses. A church 25 feet wide and 90 feet long was built with mud-and-wattle walls and a peaked straw roof. The congregation was put under Daniel Aguilar Ochoa, the pastor of the Church of the Divine Redeemer in San Cristobal. In March, 1951, during Easter week, the church was burned down. The believers built it again in August, 1951, still with mud-and-wattle walls but enlarged to 100 feet long and 30 feet wide with a roof of laminated aluminum, carried for several days over the dirt trails. It had room for 600 worshipers. As soon as construction was completed, it was used to consecrate the marriage of 225 couples. (The required Mexican civil ceremony was conducted in Oxchuc.)

In November 1953, the congregation became a full church and was named Golgota. It was the first Tzeltal Presbyterian church in Chiapas. Francisco Gomez Sanchez was elected as one of the elders. Later, he was made an "*obrero*" (worker), or assistant to Daniel Aguilar Ochoa. In 1960, he was sent to the Bible School in San Cristobal for training. In July 1963, he was ordained as the first Tzeltal pastor.

In the early 1950s, a man named Sebastian Tsul walked for three hours to Corralito from the community of Tenango carrying his desperately ill wife tied to his back to ask Florence Gerdel to care for her. She did, for a full year, but with no success. Sebastian Tsul returned home alone. By then he was a believer and brought with him a record player and a set of records. After he evangelized many of his neighbors the caciques of Tenango called them all to the community center, beat each with six strokes of a whip and put them in the community jail. They were soon released, but the hostility and menaces continued year after year. In August 1955, Sebastian Tsul went to a neighboring community with the records. As he put the player on the dirt floor and began winding the spring, the door was pushed open and three men with rifles began to shoot. Sebastian Tsul was killed instantly. He was regarded as the first Tzeltal martyr, and, a year later, the believers in Tenango built a large mud-walled church in his honor.

The Growth of the Tzeltal Church

The American Bible Society looked back at what had happened since 1949 in a small pamphlet published in 1956 titled "A Modern Miracle?" The Golgota church had become the mother church of 18 chapels that ministered to about 5,000 Tzeltals, or about half the Tzeltal population of the municipality of Oxchuc. In 1952 the Bible Society published 2,000 copies of Acts and the Epistles of John. In 1954, another 2,000-copy edition of John was published along with 1,000 copies of

A new Tzetzal translation of the New Testament was published in 1982. When it went on sale at the Golgota Church in Corralito, 1,500 copies were sold in one day and 4,000 in three months.

the Epistles of Galatians through Colossians and 500 copies of I and II Thessalonians, James and 1 and 2 Peter. The initial 2,000 copies of Marianna's entire Tzeltal New Testament was published in August 1956.

Meanwhile, literacy classes had been started to teach the Tzeltals to read their new scriptures and Florence Gerdel published a hygiene manual in Tzeltal. People began to buy wash basins and soap, and a few even began to have their stools analyzed for parasites and to receive immunizations against specific diseases. Later, agricultural technicians led by David Jarvis, a British member of SIL, came to teach terracing of the steep mountain sides, thereby increasing the yields of the staple crops of corn and beans by five times. They also introduced a greater variety of crops, including cabbage, carrots, potatoes, peanuts and onions. Once Oxchuc was considered the most backward of all the highland municipalities. After the extensive conversions, Manual Castellanos, who became director of the Bureau of Indian Affairs, said it exceeded all highland municipalities in education and the acceptance of technology and scientific medicines.

The changes, as Marianna wrote, were due to the ban on alcohol and a new autonomous internal discipline:

Florence's Tzeltal hygiene chart

Discipline was left entirely to the elders who set up even more rigid standards than I would have. Drunkenness, looked upon as a return to the old ways, was punished by a long period of being denied entry to the *Templo* itself. The offenders could stand outside and listen, but, until the elders felt they had shown true repentance and were willing to confess before all the church, they were not allowed within the walls of the chapel. Every Sunday, we had many "miscreants" milling about outside, peering into the windows wistfully but not allowed to enter. In cases of gross misconduct such as adultery, they were no longer called *hermano* or *hermana* and did not receive a handshake from their fellow Christians. But always, no matter what the offense, the elders "talked to God" with anyone they counseled.

Family and communal relations changed. Children were no longer abused but gently rebuked. Families once isolated on lonely hillsides now came into contact with one another. In a scientific paper written for a Mexico City anthropological magazine, Marianna stressed the economic gains and improvement of morale concomitant with the eradication of alcoholism.

> The money formerly expended for liquor for ritual and personal consumption is now being used for buying better clothes, for building better houses, for acquiring horses and cattle, etc. In addition, freedom from the galling debts incurred for liquor in its former multitudinous uses in their culture and personal freedom from domination by alcoholism have engendered in them a new self-respect. Public opinion, formed by the predominantly evangelical population, is now opposed to alcoholism, and the resulting social pressure is affecting even the non-Christian element in the region.[10]

Preaching and evangelizing was left to the Tzeltals themselves. One group from Golgota went twice a week to Abasolo, in the municipality of Ocosingo, where Juan and Domingo Mucha first met Martin Tsima. Pedro Santis, the first man to be converted, was briefly put in jail for his faith. On his release, he became a preacher and converted 20 others, and Abasolo become a full congregation. A second Ocosingo congregation was formed in 1956 and others in the years that followed.

Abasolo, as the first, had the premier position. In 1967 it became a full church and was named Damascus. In 1977, it had a governing board of 12 elders and 13 deacons and three separate congregations. In 1983 one of these congregations, in the community of Triunfo in the municipality of Altamirano, became the Church

Pedro Santis, the first believer in Abasolo, and his son

of the Holy Spirit, with a governing board of five elders and five deacons.

Among the early congregations formed by the Golgota mother church was one in the community of Ti'aquil in Oxchuc municipality. In turn, this congregation carried the message to the community of Cancuc, where, at first, it was received with enthusiasm. However, in 1953, when shots were fired through the wall of a house of one of the believers and then some of their houses were burned, the pace of growth slowed.

By 1957, the evangelicals of Cancuc had overcome their fear, and once again the congregation was growing rapidly. Once again, too, the caciques were aroused

---

10 Slocum (1956).

and houses of the believers were burned, but this time the guilty did not escape. A complaint was filed with the governor of Chiapas. After an investigation, 26 persons who had taken part in the arson were sent to prison.

Earlier, two brothers had been converted in the community of Pacbilna, in a narrow valley between two high ridges just north of Oxchuc. Marcos and Isidro Encin were respected political leaders of the Oxchuc Tzeltals. Their younger brother, Mariano, and Martin—the son of Marcos, who had the disability of a clubfoot—also became active evangelicals. They made long trips north to Guaquitepec, in the municipality of Chilon, and south to Chanal. At both places, they were met by mobs and were beaten and put in jail, but they were still able to found congregations in both settlements. A church that was built in Pacbilna in 1952 became the pastoral center for a large part of the Tzeltal highlands, including the areas of Cancuc and Tenejapa.

Also in 1952, a woman named Juliana Moreno told her neighbors in Guaquitepec about the marvels happening in neighboring communities. The caciques heard that she and her family were believers and burned down her house and ordered the family to leave. A complaint was filed with the Ministry of Public Order and a party of soldiers was sent to Guaquitepec. Juliana Moreno and her family were allowed to return and the caciques were ordered to keep the peace. Encouraged, the believers began to form new congregations in neighboring communities. By 1971 the growth became so large that Guaquitepec became a full church, named *Betania* (Bethany, the home of Lazarus, Martha and Mary, near which the Gospels say Jesus ascended to heaven), with a governing board of 13 elders and seven deacons and with five congregations under its charge.

A typical rural church: Canaan Presbyterian church near the Tenejapa ceremonial center

Other places visited by evangelists from Golgota included communities in the mountains of the municipality of Tenejapa. One was Tzajalch'en. There, an early believer, Alonso Luna Giron, was stripped of his clothes, tied to a post and beaten. He was later released. Their faith undiminished, the believers of Tzajalch'en built a small chapel. It was soon burned down. It was rebuilt, and three other chapels were built in nearby communities. In 1977, the original chapel became the first full church in Tenejapa and was named Messiah.

A second Tenejapa church, in the mountain community of Xixintonil, was organized in 1980 and was named Samaria, with a governing board of 15 elders, five deacons, and 25 congregations under its charge. In 1982, a church called Paradise was built in a valley in the mountain above the ceremonial center of Tenejapa. In turn, this church founded a congregation named Canaan, only a few streets from the ceremonial center of Tenejapa.

Growth in Bachajon

While all this was happening within the Highland dialects of Tzeltal, there was growth back in the lowland Bachajon dialect region, where William Bentley had first attempted to evangelize in 1939. In 1954, Santiago Gomez Hernandez, one of the remaining believers from the early days, visited Marianna in Corralito and was

given records and a record player to revive the work. The persecution was not long in starting. A Catholic priest called a meeting and told the community's caciques to get rid of the evangelicals. On the first day of May 1956, when Gomez Hernandez was holding a prayer and hymn meeting in his house, shots were fired outside. No bullets penetrated the walls but a believer named Juan Moreno Gomez, who went out to see what was happening,

Bahtzibiltic: boys Sunday School class

was killed by a blast from double-barreled shot-gun. Two women were slightly wounded. Shots were fired at Santiago Gomez and the others as they fled and then the house was burned. The believers took refuge in Corralito.

The father of one of the believers was a primary school teacher, thus with links to the government, and his complaint received attention. One man was arrested, tried and sent to prison for several years. Others were tried and released after posting bond to keep order. After that, there was peace. Those who had fled returned to their homes and built a chapel in their village of Paxilha.

Evangelists from the Golgota church established one of their early congregations in Bahtzibiltic near the community of Bachajon. By September 1959, it had become a full church, named New Jerusalem, and was responsible for 26 congregations.

In those years, migration swelled to the vacant lands of the Lacandon jungle. Evangelicals founded many *ejidos* (under the law allowing farmers to occupy vacant government land as long as they farm it communally and do not sell their holdings to outsiders) in the municipality of Ocosingo. In March 1967, in the ejido of Santo Domingo, they formed a church named Calvary, with a governing board of 22 elders and 11 deacons, and with nine congregations and two missions under their charge.

In 1963, another group formed the ejido of Damascus, one of the largest in Lacandona. In March 1968, they inaugurated a church, named Philadelphia, with a board of 25 elders and 18 deacons and 16 congregations under their charge.

In February 1977, one of these congregations, in a colony called Jol Sac Jun, was organized as the Church of the Good Shepherd, with 12 elders and nine deacons. A little later, another congregation, in an ejido called Christopher Columbus, was organized under the name Mount Zion, with seven congregations in its charge.

In 1957, after eight years of labor in Corralito, Marianna Slocum completed her translation of the New Testament and returned to where she had started—Bachajon—and there worked for another six years to complete a translation of the New Testament in the Bachajon Tzeltal dialect. Florence Gerdel continued her program of training village health workers. She wrote another medical manual in Bachajon Tzeltal and provided medical equipment for 20 village clinics. The New Testament was completed in June 1963. In the same month, Slocum and Gerdel left for the United States to supervise its printing, after which they flew to South America to translate the New Testament into the language of the Páez Indians of Colombia.

Establishment of Separate Tzeltal and Chol Presbyteries

In 1974, the Presbyterian Church in Chiapas was divided into three parts: Spanish-speaking, Tzeltal and Chol. The Spanish-speaking section, known as the Presbytery of Chiapas, which had been growing in the years after World War II, was left with 24 churches and 15 pastors. The Tzeltal Presbytery had 13 churches and 150 congregations administered by eight pastors and several hundred elders, including 13 who, along with the pastors, formed the governing board of the Presbytery. The Chol Presbytery had 10 churches and 10 pastors.

Training for Tzeltal pastors had started in 1960 at the long-established seminary attached to the Church of the Divine Redeemer in San Cristobal. Simultaneously, a shorter training period was organized for assistants to evangelize new congregations while developing the assistants' preaching skills and thus train them as deacons, elders and finally, with the approval of their parishioners, pastors.

During this period there were about a dozen American missionaries from the Reformed Church of America concerned entirely with the training of pastors and other workers. In 1966, SIL translation consultants recommended a new translation of the New Testament in the dialect of Oxchuc Tzeltal. This was done in Ocosingo municipality, at a rural Bible School known as the Tzeltal Cultural Center. The staff included Paul and Dorothy Meyerink, Samuel and Helen Hofman and Jim and Sharon Heneveld. The school was developed on a cattle ranch named Rancho Buenos Aires. In addition to biblical studies, the curriculum included music, general education, carpentry and agriculture. The wives of the students were taught child care, hygiene, sewing, knitting and bread-baking. The school became the center for the medical work, offering additional training to village paramedics. A dentist from the United States provided dental training and equipment for 30 paramedics. By 1977, there were 55 medical and dental clinics in the Tzeltal area.[11]

The Role of Evangelical Churches in Preserving Ethnicity

As mentioned earlier, the first Ladino Presbyterian church in northern Chiapas was the Prince of Peace Church in Yajalon. Later, a separate Tzeltal church was formed, called Jesus the Good Shepherd. In 1995, Irene Sanchez Franco presented a master's thesis for the University of Chiapas, contrasting these churches and commenting on the social role of the Tzeltal church. She found that even among evangelicals racism was evident in casual speech, with Mestizos described as "civilized." She called one church Mestiza and the other Tzeltal: "Although they belong to the same denomination they are not the same. Many of the believers do not know one another. Neither do the elders know one another. The Mestiza church only accepts those who are bilingual. The Tzeltal church will accept bilinguals providing they otherwise conform to Tzeltal culture." She was interested in which had the greatest influence on culture—society or the church—and decided it was the school and the work-place.

> Since teachers did not speak Tzeltal, the children had to learn *castilla* [Spanish] in order to learn to read and write. Adults also had to learn Spanish to cope with society as a whole. The main influence in preserving their culture was their faith ... We can affirm that it is possible to be Tzeltal and Presbyterian at the same time . . . Presbyterianism has contributed to the preservation and elaboration of their culture and has not been a factor in making them change it. The one place where it is not necessary to speak Spanish is in their church . . . The Tzeltals have not mechanically reproduced the Presbyterian ideology but have changed it to make it part of their identity. In this way Presbyterianism has been integrated into the daily lives of Tzeltal converts . . . The Church of Jesus the Good Shepherd is an exclusive space for Tzeltals, in which Tzeltals of different parts of the municipality can meet. It is not only a religious space but also a space for social encounters.[12]

This last point must be explained. Most Tzeltals of Yajalon earned their living as daily agricultural workers—their incomes varying with the season and the good or ill will of their employers. They lived in wood-sided shacks, often with dirt floors, and barely had one change of clothing. They were dispersed in small groups and came together only in their church. It is here that they found dignity and a sense of community. Only within the Tzeltal church could they hope to rise to a position of responsibility, as a deacon or elder and perhaps even as a pastor.

"And yet," she wrote, "evangelical religious practices were not too different from those who continued to be Catholic." Both celebrated Easter and the

11 The Buenos Aires center was occupied during the land invasions following the Zapatista uprising of 1994. An attempt to mediate the dispute, so that at least the buildings would be returned for evangelical use, was still in progress in 1998. 12 (1995): 165–66.

Nativity. In both churches the sexes were divided, with men on the left side and women on the right. She also found a parallel with the mayordomos of traditional Catholic festivals. On one side is a ranked series of traditional cargos, on the other, the "cargos" of deacons and elders.

In short, just as an American might be a Catholic or a Protestant and still think and act as an American, a Tzeltal could be a Catholic or evangelical and still think and act as a Mexican. And, like Italian Americans or Irish Americans, they would also be Tzeltal Mexicans, proud of their place in a multicultural society.

3
THE BEGINNINGS OF THE TZOTZIL CHURCH

The Tzotzil zone of the Highlands is divided into the municipalities of Zinacantan, San Juan Chamula, Huixtan, San Andres and Chenalho. For the people of these areas the designation of a single Tzotzil language is the arbitrary imposition of Mexican ethnologists. The indigenous people insist there are more languages than municipalities and that they speak Chenalho, Chalchihuitan, Pentalho, Mitontic, San Andres, Huixtan, Chamulan, Zinacantan and others.

I had read that evangelism began in the community of Chimtic in the municipality of Chenalho.[1] Its ceremonial center is the town of Chenalho, about an hour's bus ride north of San Cristobal. Chimtic was said to be another three miles from there. I was not told that the three miles were about 2,000 feet up a winding dirt road with no public transportation. With the cloud-catching mountains, it rains eight months a year in Chimtic. On mornings between November and January the temperature drops below freezing.

All traditional religions have considered lofty places as the homes of the gods. In Chenalho, two peaks were considered to be actual gods. The highest was called, in Tzotzil, *Ajaw* (ruler, king) and pilgrimages were made to there three times a year to burn incense and light candles. The Chimtic Presbyterian church is atop that peak. It is a cement-block structure about 50 feet long and 40 feet wide that can seat 500 worshipers. It was built in 1983, when each family was assessed 100 pesos (50 pesos for widows). Two men who knew a little masonry donated their labor.

The pastor, Pedro Hernandez Perez, was not there but was summoned by a man on horseback and arrived an hour later. It developed that he was only comfortable in speaking Tzotzil and the young Spanish-speaking man he brought along as a translator was little better. I asked about the church's history, its growth and things like the selection of elders and the size of the Sunday school. The answers, teased out through several dialogues between the pastor and the interpreter, boiled down to this:

✳ ✳ ✳ ✳ ✳

The evangelism began here when a man named Marcos Quentio Max came from a finca in Tapachula where he met the Word of God and was given a Bible. When he returned in 1956, he preached. I never went to school. A missionary brought some books and I learned by reading the Bible in Tzotzil. I can also read a little

---

1 Rasgado Cruz (1992).

Spanish. My father was pastor here. I went to San Cristobal to take a course at the Divine Redeemer Church. After that, I was an elder here and then the congregation selected me as pastor. The Gospel spreads when people are sick or drunk. They come seeking help and stay in the church. After that, they don't look for doctors any more. They just let God heal them. Some have come when they were deaf or could not talk. After praying, they began to hear and talk. Not everyone will be converted. Some are accustomed to being Catholics. We cannot make them change. It has to be their own will. When I began in 1980, there was just this church and seven congregations and missions. Others were built until we had 42 congregations. That was too many, so it was decided to form another church and divide the congregations. Now I have 10 congregations and 10 missions. I visit these congregations on Sundays and an elder leads the services here. We also have a Sunday School here. Sometimes 60 or 65 children come, but when it rains and there is a lot of mud or it is cold, only 10 or 20 come. First they draw pictures, and then we read the Bible. After that, they sing songs in Spanish and Tzotzil, and then they give a little offering. After that, they play for a little while, and then they pray for a little while.

✳ ✳ ✳ ✳ ✳

Extracting information was proving to be difficult. It was getting late and I still faced the knee-jolting decent. Pastor Hernandez seemed relieved when I said thanks and goodbye. I was not disappointed. The purpose of my visit was really just to see the church. I knew from reading Esponda's history of the Presbyterian Church in Chiapas that the most noteworthy evangelical events of Chenalho happened in the 1950s and 1960s.[2]

Chenalho, even more than Oxchuc, illustrates the grassroots growth of evangelism in Chiapas—a reaching out for the Bible by those marginalized by Ladino society and how the diaspora facilitates this outreach.

In 1952, Marcos Quentio Max of the Chenalho community of Shunush went to a plantation at Huehuetan, near the Pacific coast, to join his elder brother, who, like many Highlanders, was working on a coffee plantation. His brother told Marcos he had met an all-powerful God and gave him a New Testament and a few pamphlets in Spanish, including the familiar "*Padre Nuestro*" (Our Father). Marcos could not read Spanish or any language, but, when he returned to Shunush a month later, he was so enamored of the pamphlet that he slept with it in his hand.

He described his inner awakening to two brothers, Agustin and Victorio Perez Gutierrez (of an extensive clan known as the Pasciencias in the community of Chimtic), who could read and speak a little Spanish. They wanted to know more. In 1953, Victorio heard there were people who knew the Bible in Mesbilja in Oxchuc. He went there with Marcos and they met Francisco Gomez Sanchez. Since Gomez Sanchez spoke Tzeltal they could learn little from him, but Francisco volunteered to take them to San Cristobal where, he said, there was a church. There they met Kenneth Weathers, a member of Summer Institute of Linguistics, who understood a little Tzotzil. He gave them a pamphlet in Spanish: "You shall have no other Gods before me. You shall not make for yourself an idol in the form of anything in heaven above or in the earth beneath or in the waters below. You shall not bow down to them or worship them" (Exodus 20:3–5).

2 (1986).

When they returned to Chimtic, they began to think of themselves as Presbyterians. Little by little, the Perez Gutierrez brothers improved their ability to read Spanish by studying the New Testament that Marcos had brought from Huehuetan. They had an elder brother named Sebastian who was the curandero/shaman of Chimtic. At first, he refused to join them, but then he did. The three prayed together outside their house because their father, despite their urging, had refused to accept the new faith. Finally, he relented, and that night he joined his sons as they knelt before the fire in their kitchen and recited "Our Father...," which the three brothers had memorized. It then became a family custom to join, with their mother, in afternoon readings of the Bible.

Slowly, the Gospel spread to other communities, so that by 1957 there were 10 families of believers. Their absence from the traditional ceremonies in Chenalho could not be overlooked and the inevitable persecution began. The municipal president, whose name was Antonio Lopez, went to the house of the Pasciencias to ask them to rejoin the worship of the traditional gods. Their mother replied that mountains, springs and the sun were not alive but were created by God in heaven. Furious at this defiance, Antonio Lopez struck her.

When it was known throughout Chenalho that these families did not believe in the traditional gods, rumors spread that they were children of the devil and that they ate human flesh. Three policemen were sent to Chimtic and brought Augustin and Victorio to the municipal center for trial before the entire municipality. The president asked Victorio if it was true that he would no longer pay tribute to the gods. He answered that it was true, because the mountains, caves, springs, sun and moon were created by an all-powerful God in heaven. He said there was only one God who could save everyone and that if they too heard the Word of God and repented their sins, they would be pardoned and received by Jesus Christ.

The crowd shouted "Seize him. Tie him up. Kill him." Victorio took out of his pocket a pamphlet of the Mexican Constitution. He said, "It says here that everyone has the right to his religious belief. Do you not respect this?" The municipal president was furious. He took the pamphlet and tore it to pieces, but still let the brothers go free.

Part of the mob was not so forgiving. One night, later in 1957, groups armed with rifles and machetes began to attack the house of the Pasciencias from two directions, but were scared off by their barking dogs. Then witchcraft was tried. Three men experienced in the craft went to the mountains of Chimtic and burned 13 candles—the symbol of a death sentence. They went away and waited. Nothing happened, so they tried again. They went to the family's fields and prayed and sowed charms so the plants would not germinate and grow. Again, nothing happened.

Finally a direct blow fell. One night, a distant relative of the Pasciencias, named Amporox de Chimix, was ambushed on his way home from a store. He was struck dead with a machete. He carried a Bible in his knapsack. This was taken out and placed on his chest to show the reason for his death. The authorities did nothing, but Victorio Perez and his brothers asked in many places and learned the name of the assailant. One midnight, they seized him and took him to the police, who took him to San Cristobal, where he was tried and sentenced to ten years in prison.

In 1958, some members of the Pasciencia clan walked to San Cristobal to meet Kenneth Weathers, who gave them more leaflets of biblical verses in Tzotzil, including Leviticus 26:1: "Do not make idols or set up an image or a sacred stone for yourselves, and do not place a carved stone in your land or bow down before it. I am the Lord your God."

The Pasciencias used the leaflets to teach to their neighbors. This began a general rejection of ancestral gods and the separation of evangelicals from their neighbors to form a new community. In 1960, a mission was established in the community of Pechiquil. In 1961, another mission was formed in Acteal, five miles from Pechiquil. To walk from Chimtic to Pechiquil took six hours. This isolation heightened the fear of sudden attack or ambush. The believers asked Weathers to live with them to demonstrate that they were not alone. Instead, he advised them to remain calm and strong. Because there were so few roads, the Mission Aviation Fellowship was organized to link translators living in isolated mountain communities. There was no landing strip in the steep-sided mountains of Chimtic, but one day he asked the pilot to fly him over the community at a low altitude and dropped a note in Tzotzil saying: "Do not be afraid of enemies who may kill your body. They cannot kill your soul." Of course, the mere fact that the evangelicals could summon the plane was a demonstration that they were not alone.

The believers had good reason to be wary. In 1961, three former municipal presidents of Chenalho filed charges accusing them of not sending their children to school, not working for the benefit of the community, not taking the traditional cargos and, instead, wanting to burn the images of the saints in the church. Victorio and Augustin Perez of Chimtic and leaders of the congregations in Pechiquil and Acteal were ordered to appear before Manuel Castellanos Cancino, then assistant director of the Bureau of Indigenous Affairs in San Cristobal. There was no road, and they had to walk much of the day. School officials were also called but did not appear. The evangelists once again recited their beliefs and cited freedom of religion and called, as a character witness, Daniel Aguilar Ochoa, who was well known as the pastor of the Presbyterian Church of the Divine Redeemer in San Cristobal.

When the three accusers could not produce a witness, Castellanos dismissed the charges and fined them, warning that if they continued to harass the evangelicals, thus violating Article 24 of the Constitution (which gave freedom of religion), he would put them in jail.

In 1962, a Canadian Presbyterian group financed a health clinic in Chimtic to train community leaders to teach, along with the Bible, such health practices as boiling water and washing hands before meals. The clinic also sold medicines at low prices. In 1965, the Pasciencias asked the Bureau of Indigenous Affairs to build a school in Chimtic. By then, a fourth mission had been established in the mountains, in the community of Yabteclum, where believers decided to build a church. Five teams worked two days and built a church measuring about 12 by 15 feet with mud walls and wood roof.

In addition to Sundays, those who lived close to the church in Chimtic came on Monday and Wednesday afternoons to pray and read the Bible. Worshipers from the scattered congregations left their homes on Saturday, bringing their food with them, and spent the night in the homes of the Pasciencias so that the entire evangelical community was united on Sundays.

In 1966, there was a drought, and, despite the warning not to harass the believers, Chenalho's president, Domingo Luna, spread rumors that the gods of the mountains and wells were angry and would not give enough rain for the crops. By then, Manuel Castellanos Cancino was head of the INI office in San Cristobal. He summoned Luna to explain what he was doing. As he entered Castellanos' office, Luna said, "We do not want these evangelicals because they do not respect our customs." Castellanos refused to listen and repeated his warning of jail terms if harm was done to the evangelists. With that, the persecution of the believers in Chenalho ended.

Kenneth Weathers continued to nurture the Chimtic evangelists. When the requested government primary school was built, he arranged to teach those who had finished their elementary studies to read and write Tzotzil. Eleven were sent to the town of Ixtapa, where they first learned the alphabet and then how to use this to write Tzotzil stories and then to translate these into Spanish. The final test was for them to learn to translate other Spanish stories into Tzotzil. They were also given a three-month course in typing. The entire course lasted two and a half years.

By then, Gospel Recordings had established a studio in Mexico City. Weathers gathered some of his students and recorded hymns in Tzotzil and gave five Victrolas and sets of records to the Pasciencia family for use in their evangelizing. He also had a calendar made with the Bible verses in Tzotzil and sold them at a cheap price. The idea was for a believer to memorize verses on the calendar. He was not well and moved to San Cristobal in 1972 and lived there until 1980. Another SIL translator, Marion Cowan of Canada, took over the translation of the Gospel for the Tzotzils of Chenalho. She asked for volunteers who felt the call to translate the Word of God into their language. Three of those who had completed the course in typing responded and joined her in her house in Pechiquil. Together, they completed the translation of the New Testament along with a summary of the history of the people of Israel and a book of some 160 hymns. Ms Cowan left Pechiquil in 1980. Her early experiences are told in the next chapter.

4
PASSING ON THE MESSAGE

In an article in the missiological magazine *Practical Anthropology*, Marion Cowan recalled her first contact with Tzotzils of the municipality of Huixtan in the days before roads. Huixtan, she wrote, was three-to-four hours by foot north-to-south and four hours east-to-west, with a population of 3,000 to 4,000.[1] It was a four-hour walk from the northeast corner of Huixtan to Corralito, in the municipality of Oxchuc, where evangelism had first blossomed among the Tzeltals in 1949, and another half day's walk through Huixtan and Chamula to San Cristobal. The Tzeltals continually made the nine or ten-hour trip, bringing chickens, rope, blankets and flowers to sell and returning with salt, sandals, hats, bread and yarn

1 (1962).

Marion Cowan talkling with Huixtec believers in 1956. Martin is on the right

for weaving clothes. The evangelicals of Corralito were eager to gain new believers. One man in particular was always willing to take the Victrola and records to play in someone's house or to accompany someone else on a similar mission. In December 1955, he was walking on the trail to San Cristobal when a Huixteco stopped him to chat. Although the Tzeltal of Oxchuc and the Tzotzil of Huixtan are different languages, the municipalities are adjacent and there was a degree of mutual intelligibility.

The Huixtan man, whose name was Martin, was accompanied by his son in law, Nicholas. When Martin offered the Tzeltal a cigarette, it was refused. That was unusual: no one was supposed to refuse a gift. When Martin asked why, the Tzeltal said he no longer smoked or drank alcohol and never attended the festivals of the saints because he had found the one true God. It was late, and the Tzeltal still had four hours to walk, so they parted, but the Tzeltal agreed to meet again when he returned.

In San Cristobal, he told friends what happened and they were surprised. They had long wanted to spread the Gospel to the Huixtecos, but were afraid: they thought the Huixtecos were killers. The Tzeltal did his business and set out at four the next morning to have more time to talk with his new acquaintance. At the point on the trail where the meeting had occurred the previous day, he called out.

Nicholas appeared and took him to Martin's house, where others were also waiting. Martin had told his brothers and his wife's relatives of the planned meeting and urged them to come to listen. The group included some of Martin's brothers and a nephew, all of his own family and many of his wife's relatives— 16 in all.

Martin was an unusual man. He was 40 or 45 years old. At one time, he made and sold chicha, the cane-sugar beer. He owned three houses, at least six oxen, a horse, 10 or 12 sheep and was a money lender. His wife had 10 children, of whom seven were still living. All of this was seen as a sign

Pedro and Nicolas, two preachers among the Huixtecos

Christmas pageant in Corralito

that he was favored by the gods. Nicholas, his son-in-law, was 22 and was the only literate man in the community.

The Tzeltal explained his faith and invited them to come to Corralito in about two weeks for the Christmas celebrations. The subject was discussed, after which nine said they would accept and seven said they would not. Later, the nine who accepted set out for Corralito, but four turned back: they had heard the Tzeltals were killers and were afraid. Four men and one woman persisted and were amazed when they were met and befriended by more than 2,000 evangelicals.

Of the seven who initially refused to believe, there was one man who openly derided the decision. He even hired a killer to assassinate Martin. The attempt was unsuccessful, and that was taken as a sign of the new God's protection. Soon, another event was seen as a stronger sign: the man who had derided the believers was himself killed and mutilated with axes and machetes.

The initial difference persisted between those who would believe and those who would not. None of Martin's brothers or sisters believed, but his sons and daughters did and almost all of his wife's family. The men of these families were linked by an agreement to work with their oxen at the rate of three pesos a day—one peso for each ox and one for the driver. A neighboring cooperative group usually charged 10 pesos a day.

Then the message spread to a family that lived 10 minutes down the mountain. Two younger men of this family were told of the conversions while walking home from the market with some of the new believers. They agreed to accept too. There were also two families who worked fields adjoining those of the believers. When one man of these families decided to accept, all members of both families accepted. Then there was a son-in-law who lived about a 20-minute walk away. He had been a companion of the man who was killed. When he heard this, he and his wife came

Huixtec harvesting wheat

to believe, and later his son by his first wife was converted.

In 1956, after the Corralito Christmas celebration, a group of Tzeltals, faithfully, every Saturday, walked eight hours to Chenalho, spent the night there to teach the Gospel on Sunday, and then, on Monday, walked the eight hours back home. Some Huixteco believers also walked to San Cristobal to help in translating evangelical literature into their version of Tzotzil.

Twice over the years, the SIL had asked for permission to set up a base in Huixtan, but it was refused. Then, the governor of Chiapas sent a letter of permission, and, on February 20, 1958, Marion Cowan and another woman translator moved into the house owned by one of the believers until a new house could be built for them. There were difficulties. Soon after they arrived, a violent wind storm blew the roofs off houses and knocked some down. There were also rumors. It will be recalled that when Marianna Slocum and Florence Gerdel arrived in Yochib it was rumored one of them was a man wearing false breasts. The same rumor spread against Marion Cowan and her companion and people gossiped that maybe little girls would soon be pregnant. People were afraid to enter their house. Some, when they did come in for medicines, trembled with fear.

There were also false charges. Six new believers were accused of murder and were taken to the community jail. Huixtan did not have an airstrip, but a Mission Aviation Fellowship plane regularly flew over at a low altitude to drop messages. The planes were seen as guardians of the two foreign women and all the believers. By chance, it flew over when the six believers were in jail, and men ran immediately to the prison to see if they were still there. They were and were soon escorted to San Cristobal, where the charges were dismissed as unfounded and the men were released.

In the first year, there was a Christian wedding, a Christian funeral, the first Christmas festival and the first translations. These were a short life of Christ, the Ten Commandments, several incidents from the Old Testament, including the Creation and Fall, the murder of Abel by Cain and the fiery fur-

Women reading the new Christian literature

nace, along with a few excerpts from the New Testament and 21 hymns. Typewritten copies were given to Nicholas and two other Christians who had learned to read Tzotzil.

Later came the Sermon on the Mount, the Gospel of Mark, the book of Acts, a longer life of Christ and 12 more hymns. A set of three primary school books was prepared to teach the Tzotzils to read their own language. Classes were held for men, women and children in the home of the two women. In addition, some men spent many hours a month teaching others. By the end of the year, 20 men, women or children could read scripture portions, while four men were regularly engaged in helping with the continued translations.

Gradually, a new society and new customs came into being. A gift was still given to a bride's family and the amount spent did not change, but an evangelical gave meat, bread, cane sugar and cocoa. Nonbelievers gave liquor, bread, cane sugar and cocoa. Furthermore, before going to ask another family for a wife for their son, the parents had to be instructed about the new customs the girl would encounter.

When Marion Cowan and her companion went on home leave, they received letters from Huixtan saying that prayers were being said for them and asking for their prayers in return. By June 1961, there were 82 adult believers. Cinder blocks, mortar and lumber had been bought with savings from the Sunday offerings, and, with donated labor, a church was built. Marion Cowan, an anthropologist as well as a linguist (her Spanish-Tzotzil learning text was published in 1956 and her Tzotzil grammar was published in 1969), recorded the relationships of who converted whom. She listed:

Husband to wife, 26
Brother-in-law to brother-in-law, 9
Father to daughter, 8
Father to son, 5
Son to mother (father dead), 4
Older brother to younger brother, 4
Son to father, 3
Younger brother to older brother, 3
Older brother to younger sister, 3
Grandfather to granddaughter (in household), 3
Neighbor to neighbor (men), 3
Older sister to younger sister, 2
Grandson to grandmother, 1
Wife to husband, 1
Father-in-law to son-in-law, 1
Son-in-law to father-in-law, 1
Mother to daughter, 1
Younger brother to older sister, 1
Younger sister to older sister, 1

Looking at the relationships in another way, she broke this down into groups:
Consanguineous kin (blood relatives), 19
Affinal kin (relatives by marriage), 38

Non-kin, 3
Man to woman, 46
Woman to man, 2
Man to man, 29
Older to younger (same sex), 13
Younger to older (same sex), 5
Older man to young woman, 14
Younger man to older woman, 6
Younger woman to older man, 1

From this she concluded that conversions spread equally through consanguineous and affinal ties—mainly from men and from older to younger. Rarely did a woman believe before her husband, but usually when a man believed, his whole household followed suit.

5
CACIQUES AND LIBERATION THEOLOGY

Tzotzils and Tzeltals, who migrated to the coffee plantations encountered the Bible and returned to evangelize relatives and friends who, in turn, evangelized others. This is a spiritual, social and cultural process, inextricably mixed with the metamorphosis of *Indios* into Ladinos. Post-revolutionary Cardenista policies were designed to accelerate this process. Moises Saenz, the pioneer of rural education who invited William Cameron Townsend to Mexico, once said: "The logical exit for the Indian is to become Mexican." In 1969, INI director Alfonso Caso said his institution was "concerned . . . with taking the improvement of modern civilization to the Indians."

This was not mere do-goodism. The aim was to incorporate educated indigenous leaders (known in Chiapas as "scribes" because they began as bilingual promoters of government policies) into the ruling Institutional Revolutionary Party. They were rewarded with what Jan Rus has described as a "federally financed payoff":

> Cooperative stores . . . were now turned over to their managers and became private businesses, trucks that had at first been entrusted to community cooperatives were increasingly owned individually by former scribes and their families, and agricultural and other demonstration projects that had originally been conducted on community land were now relocated to private holdings . . . Throughout the 1950s and 1960s . . . wealthy Ladinos helped the *principales* of most of the communities of the highlands buy land, acquire trucks and become soft-drink and beer distributors. In return, the recipients of these favors quietly blocked agrarian reform petitions, guaranteed wholesalers sole access to their community's stores, and looked the other way as *coyotes*—sharp dealing commodity merchants—short-weighted the produce they bought from community merchants. By

such means, carefully dissembled, the scribes had become, by the 1960s, not just powerful, but often quite wealthy.[1]

The expulsions from San Juan Chamula were a ruthless attempt by the caciques to retain power. They insisted they were defending sacred geography and ancient traditions and that to allow dissidents to remain in their midst would cause the gods to withdraw their protection, resulting in drought, crop failures and epidemics. It was a sham. At the bidding of their PRI bosses, they squelched local objections to the building of roads across their sacred territory and the construction of communication towers atop their sacred mountains. In the early 1970s, they permitted PEMEX (the national oil company) to bore test wells into their vaunted "Mother Earth."

Although the heaviest and most sustained persecution would affect evangelicals, the first to feel the blows were reformed Roman Catholics. In January 1960, a new Catholic Bishop, Samuel Ruiz, arrived in the diocese of San Cristobal. He had studied philosophy and theology at the Gregorian University in Rome, was ordained in 1949 and studied scripture for a further three years in Rome and Jerusalem. He returned to Mexico and was soon appointed as rector of the seminary in Leon, in his native state of Guanajuato. He was just 34 when he was named Bishop in Chiapas and had been a priest for only 10 years.

The Catholic Church in Chiapas was recovering from more than 20 years of revolutionary repression. When Victorico Grajales became governor of Chiapas in 1932, he expelled all priests, including the bishop, and began *la quema de santos* (the burning of the images of the saints) or, simply the *quemasantos*. (When mobs later accused evangelicals of conspiring to burn their saints, this was the subconscious base of their fears.) Some images were seized and hidden by indigenous leaders who perceived them as their gods. The last of these "rescued" images were not recovered by their churches until 1990.

The law is always bendable in Mexico. With tacit official approval, a process evolved in which the Catholic Church, through *prestanombres* (borrowed names), held property, operated schools from kindergarten through the university and owned publishing houses. The most difficult handicap was the shortage of priests. In the late 1950s, when the population of Chiapas was about one million, there were only 13 priests in the entire state.

One of Bishop Ruiz's first acts was to explore by muleback most of the major towns of his diocese, seeing for himself the miserable lives of his parishioners and, more relevant, the fact that the Catholic Church hardly existed except among Ladinos. As a quick fix, he asked the help of religious orders. Jesuits were already established in Bachajon in the municipality of Chilon. In 1961, other Jesuits founded a base near Palenque. In 1963, Dominicans from California came to Ocosingo. There were also Marists and Brothers of the Divine Shepherd. Nuns from South Dakota established a medical mission and hospital in Altamirano. Evangelists believe it was not simply the absence of priests that motivated Bishop Ruiz: these were regions where the Summer Institute of Linguistics had started work among the Chols in 1940 and among the Tzeltals in the early 1940s.

---

1 (1994): 289, 292.

Ruiz and the Theology of Liberation

For Bishop Ruiz, priests were only the starting point. There was also the question of what they would teach and how. Technically, the Theology of Liberation did not receive its name until 1971, when the Peruvian Gustavo Gutierrez published a major text under that title. However, Gutierrez was merely putting into written form an ideology long in gestation. He cited documents from Vatican II (1962–65), which spoke of the birth of a "new humanism" and "reading the signs of the times."

All earlier trends, he wrote, came into focus at the Second Conference of the Latin American Bishops (CELAM II) in Medellin, Colombia in 1968, with its "urgent" call for

> . . . concienticizing evangelization . . . The God whom we know in the Bible is a liberating God, a God who destroys myths and alienation, a God who intervenes in history in order to break down the structures of injustice and who raises up prophets in order to point out the way of justice and mercy. He is the God who liberates slaves (Exodus), who causes empires to fall and raises up the oppressed . . . Evangelizing action ought to be directed preferentially [to the poor], not only because of their need to understand their life, but also to help them become aware of their own mission, by cooperating in their deliberation and development.[2]

Those familiar with the "Post-Marxist" debates of the 1960s will recognize, in the final sentence of this quotation, Antonio Gramsci's teachings on the role of "organic intellectuals" in using their talents to enlighten and lead the masses.

In 1967, at a preparatory conference in Melgar, Colombia, Ruiz was elected president of CELAM's Department of Missions. He then attended the Medellin conference where, as he later recalled, "we started to discover that the marginalized are not that way because they want to be, but it is the system that marginalizes them . . . It is there where the church has to take an option."[3]

The option he chose was "the option for the poor." With the fervor of a crusader, Ruiz sent his first phalanx of Liberation Theology warriors into San Juan Chamula—the most zealous of all the highland communities in guarding its way of life. Until the mid-1930s, no Ladino was permitted to live in Chamula except within the small precincts of the municipal *cabecera* (the ceremonial center, with its church, "city hall" and open space for a market). When the state government built a school near the cabecera, it was burned down and never rebuilt. A foreign woman who lived in Chamula and wore the costume of local women was expelled because she might have a bad influence on indigenous women. For years, the municipal elders allowed only monolinguals to hold office. When the government said it would deal only with bilinguals, the caciques established a two-tier structure: bilingual for dealing with outsiders, monolingual for internal affairs.

From 1936 on, as Rus writes, Chamula was "solidly part of PRI machinery." Ballots for state and local elections were handed to the cabecera and later handed back appropriately marked. By about 1965, "the principales and their closest relatives held all the best government jobs, owned most of the stores and trucks and

---

2 Gutierrez (1973): 8, 116–117. 3 Reyes and Zebadua (1995): 21.

possessed a disproportionate share of community land." They were also aware that if new men or new ideas "were not subordinated to the group... they could easily become rivals, whether as cultural brokers, sources of loans, or even informal authorities themselves."

Under the guise of maintaining traditional purity, dissidents had to be crushed or expelled. The caciques could strike without fear of government retribution: "The state, hoping to retain control of Chamula through its alliance with the scribe-principales and their successors, made itself an accomplice in these actions, by retreating to its pose of non-interference in 'internal community affairs.'"[4]

A new government organization was formed in 1971—the Socioeconomic Program for the Highlands of Chiapas (PRODECH)—ostensibly to integrate the indigenous people into a coordinated federal and state development program. With funding from the United Nations, Chamula and other Highland municipalities were supplied with trucks, machinery, health equipment and food. It quickly became a new source of wealth for the caciques and a shield for the Chamulan bosses in their purge of dissidents.

Misión Chamula

Chamula had long been without a resident priest. One, named Juan Cabrera, came from time to time to baptize—the only Catholic ceremony that interested most Chamulans who believed baptism was vital to attach the soul to the body. The community liked Father Juan because "he did not mix in political affairs."

In 1965, when an evangelical congregation began to grow in Chamula, Bishop Ruiz removed Father Juan as ineffective. On November 1, 1966, he sent a new priest eager to institute the reforms of Liberation Theology. He was Leopoldo Hernandez, whose mandate was to live in Chamula to conduct what was called Misión Chamula. Ruiz knew he was throwing down a gauntlet: the caciques had already burned the houses of evangelicals. Pablo Iribarren, a Dominican who later wrote a brief history from which most of what follows is drawn, noted: "For four centuries, that is since Hernan Cortes, they have lived independently and are ruled by their own laws. They obey only their elders."[5]

Father Leopoldo—or Padre Polo as he was quickly called—had a team of three nuns of the Sacred Heart of Jesus and Mary, two male catechists to teach tailoring and reading, two indigenous female catechists and two housekeepers. They established a health center to foster better hygiene, a school of domestic economy and a night (Spanish-language) school for boys and girls to train them as promoters and as tailoring and artisanal leaders. He also started a credit union in direct competition with the 10- or 15-percent-monthly loan business of caciques. These activities were carried out in the Marist Seminary in San Cristobal and in new chapels built in communities away from the municipal center. This decentralization of religion was revolutionary, since previously religious activity had to take place in the cabecera under the vigilance of the principales.

Padre Polo denounced them as blind and deaf to the true Christian religion, comparing them to the Sanhedrin when confronted by Jesus. In return, everything he and his team did was viewed with suspicion. People asked Padre Polo to accompany them when they went to the municipal office to complain and the caciques

4 (1994): 271–299. 5 Iribarren (1980).

were furious: "Here, the municipal authorities determine constitutional questions and the church determines religious questions and does not mix in civil affairs."

When Padre Polo suggested that a request be made for help to electrify the municipal office, it was opposed because that would end the sale of oil for lamps, a cacique monopoly. The caciques forbade him to celebrate mass in the church and, in November 1966, they destroyed a chapel he had built in a community on the east edge of the ceremonial center. His car tires were slashed and rumors spread that he was having trysts with indigenous women in the mountains.

The confrontation became openly political in 1968, when caciques levied a tax to pay for reconstruction of the municipal administrative building. Activists, mainly college students from San Cristobal and Tuxtla Gutierrez, charged this was a cacique trick to enrich themselves and their friends. A protest march of 3,000 was staged in San Cristobal to demand the removal of the council president. The state government, eager to avoid trouble, agreed to pay for the reconstruction itself.

In February 1969, a group of catechists and "new Christians" went to San Cristobal to sing hymns and celebrate the Eucharist with Bishop Ruiz. In his memorandum, Reverend Iribarran commented: "At the same time, in the church of San Juan, it was all Babylon: some danced, others practiced healing services, some drank alcohol, others cried and sang, and the air was filled with dust and the incense of copal."

(To clarify the reference to dust: the church contains no pews or chairs. The dust rose from a dirt floor covered with a layer of pine needles. Then, as now, the image of San Juan (the patron saint) was above the altar, with about 20 other images of saints arranged along the sides of the nave. On crowded festival days in the 1960s, it was illuminated by small candles before the saints and on the dirt floor where the curanderos sat, chanting and singing prayers over their patients and administering posh as medicine. It was certainly Babylon in the eyes of a sophisticated European priest. Nowadays, the church is virtually empty except on Sundays when tourists are ushered through. The floor has been paved but is still covered with pine needles, a symbol of purification that invariably accompanies even civil ceremonies.)

While lamenting, Padre Polo had the consolation of knowing that the training of catechists was going well. In June 1969, the first group of 30 was formed for a course lasting 15 days. A little later, four young men were sent to the Marist seminary to be trained as sub-deacons—the first step toward the formation of an autochthonous clergy. A summation issued in April 1969 reported 830 "Christians," 15 catechists, one ceremonial temple and five centers for open-air meetings where there were no chapels. The catechists met every three months to review progress and plan for the future—a further indication of indigenous leadership in the making.

Now the caciques acted. In September 1969, Padre Polo was denounced for disparaging the gods, for introducing people from outside the region and for building forbidden chapels. In October, he was given a month to get out of Chamula. A mob of 200 persons shouted for his expulsion and there were muttered threats: "We are going to kill you. You are an evangelist and a Protestant."

Father Polo did not wait for the ultimatum to expire. On October 26, he announced the withdrawal of his mission, saying, "There will remain a church without a priest and it will return to the control of curanderos and witches." The following November 19, the Mexico City newspaper *Excelsior* reported: "Most of the people celebrated a new triumph over *los conquistatores.*"

On January 1, Ruiz retaliated with an announcement that baptisms would only be administered at the church of La Caridad in San Cristobal. The following June, it was announced that no baptisms would be administered without preliminary instruction in the faith. The notice read: "The people of Chamula speak of Christ but do not know him. They ask for the baptism of their children but they do not ask for the sacrament of baptism. It is a rite imposed by custom that has degenerated into superstition."

To teach the "true Christian religion," Catholics were told that baptism would be administered only to families who had been evangelized by the catechists. For others, the meaning of the sacrament would be explained in Tzotzil by a catechist, who would then "administer the sacrament, but only to those who had changed their attitude and were disposed to receive the Word of God." To make sure they understood what they were doing, parents and godparents had to come to La Caridad for four successive Sundays for instructions.

To cap it all, the diocese struck directly at cacique political power. Although Padre Polo had left, his catechists were still in the field. With their support, an opposition candidate, Professor Mariano Gomez Lopez, was elected municipal president for the 1971–73 term. In April, only a few months after his election, he asked Father Leopoldo to return to baptize during Holy Week. He did, and for the next three years returned every Sunday and on Holy Days to administer baptisms and the sacraments. During these years, as Reverend Iribarren later wrote, "Christian leaders intensified their work as catechists and enjoyed all liberty." Intensive courses for catechists were held in the seminary in San Cristobal. "First we form the apostles. Then they form the communities," Iribarren noted.

With the help of Dominicans and Brothers of the Divine Shepherd, catechists, using their own houses for meetings, became strong in 10 communities. A chapel was built with a loan from a state bank and a health clinic (with two-month courses) was organized with help from Oxfam and Catholic Charities. There were also housekeeping courses for women. When Cardinal Angelo Rossi visited Chamula, the large doors of the church were opened wide and he entered in a procession accompanied by principales with their batons of office and bands with drums, strings and flutes.

Meanwhile, Father Polo prepared for the next elections. In August and November 1972, he sponsored leadership courses, paid for by Catholic Relief Services. The first course lasted three days, and the second for 10 days. In the early months of 1973, he had four courses of 10 days to study the Constitution, public offices and their functions, rights and obligations of students and guarantees of individual rights. He discussed the courses in a letter written in March 1973:

> This was of great interest for the leaders, especially in this year, because of the triennial elections ... We devoted most of the time to study ways to channel government programs in favor of indigenous collectives for agriculture and for betterment of the lives of the peo-

ple. The leaders need to discover community action, so that they can, more urgently, take action together to develop concientization and to direct this toward true growth.

Father Polo's boldest stroke was to sponsor an opposition candidate from the National Action Party (PAN) for the 1974 municipal elections. When the votes were counted, his candidate won with 1,628 votes, as against 425 for the cacique's candidate. For the PRI, this was unthinkable and insupportable. It was bad enough that an opposition candidate should gain a toehold in their traditional stronghold, but for him to come from their national rival—the PAN—was the crack of doom. The PRI manipulated a new election, and, with massive help from INI, had the results declared invalid. A new election was called and the votes were counted in such a way that the PRI won, returning Chamula to the fold. When the PRI candidate was installed in office, he was surrounded by soldiers and INI officials. Seven persons bold enough to stand up to denounce the robbery of votes were arrested and taken to the municipal jail to cool off.

The catechists, however, were still not ready to admit defeat. They asked the PAN to intervene. It obliged by setting up an office in the cabecera. In August, the governor warned that if the people continued to follow PAN there would be no further state projects in Chamula. Father Polo was asked to come to the Chamula ceremonial center to conciliate. When he arrived, a cacique-inspired mob beat his car and punctured its tires.

On November 1, All Souls' Day, all men identified as members of the opposition were called to the cabecera and beaten while mobs went to their houses, stripped them of possessions and burned them. On November 6, chapels in the communities of Yalhichin, Majomuth and Bautista Chico were totally destroyed. Finally, about 200 men, women and children were loaded into PRODECH trucks and dumped on the outskirts of San Cristobal.

There were fitful peace negotiations in 1975, and, for a while, priests and nuns returned to Chamula for the traditional saints' festivals and for baptisms. Later, when a letter was sent to the caciques asking for another agreement on the return of priests and nuns, it was ignored.

The following year was one of the most violent. From August 15–25, 1976, 600 men, women and children were rounded up and loaded into PRODECH trucks that were clearly labeled as gifts of the United Nations. They were taken in convoys, with federal soldiers in the lead, and dumped before the offices of PRODECH in San Cristobal, to be later funneled into refugee colonies.

There was no doubt of the government's complicity, with PRODECH as the instrument. On October 4, a group of priests and nuns sent an open letter via the newspapers, saying: "We are 1,750 people exiled in different parts of San Cristobal. We want PRODECH and the Chamulan authorities to allow us to return to our houses and our communities. We want respect for the right to live in peace. PRODECH wants to send us to the *tierra caliente* [hot lowlands] only to die."

There were public demonstrations in San Cristobal on October 21, 22 and 30, then another, in Tuxtla Gutierrez, on November 3, in which two men were killed in a clash with police. A note was sent to the newspapers, which said: "They have killed two of our companions, and the killers have not been punished and we have been told by the judicial police that we should not keep making complaints." A notice was given that, on November 18, some of the expelled would return on their own. When they did, they were beaten and held in jail for five days without food. The INI said it could not allow them to starve so they were again loaded into the UN-supplied trucks and dumped back in San Cristobal.

In December, the government had a meeting with two representatives each from the Catholics, Presbyterians and Seventh-Day Adventists who had been expelled on August 15. They reviewed what had happened and called for a new meeting at the end of January 1977—this time along with representatives of the PRI caciques of Chamula and agents from all its communities. The hope was to agree on the return of those expelled and a guarantee of their constitutional right to freedom of religion. The meeting never took place.

This became the scenario for the next 20 years. There were more expulsions in 1977, more requests for peace dialogues, more promises, more letters, more replies and still nothing happened. Bishop Ruiz finally admitted defeat: He announced that all priests and catechists would be withdrawn, thus ending the presence of the Catholic Church in Chamula. In 1980, Pablo Iribarren ended his review of *Misión Chamula* with the lessons learned:

> The caciques control the economy, the services and the commerce of the municipality. The caciques, in conjunction with official organs (INI, PRODECH) control political power through state organizations such as health and education. The caciques control the ideology of Chamula, its economic interests, its cultural values, and its customs. Because of their control of civil authority and the civil cargos, the caciques' control extends from the municipal center to all the communities. Today we can see clearly that in Chamula religion is subordinate to and sustains the economic system. The Chamula authorities fight so they will not lose control of the Church, because the community has not lost its faith in it. They also fight to control, through the Church, a great part of the economic structure. To control ideology is to control all the social, economic and political life of Chamula.

The diocese made a final attempt to negotiate a settlement in mid-1982, when Dominicans and Brothers of the Divine Shepherd, who had maintained an interest in Chamula since 1966, formed a "Committee for the defense of those threatened, persecuted and expelled from Chamula." Although priests and nuns had been withdrawn from Chamula, there were still catechists living quietly, evangelizing in their communities. Now they became active again, and organized popular support within Chamula for the committee's efforts. Gaspar Morquecho, the historian of these events, described what happened. (His account is abridged):

> The Committee wanted to denounce the cacique aggression and sought an audience with Juan Sabines, the governor. The Bureau of Indigenous Affairs [INI] offered its help in obtaining the audience, but on the condition that no complaint would be filed. This showed the

political role that Indigenous Affairs played. The meeting was held in October in Tuxtla Gutierrez with wide press coverage. Five hundred Indians went with members of the Defense Committee and Dominican priests and met with the governor and all of his cabinet. They pleaded their right to live on the lands where they were born and called for religious peace. They said they would respect San Juan and the good customs of the municipality, but they wanted an end to persecutions, jailings, fines and forced signatures on documents, the imposition of religious cargos and guarantees for their safety in the face of death threats. All of this was put down in writing. Juan Sabines affirmed that he was not in accord with the expulsions, but said he had to respect Chamulan customs and offered the expelled land outside their munic-ipality. At first, the expelled rejected it, saying that they would not "sell their liberty." However, after thinking it over, they thought it best to accept the land because they realized they would never be allowed to return to their communities. The caciques returned to San Juan to celebrate, saying they had "won the war." The government's response was clearly help for the Chamula caciques. With this, the catechists finally withdrew from the problem of the expelled of Chamula.[6]

It was an extraordinary development: the diocese was surrendering its obliga-tion to evangelize and to comfort those who were persecuted for their faith. Evangelicals were left—alone and exposed—to teach the Bible and to suffer the consequences. It took several years for the caciques to find a way to replace the Roman Catholic Church, but eventually they did in the person of a former priest, married, with children, who lived in Tuxtla and called himself Bishop of the "Orthodox Church of San Pascualito." This had no connection with the Orthodox Church of Eastern Europe. In reply to a questionnaire from the diocese, the bishop said he had been consecrated in a community in the state of Veracruz in January 1959, but left the Roman Catholic church in 1965, after which he served in various churches in Veracruz and Guatemala.

In July 1984, he was welcomed to the cabecera by an estimated 5,000 people and was given a gold cross valued at 1.5 million pesos. After that, he came to baptize, per-form marriages and serve mass every two weeks and on festival days, using tortillas and posh for the Eucharist. He remained until August 1994, when Bishop Ruiz nego-tiated a compromise with the caciques. The Orthodox Bishop was dismissed and Bishop Felipe Aguirre, of the Tuxtla Gutierrez diocese, appointed a conservative Tzotzil speaking priest, Gonsalvo Lopez, to attend the religious needs of Chamula Catholics. However, it amounted to little more than making a presence, since the caciques would not let Lopez do more than celebrate mass and perform baptisms.[7]

6 1992. 26–27. **7** Jeffrey (1997).

6
THE FIRST TZOTZIL MARTYR

Several evangelicals were murdered in the early years of the new faith among the indigenous people of Chiapas, but none was as defiant of the persecutors as Miguel Gomez Hernandez. When he was tortured and killed, thousands of Tzotzils mourned, and he came to be known as the First Tzotzil Martyr. What little we know of his early history we owe to a short article by the anthropologist Gary Gossen, in which he calls him the "founder and leader of the post-1965 Protestant movement of San Juan Chamula." As he wrote: "This biography developed over the 20 years of my association with the Harvard Chiapas Project as an almost clandestine undertaking, for any public association with Tzotzil Protestants would not have been politically appropriate for me in my dealings with Chamulan traditionalists with whom I had friendships and good working relationships. My association with the Chamula Protestant Movement has never been open or close, yet my interest has been nothing short of intense, for it was hard to hear hymns that I had known as a child in Kansas translated to Tzotzil and sung with the abandon of a full-blown revival, without feeling some deep sense of *dejá vu.*"[1]

Miguel "Kashlan" Gomez Hernandez

Miguel Gomez was born in 1912 in a community near the ceremonial center of San Juan Chamula. His parents died shortly after his birth and he was raised by a paternal uncle. When he was eight, he was sent to Chamula's first (and later to be destroyed by the rising breed of new caciques) public school. He was such an excellent student that he was given the honor of raising the flag when the school was visited in 1922 by an official of the federal Ministry of Education. The visitor was so impressed by the scholarship, in Spanish, of an indigenous boy, and so appalled by the boy's tattered clothing, that he gave him a complete new outfit in European style, including his first shoes.

With this clothing, Miguel earned the appellation of "Kashlan," the Tzotzil pronunciation of *castellano* (Spanish). Kashlan is often translated as Mestizo but this mistakes the intent. Kashlan, from the Tzotzil point of view, is a cultural designation, not a genetic reference.

In 1925, he went to a secondary school in Tuxtla Gutierrez and there perfected his command of Spanish. There too, at the age of 15, he met and took as his wife a girl from an exile Chamula family. Among the indigenous peoples, such liaisons were (and are) casual affairs. When he was 17, he left his wife to study in Mexico City. How he managed this—who paid for his clothing and travel and who sponsored him—Gossen does not say.

He lived, and presumably worked, in Mexico City for the next six years, until he fell ill and was given an injection that temporarily left him paralyzed in one arm.

---

1 (1989): 217.

In 1931, he returned to San Juan Chamula and his uncle allowed him to farm land that had been his parent's but which, as was the custom, had reverted to the uncle. Miguel took a second wife and they became potters and had six children. Not different from other Highland men, he drank heavily and beat his wife so that there was little money to feed and clothe his children. The youngest ran around nude.

In 1940, he left his wife and children to the care of his uncle and went to work in the coffee plantations of the Pacific lowlands. Again, his early promise showed itself: at one plantation where he frequently worked he was made a foreman. In 1947, he returned to Chiapas to work as a day laborer on the Pan American Highway, then under construction to link San Cristobal and the Guatemalan border. During these years he took another wife, this one from the neighboring municipality of Zinacantan.

In 1951, when the highway work ended, Miguel Kashlan returned to his second family in Chamula. In traditional households, there was a separate structure of piled stones where water could be boiled for a steam bath. One day, while Miguel was sweating some of the poisons out of his system, he had a vision. A spirit called him to a new career as a shaman.[2]

By then, the evangelicals had reached Chamula in the person of Domingo Hernandez Aguilar, Miguel's brother-in-law. In 1952, Domingo, who previously was known as a curandero under the name Domingo Max (pronounced Mash), enrolled in a Spanish-language adult school in San Cristobal where he met a Presbyterian Chol named Cristobal Trujillo Diaz, who persuaded him to join a Sunday School that met next to the Presbyterian Church on National Army Street. Domingo Hernandez had attended the school every Sunday for a year without telling anyone in his community where he was going.

In 1953, he finally told Miguel Kashlan what he was doing. Kashlan knew of the Bible—he had met evangelicals on the coffee plantations—but it had not interested him. Domingo Hernandez worked as a gardener in the house of Kenneth Jacobs and his wife Elaine, a Summer Institute of Linguistics team who were just beginning to translate the Gospel of Luke into the Chamula Tzotzil dialect.

Domingo Hernandez had been given a Spanish-language Bible at his Sunday School. One day, Jacobs came upon the two in his garden discussing the Bible and began asking them questions about the translation of Spanish phrases into Tzotzil. In turn, they began to learn how to preach in Tzotzil. When they became evangelicals, their lives changed: they no longer took alcohol or smoked and were outwardly sedate and serious. Others asked what had caused these changes and slowly a congregation began to form, including Domingo Max. In 1956, when they were about a dozen, there was a threat that the house where they met would be burned.

Miguel Kashlan made a formal complaint to the Attorney General's office in San Cristobal. The assistant director of the INI in San Cristobal was Manuel Castellanos Cancino, who would later protect the Tzotzils of Chimtic. The complaint had its effect. When the caciques of Chamula were told to ensure that Constitutional protections were enforced, the mystique of Miguel Kashlan began to form. His neighbors and friends saw him as someone with spiritual power: under God's protection. Little by little, they stopped calling him Kashlan. He became *Jmol* (Elder) Miguel.

2 At this point Gossen's detailed history ends. From here on his story is drawn from Esponda (1986) and Lopez Meza (1992).

When some came still thinking he was a curandero, he told them they could be cured without spending money on candles, posh and chickens. Jmol Miguel and the small congregation gathered over the sick and prayed. They said if the sick man or woman believed in the Word of God and gave up posh and tobacco and lived good family lives, they would be permanently cured. There were cures and new believers.

In March 1965, by which time the evangelical community had grown to 35 they were called to the Chamula municipal office to explain what they were doing. They said they sang hymns to God, prayed, read the Bible and did no harm. Their explanation was not accepted. The municipal president and council ordered them to abandon their faith and threatened to kill them if they disobeyed.

In 1966, (the same year that Padre Polo began *Misión Chamula*) the houses of evangelicals were burned in three communities. The believers fled to San Cristobal. All, except Miguel Kashlan, were permitted to return and were promised legal protection. Kashlan, with his knowledge of Spanish, found work in a hotel. By then, a small Tzotzil congregation had been formed in San Cristobal. On Sundays, it met in the compound of SIL translator Kenneth Jacobs, with Kashlan as its pastor.

In 1967, when the number of evangelicals in Chamula had grown to more than 100, the small wooden house of Pascuala Lopez Hernandez was set on fire. As she fled through the door she was hit by a blast of shotgun pellets. She managed to escape but two nephews and a niece, were killed. (Her narration of this incident and her subsequent history will be told in the next chapter.) Other houses in several communities were burned and the believers fled in fear to San Cristobal, where they took sanctuary in Jacobs' compound.

After a complaint to the authorities in San Cristobal was ignored, Kashlan led a small delegation to Mexico City. He returned with a letter from the Secretary of State ordering the governor of Chiapas and the municipal president of Chamula to allow the evangelicals to return to their communities. The deaths of the three children in the attack on Pascuala's house had drawn international attention. Moreover, a fourth badly scarred girl was taken on a tour of the United States to call further attention to the persecution. Manuel Castellanos Cancino was still the director of the Bureau of Indigenous Affairs in San Cristobal. He quietly let it be known that any further violence against the evangelists would be severely published. There was peace for seven years and the numbers of evangelicals grew until there were about 1,200 believers in 18 communities.

Then came Padre Polo's political attacks on cacique rule. After the first victory of an opposition candidate, Manuel Castellanos Cancino, who had done so much to protect the evangelicals, was replaced by two lawyers who sided with the caciques and, with government help, the victorious PAN candidate was ousted and those who campaigned against the PRI were arrested and deported. Miguel Kashlan, as the only evangelical with wide experience outside Chamula, had supported the PAN candidate and had filed a complaint with the Supreme Court in Mexico City. In January 1975, the court sent a letter to the governor of Chiapas saying that it had nothing to do with Kashlan's charges.

Since there were far fewer catechists and new Catholic believers in Chamula, almost all of those who had been rounded up and trucked away when the mass expulsions began were evangelicals. Miguel Kashlan advised believers that it was a waste of time and energy to petition the authorities for their safe return to Chamula and it was decided to buy a place where they could build permanent homes. Funds were raised to buy, on extended payments, about 10 acres of land at the foot of the mountain on the northern outskirts of San Cristobal and there the community of *Nueva Esperanza* (New Hope) was built.

The expulsions continued and so did the increase in number of new believers. Many left simply because they were afraid. In 1978, a new community was started on the Pan American Highway about 15 miles south of San Cristobal. It was called *Betania.*

Since threats and expulsions did not end evangelical growth, the caciques decided they must get rid of Jmol Miguel. First, he was accused of murder. A Chamulan was paid half a million pesos to a file a charge that Miguel had once killed someone. He was arrested, but, at the first hearing before a judge, the accuser confessed that the authorities of San Juan Chamula had paid him to file the charge. Miguel Kashlan was absolved and continued his ministry.

Next, he was ambushed in an arroyo between San Cristobal and Chamula. Several shots were fired, but they missed. Then there was a roadside ambush. Three gunmen pointed pistols. One aimed at his head, the other two at his body. When they pulled the triggers, none of the guns fired. The attackers fled. In the next attempt, people who lived near his house were incited to surround him and kill him. Miguel, seeing the people gathering, dressed as a woman and walked out his front door with a *rebozo* (scarf) covering his head.

All this was seen as proof that he was under the protection of God. On Sundays, greater and greater crowds came from Chamula to the church that had been con-structed in Nueva Esperanza to share the blessing of the new faith. One day, a man named Pedro Acobal sent word to the hotel where Miguel worked saying that he wanted to see him about some property. He was the Judas. On July 24, 1981, at about one in the afternoon, Acobal was standing on the street as Miguel approached. As they met, Acobal's brother and three others jumped out of a taxi and seized him. He struggled and threw two of the men to the ground but the others forced him into the taxi and it sped off.

A woman from Nueva Esperanza happened to be passing and telephoned a friend to say what had happened. The man jumped on his motorcycle and raced to Chamula, where he found the taxi. He detained three of the assailants but Miguel had been removed. It was later learned that he had been gagged and thrown on the floor of the taxi. When he continued to struggle, they stabbed him with an ice pick.

He was taken first to the municipal hall of San Juan Chamula and then to the house of Javier Lopez Perez, the son of Salvador Tushum, the richest and most ruthless of Chamula's caciques. It was Tushum who had paid the half-million pesos to bring the false murder charge against Miguel.

Miguel was first tortured. He was scalped with a machete and then the skin was pulled from his face. His right eye was gouged out and his tongue and nose were cut off. He was also emasculated. His body (no one knows if he was dead or alive by that time) was taken to a mountain and hanged from a tree. Because the search had started promptly, his body was found and retrieved the same day.

Three days later his coffin was carried in a procession through the main square of San Cristobal. An estimated 4,000 of the expelled followed it to the cemetery. Three of his assailants were tried and sentenced to prison. His brutal murder did not stop evangelical growth in San Juan Chamula.

Pascuala, at the age of 20, before the murder attempt

7

Pascuala's Story

Pascuala Lopez Hernandez was one of the first Tzotzils of Chamula to follow Miguel Kashlan and paid a heavy price. In 1967, her house was burned, and she was shot and seriously wounded but survived. A girl also survived, but three other children were killed. More than any other, Pascuala symbolizes both the willingness of evangelicals to risk their lives for their faith and their courage in rebuilding their lives after being persecuted. Pascuala told her story as we sat in the kitchen of her general store and restaurant in the colony of Betania.

* * * * *

I am originally from the community of Zactzu in San Juan Chamula. My mother taught me to adore idols and *j'ilols* [shamans] who use candles, chickens, money and liquor to cure people. My mother and father died when I was young and I was left with two sisters. In 1967, I was living with my older sister, Rosa, and her five children. My nephew and nieces often got sick and were taken to a j'ilol. By this time, Rosa had lost three children and now a son was very sick. Rosa thought the boy was about to die because he could not nurse at her breast. There was a j'ilol named Domingo Max [monkey: indigenous people often had a duel name, including that of an animal]. When my sister took the boy to Domingo Max, he said, "Rosa, I'm not a j'ilol any more. I don't cure people with candles, chickens, money or posh. I am an evangelical. If you want your son to be cured, I can ask God to do it. He can heal him."

Domingo Max put the child down on a comfortable mat. He prayed once. Nothing happened. He prayed twice. Still nothing happened, but after a third prayer the child stirred and reached for her breast to feed. After that, Rosa began to believe. Domingo Max told her of a preacher in San Cristobal and she went there and joined his meetings and learned about God.

At that time, because I did not have a father or mother, I had gone to the *tierra caliente* to look for work. When I returned, Rosa was a Christian and she told me what had happened. To her, everything seemed so beautiful: the songs, the friendship and the advice. She said the preacher was from the community of Yalnunacash but was now living in San Cristobal and that his name was Miguel Kashlan.

I went with her one day and liked the message so much I went to the meetings every Sunday, even though my community was three hours [by foot] from the city. I stopped drinking posh and tried to live a better life. Brother Miguel warned us of danger. He said people in Chamula did not like evangelicals and might even try to kill us. He also said if God did not allow it, the people could not do us harm. I listened to his warning, but I felt a great desire to tell people about my new life and about God. I was not afraid.

We had an aunt whose name was Maria. She was a j'ilol in our community and people used to call her to different places for cures. I met her on the road one day. She had injured her leg when she was drunk and fell down. I said I knew an evangelical man in San Cristobal who could cure her with the Word of God. She became angry and asked, "Have you become an evangelical?"

I said I loved God and that God does not want money or alcohol or chickens. Only prayer can cure. I said my sister's son had been made well by prayer. And so time passed. Since she went to different places she heard what people were saying. One day Maria said to me: "Pashcu, be careful. People are going around saying they are going to burn down your house. Cashtuli, (that was the name of a man in a community about two kilometers away) has already bought two drums of gasoline." But I was not frightened. I heard the Word of God from Pastor Miguel. He said Jesus Christ had also suffered and had died on the Cross for our sins and that we will also suffer if we take *trago* [liquor] as medicine and believe in idols. He said, "People who do not love the Word of God may try to kill us but *El Señor* also suffered." I was not afraid because I was sure it was like Brother Miguel Kashlan said: "If God does not want them to kill me they will not be able to."

We loved and had faith in Brother Miguel. He helped us a great deal when we were in San Cristobal. We were about 20 believers. We went out at night to the hills to pray to God to help the people of Chamula and to make more of them believers. He carried a Bible. One night he would take us to one hill, the next night to another hill and on the third night to a third hill. Brother Kashlan almost never slept. If we fell asleep he would say: "Get up! Let us pray to God. Let us pray and not sleep!"

We knew that when he was young he was a bad man. He worked on fincas and drank but when he heard the Word of God he changed his life. He did not drink posh and came to San Cristobal with his family. After he was killed, and his body was carried through the city for burial, no one could pass through the Zocalo, it was so full of people. They asked: "Who has died? Was he a priest. Was he a king? Why are there are so many people?" He was not a king or a priest. He was just a good man. He helped people with food, medicine and houses and preached everywhere. For this reason, all believers came to his funeral.

After I got home, I told my nephew and nieces what aunt Maria had said and we started praying as we had been taught. We also fasted for three days. On Friday, I gathered some firewood to sell the next day in San Cristobal because on Saturdays Brother Miguel would teach us and read the Bible to us and, I would stay in the city for the regular Sunday meeting.

Friday night we sang a hymn, prayed, and lay down to sleep peacefully. My nephew and three little nieces lived with me because their mothers were widows and had gone away to look for work. At about midnight or one o'clock (we did not have a clock so I do not know exactly at what time), a dog began to bark many times. I called out, "Who is there?" I got up, and, through the bars on the door, I could see a light outside and another coming from the back of the house. I realized they had set fire to one corner of the house, and, because the roof was made of *jovel* [dried grass], the fire quickly spread.

I opened the door, and two men were standing there. They shot me, and I felt like I was being covered with hot water. I did not have any clothes on. It was then our custom to sleep without clothes. I grabbed a blanket and shouted to the children, "Get out." I was shot but did not fall. I ran out and the man who shot me tried to grab me but could not because I fell in a hole. I crawled to a field and became unconscious. The last thing I remember was looking back and seeing the house on fire.

After a while, I woke up but could not walk. I felt tired and felt as if warm water was running over my body. I then realized this was blood. I felt I was going to die. There was blood all over my face and arms and body. I began to crawl on my hands and knees to try to reach the house of a Brother named Salvador, but it was about a kilometer away and my arms could not move any more. I found an abandoned house and decided to stay there until daylight. I was sleeping and could not go on. Then I called out to God and could feel Him giving me strength. I got up and began to walk. I became thirsty as if my throat was plugged. Sometimes I fell and then crawled. Sometimes I had to pull myself forward by grabbing at grass.

Finally, I reached the house. I knocked on the door, but they did not want to let me in. I called out, "It's me, Pashcu. Open the door." They were frightened when they saw me without clothes and covered with blood. They gave me something to cover myself and something to drink. Little by little, I calmed down and told them what had happened. They asked me what had happened to the children and I said I did not know.

Brother Salvador went to find Brother Domingo to help to decide what to do. He returned with four other Brothers and they prayed for me. Each time, I could feel God giving me peace and strength. They decided to carry me on a sort of stretcher but my entire body felt so painful it hurt if someone touched me so I said I would walk. We walked for three hours. At eight in the morning, we arrived at the house of Brother Miguel in San Cristobal. My face was swollen so I could not see, and I was still bleeding. Brother Miguel took me to the Ministry of Public Affairs to make a legal report. We were very worried about the four children. They asked me many questions and then I was put in a hospital. The doctors found 21 bits of shotgun pellets in my face, neck and arms. Ministry of Public Affairs officers and officials of San Juan Chamula then went to examine the house.

They found little Domingo, who was 10, with his head cut off in the *Baño Temazcal* [steam bath]. It seemed he was trying to hide there and they found him. Little Dominga, who was 12, was found in the house almost completely burned up. Angelina, who was seven, was found unconscious. One of her arms had been hacked with a machete and she had other wounds on her body. Angela was four. Her skull has been split by blows of a machete. She was barely alive and died on the way to the hospital. Angelina was also alive and was taken to a hospital where she recuperated and is still alive.

There were three men responsible for the murders. One was tried, convicted, and sent to jail for three years. Another was sentenced to only six months. The third escaped completely. The president of San Juan Chamula said he knew nothing about the crimes. Other people said they were not sorry and that more believers should be expelled, killed, or burned.

I was in a hospital and recovered quickly. My greatest pain was the murder of my nephew and two nieces. I felt so sad I wanted to die, but I prayed and, little by little, became peaceful. After I left the hospital, the doctors said I should return to have more of the pellets removed, but I had enough of hospitals. I still have bits of metal in my face and chest. I married the man who was my fiancé in Chamula and worked for 19 years as a maid at a church [SIL] residence in San Cristobal while my husband worked on the coffee plantations. We earned little and could not save money but when the Americans left for the United States they gave us eight hectares [about 20 acres] of land worth 400 pesos near Ocosingo in the tierra caliente. My husband grew oranges and vegetables, but prices were low. He also grew corn, but we still had little to eat and little money to buy food.

We had three daughters and then a son. I was not used to the tierra caliente. I became sick and sweated a lot and lost more than 15 kilos. People told me not to work so hard, but we needed money. I had to sell my woolen Chamula skirt and *huipil* [traditional blouse]. I had no energy so we thought we should return to San Cristobal. We sold our land and bought a small plot in Nueva Esperanza. Then we sold that and bought a larger piece of land here in Betania, where my husband's father and mother lived. Here we planted corn and beans. This gave us just enough to eat but we still had no money. My husband wanted to go to the tierra caliente to work on a farm, as he used to do, but his back hurts him and he can't do hard work. Besides, I needed his help with the children.

The girls were going to school and needed money for pencils and workbooks. We couldn't afford the school supplies so we made some *chicharrones* [fried pork skin] for the girls to sell outside the school for the other students to eat at lunch time. I also made tortillas to sell in San Cristobal. I had only a small mill to grind the corn. I got up at two o'clock in the morning to grind the corn and went to San Cristobal at half past six. My husband dressed the children to send them to school. At recess, they came home for the chicharrones to sell to the other children. One day, they stole some money to buy candy. The school committee got very angry and would not let them sell chicharrones any more, but they were allowed to sell tortillas.

One day in winter, when it was cold, I began to feel very sick from the labor of grinding corn for the tortillas. I still have bullets in my body and I felt a strong pain in my back. I could not work and we had no money. Our land was up on a hill. I thought if we had land near the highway we could sell things there and I would not have to get up so early to go to San Cristobal. We had saved some money from my work selling tortillas. There was a piece of land without a house owned by a Brother who lived in San Cristobal. We bought it for 540 pesos. My husband cleared it and cut away part of the hill to serve as the back wall of our house.

My children were hungry and asked for chicken soup. I prayed to God: "Please help me." Just then there was some work at the school. They asked my husband to help unload some things. He did that and they paid him two pesos. He gave me the money and said: "The children want chicken. Buy some chicken heads because they are the cheapest things in the market." At that time we had only a small market in Betania so I went to San Cristobal to buy the chicken heads.

The next thing that happened was this: We knew an American missionary in San Cristobal named *Esteban* [Steven]. He hired my husband to work two days a week washing windows, cutting the grass and other things. When I was on my way to the market to buy the chicken heads, I began to think: "We will always be poor and never have enough to eat." I began to pray again. God is merciful. I remembered there was a Brother who lived on Almolonga Street in San Cristobal who sold live chickens. I went to him and asked if he would sell me chickens on credit. He said he could not do that, but he would sell me chickens at the cheapest price. He had no chickens then and told me to come back. I prayed three times and went to Brother Esteban's house that afternoon. I asked him to lend me money. He asked me what I wanted it for. I told him to buy chickens. I said nobody was selling chickens in Betania and I had a piece of land near the highway where I could sell them.

He said, "Come next Monday." I went and he lent me 30 pesos. The next day, I went to the Brother who was selling chickens and he said he would he would bring 30 chickens to my house but, with the cost of transport, I would have to give him 33 pesos. I said I only had 30 and he agreed to give me credit for the rest.

I began to pray about how I could repay all that money, but in five days all the chickens were sold and I had a small profit. One of the Brothers here in Betania told me, "If you had a small profit it shows you are able to earn more. Don't be bashful. Ask for more chickens." He took out his wallet and lent me some money. I used it to buy even more chickens and again sold them all. I had enough money to pay back Brother Esteban but I used it to buy a scale. I went to him and told him what I had done and how I had made a small profit. He said I could repay the 30 pesos by giving him two chickens a week.

We then regularly bought and sold chickens. My daughters wanted to eat some, but we never ate any, not even a leg or a neck. My husband began to break up stones and we made a better house. I put a small table under a tree and I bought things to sell like soda, fruit, sugar, or eggs. My daughters wanted to drink some of the soda, but I told them no. I gave them rotten fruit to eat so there would be more profit.

My husband broke more stone and built a small store. I told him to put up brackets and I sold candies and gum. I sold many different things like mangos and oranges, but I never sold liquor or beer or cigarettes. I also bought meat here and sold it in Teopisca: at first three kilos each Saturday, then five, then 10 and then more.

A Brother came to visit us and lent us 200 pesos so we could build a bigger house as part of the store so I could watch the children while I was in the store. We also built a kitchen and a room to serve food. My daughters cooked the food and served the customers. We also borrowed money to buy a refrigerated display case to sell cold sodas and frozen ice sticks. Now if we need money we can borrow it with no trouble

My son is now in high school here. As we made more profit, we bought more land here and then we bought eight hectares in the tierra caliente. We have a store there and orange and lemon trees. We also grow corn and vegetables. It was a three-hour bus trip, but then we bought a car. Then we sold that, and we now have a three-ton pickup truck. The fruit and vegetables we grow there we sell here in Betania. Some people say our lemons are the best in any market. We sell fruit and vegetables from here in our store in the tierra caliente. Sometimes my husband works in the fields there. When he grows corn he is happy remembering how we began. God is good.

8

HOW EVANGELISM GROWS

Salvador Patishtan Diaz was among the earliest of the evangelicals expelled from San Juan Chamula. He is the pastor of the church *El Puerto del Cielo* (The Gate of Heaven) in *La Hormiga*, the largest of the refugee colonies along the northern Ring Road. I kept trying to see him but he never seemed to be at the church. Finally, I came on a day when I was assured he would be there and he was, but when I told him who I was and what I wanted to talk with him about, he said he was busy. Still, he took out a large monthly calendar to search for free time. He explained he was not only the pastor at this church but also at a church called La *Nueva Palestina* (The New Palestine) in San Cristobal and at the church of *Jesus El Buen Pastor* (Jesus, the Good Shepherd) in the settlement of Vistahermosa, where he lived with his family. Furthermore, there were a number of missions and congregations that he was obliged to visit once a week. He could not find an opening in his schedule, but he said if I came to his home before eight o'clock in the morning we might talk for a while. Vistahermosa (beautiful view)—about 25 miles south on the Pan American Highway—lived up to its name: up a dirt road leading to a small hill with a sweeping view of cloudbanked mountains on one side and the wide, flat plain of Venustiano Carranza on the other. His church was small, seating perhaps 300 worshipers. There was also a primary school and basketball court. Pastor Patishtan lived a short distance away in a stone house built on the downward slope of the mountain. It appeared to have only two rooms, one of which he used as an office.

When we had met at his church in San Cristobal, I had noticed about a dozen women of various ages sitting quietly on the floor in the space before the platform and podium that served as an altar. Their hands were joined to form a circle. People talked and walked around them, but their eyes were closed in prayer and they seemed not to notice. I told Pastor Patishtan I wanted him to tell me about church growth, but asked him to first explain about the women in the circle.

✳ ✳ ✳ ✳ ✳

The power of the Lord was with them. They have faith that the Lord is near. They sit in a circle holding hands—a symbolic chain of faith in Jesus. This frees them from fear of death or persecution. They don't do this every day, or every week, only when they feel times of affliction or times of trial. They pray for their companions, but also for those who are outside. If they hear a report that a community is surrounded by bad people who want to kill a Brother, they form a circle and they pray to God. They ask His angels to go around to protect those who are sick and in danger of dying. They pray that people will not be afraid, even if someone comes with a high-powered gun. God doesn't work with guns. He works with power and with faith. That's how a person is saved—with faith.

Now I will tell you how the Word of God came to San Juan Chamula. It came first to a place called Bimiktum near the community of Nichen in the year 1964. People then didn't know if there was or wasn't a Bible, they only knew their cultures. Their cultures were everything. There were no Catholics or anything in San Juan Chamula. When they came to know the Gospel they were called Protestants, but they were not protesting. They were not against politicians. They did not want to harm anyone. They only wanted to believe. Are they not free to do so?

I finished the six years of grammar school and then, in 1974, I began to understand the Bible. I was the first in my community in Chamula to know the Lord. I began to talk to others, to read the scriptures and to pray. They asked, "How do you heal?" I said, "We have a book and here it says that the Lord heals. Listen to what it says. It is true."

I later studied at the Villahermosa Seminary, in Tabasco, and at a Getsemani Seminary in Tapachula; however, I can't say I am a professional, although I am now working with the Bible Society of Mexico on a translation of the Old Testament. We have almost finished it. Translators began with the New Testament. It was translated into the Tzotzil language of Chamula and afterward there was a translation in Tzotzil of Zinacantan. Much later, there was another translation in Tzotzil of Chenalho and another in the Tzotzil of Huixtan. They are all Tzotzil but there are certain slight differences in definitions so they are not the same. Today, each has the Bible in his own language. They are reading it in their churches. That's why in every place you see evangelicals.

Evangelical faith began in Chamula with Miguel Gomez Hernandez and his family, including his brother-in-law, Domingo Hernandez. They began to talk to their companions in the community and the effect of their believing was that others believed. It was not like a fool, who believes because of words. It was because they saw the effect. As the Scripture says, "Those who believe in the Lord will be saved."

At first, the Word left the others astonished. They didn't know if it was true, but they saw. The municipal president and his companions came one night to surround the house of Brothers Miguel and Domingo. They threw gasoline and they fired shots but the Brothers did not die. That's how the people could see the truth of what the Bible says, "The Lord protects those who believe." When they didn't die, many of the neighbors came to ask, "How was it that you didn't die? How was it that the house didn't burn if they threw gasoline and fire?"

Brother Miguel was known as Kashlan. He was once a bad man, but the Word of God says that if you want to live a long life on earth, do what the Lord says; behave as the Word says. Miguel began to believe. He began to humble himself in the way of the Lord. He changed little by little, to behave well and not do what his thoughts once told him to do. He changed little by little, because many of the new ones don't understand. That's why many say, "I don't know if the Word of God is true or not. It's something crazy." However, after a time, when they read, little by little, they come to understand. What is most important is that they ask the guidance of the Lord and the Lord gives light. He gives blessing and fills a person who desires it with His presence and fills him with the Spirit. The person who seeks perfects himself, not by himself but with the help of God.

God lives. We can't see Him but He lives. We believe. Evangelical faith has a real effect. It is not words of deceit. I have seen that God does exist. I have not seen His face, nor His size nor the color of God, but I have seen His power. In the past they wanted to kill me and now these same people believe in the Lord. They call me Brother; they don't call me enemy. They say: "Brother, forgive me because, when I didn't believe in God, I was ready on the road with a bullet to kill you. I saw you at a distance and I prepared my gun but, when you came near, I saw many persons. My hand began shaking. Then I felt strong, but you had already passed. That's how I came to know God is Great. Now we both believe in God. We are companions. Let's go to preach the Gospel."

There are two points that make people stronger in their belief. The first is when they come to know the Word doesn't lie. It keeps its promise. The second is that Jesus healed many sick people with no medicine and no curanderos. Only with faith were the sick healed. So they began to pray to God asking Him to heal the sick and protect them from perils and He keeps His word. Although many persons have gone to jail, and many have been beaten, most have not died, but some have. It isn't that a person will never die. A person has to die. That's the destiny God gave us. We know that the little children who were in Pascuala's house died, except one who was saved.

We are not looking for trouble. I came to believe the Gospel in 1974 and to this day I am not against the government nor am I against political parties. Our colony here in Vistahermosa is not a product of invasion. When we bought this land in November 1982, it was just a small wood. It is not large, only 60 hectares [about 150 acres]. We were six families. Now we are 130 families. We left Chamula at different times: first eight, then maybe 30 families, then 40 or 50. The number is not increasing now because many Brothers have returned to their communities even though there is not much peace.

Evangelical faith is growing because it is not only written in words like other documents—a story with no basis in facts—it is written in deeds. The Word of God has a base; it has value; it has an effect. That's why people come to us. We don't have to seek them out. They look for the Gospel themselves. In the afternoon and at night, they come and say, "We want to know. We want you to talk about the Gospel. We want to know how to receive it." It begins with one and then it spreads.

Now, I don't work much. I preach in the churches on Sundays and visit other congregations but it is the people themselves who are saying, "The Lord helps. He helps the poor, the sick and the afflicted. He protects everyone."

9
THE GROWTH OF THE TZOTZIL CHURCH

The expelled from Chamula and the other Highland municipalities have established thirty-six refugee colonies. Nineteen are on the Ring Road that runs along the northern edge of San Cristobal at the foot of a mountain that forms one side of a wide valley. Half the colonies are on the mountain side of the road and climb steeply up its slope. The other half are on the swampy southern side of the road. The remaining seventeen refugee colonies, including Betania and Vistahermosa, are strung out along the Pan American Highway, which leads to the municipality of Teopisca and on to Guatemala.

These colonies are what Puritan "Separatists" might have thought of as places of "Purity." They also resemble the democratic social structures devised by the Puritans to preserve their individualistic, yet communitarian, way of life. This is not to imply that evangelical societies in Chiapas are clones of Puritan structures. They are a reformulation of the cargos through which traditional societies divided civic, social and religious responsibilities.

The first church for the expelled is the Presbyterian Church of the Divine Savior in Nueva Esperanza, with Salvador Lopez Lopez as its pastor. The church is huge, with row after row of plain wooden pews, and can seat about 1,000 worshipers. Except for its size, the Puritans might have nodded in approval. It is utterly plain, with bare concrete-block walls and not a single decoration: not even a cross. The altar is simply a platform with a podium, enlivened only by vases of flowers.

A dusty press release, dated March 6, 1990, is posted amid a jumble of papers on a notice board in the entrance vestibule. It was issued after a meeting of Baptist, Methodist and Presbyterian leaders at Los Piños, the official Mexico City residence of Mexican presidents, with the then-President Carlos Salinas de Gortari. It seems to have been tacked on the gesture of faith in government promises. That it remains is an ironic reminder of the many blank shots fired by the Mexican government to give the sound, but not the substance, of a resolve to end the expulsions. It says:

1. The doors of the Presidency are not closed to Protestants and will remain open in order to hold a frank and sincere dialogue.
2. We live in a world of continuous change. Our country has to change, but these changes must preserve human liberties, including the liberty of thought and the liberty of belief.
3. Mexico has begun to advance with the Solidarity Program in which we seek justice and liberty.
4. We live in a constitutional regime that must not change.
5. I welcome you to this meeting and the document you have given me. I take into account that we should treat religious matters seriously but in a profound national sense.
6. I am convinced that you, different from other religious expressions, do not cause problems for the state.

The principles of liberty of belief, secular education and separation of church and state are irreversible because what has been won with so much effort can not be ended. The Secretary of State has told the press that the Protestants do not put at risk national sovereignty. Rather, they help us in the formation of a more dynamic people.

Reading it, I thought of those who, subsequent to the meeting, would continued to be killed, beaten and expelled.

Pastor Lopez is a busy contractor. He lives down the street from the church in a small house with a courtyard of odds and ends of past jobs. Except on Sundays, he always seems to be dressed in paint- and dust-spattered work clothes. He had no set schedule, and so, after several fruitless attempts, I ambushed him one afternoon at the time when Mexicans eat the main meal of their day. He came late and said he was too busy to talk, but he agreed to see me at about the same time a day later. I was eager to hear him tell of his experiences, since he is a living bridge between Miguel Kashlan and the present day.

＊ ＊ ＊ ＊ ＊

In 1974, when I was 17, believers came to my community and talked to me about Jesus. They told me that God died for all men and said that only by believing in Christ can we be transformed. My father and I worked making alcohol. We used to sell it in the municipal center to all the officials in the ceremonies. The believers told me to accept Christ: to finish with all the evil of liquor. I believed, and they gave me a leaflet. I read and read and began talking to my father and mother and all my family. I told them that Jesus Christ is good. He changes the lives of men. My father accepted Christ and sold his posh factory, and we worked our fields, cultivating lettuce and other vegetables. God changed our lives. He changed our minds. We no longer took part in fiestas or in beating people. We no longer divorced our wives, or robbed or cheated. We no longer accepted spiritualists or curanderos. We believed in the one true God, the only one who saves.

Before we accepted the Word of God, my father and I used to play the harp, the guitar, an accordion and traditional instruments while we drank. When I went with other believers, I played the guitar while we sang. We evangelized 36 families and 12 of those families accepted Christ. Then, in August 1976, the caciques authorized our expulsion. They put us in jail and some women were raped. When they took us to jail, they asked me to bring my guitar. Then, when they took us to San Cristobal, just at the outskirts, they took it and tore it apart. I was very sad.

Before we were taken away, we were made to sign some documents giving up our land and fruit trees. In another community, called Chiotic, a Brother named Childish was killed. His body was thrown into a river and has never been found. In the community of Muquem, they burned more than 20 small houses. The people lost their clothes, their belongings and the corn and beans in their fields. We didn't know where to go or what to do. It was difficult to start over. In the city, you have to buy food and wood for fires, but you need money and we had none. We suffered. Some of us took work as street sweepers and garbage collectors. Others made candies or ice cream to sell on the streets. Others worked as day laborers for construction work or went to fincas in the tierra caliente. Women made skirts or embroidered blouses and offered them for sale on the streets. The police said they were not allowed to do that and stole their things. We suffered in many ways.

We were scattered in different places and had no place to live. So in 1978 we founded this colony. Miguel Hernandez Kashlan met the owner of this land and we signed a contract and made a down payment for 10 acres. We called it Nueva Esperanza because we had hope (*esperanza*) in Christ and divided it into lots with biblical street names. God blesses us in many ways. There was no Bible in our dialect of Tzotzil in those days, but there was a translation of the New Testament in the Huixteco dialect of Tzotzil. We could understand only a part of it, but that was enough for a start.

After 1980, we knew we would never return to Chamula even to visit our relatives. We began to pray and fast for three days, without even water. People heard of this and came and there were many cures, many miracles. Every week, they came from Chamula to this church. At that time it was much smaller, 15 by 50 feet. Every Sunday, 10, 15 or 20 came and accepted Christ. They brought their sick relatives, and, through prayer and fasting, they were healed. The Word of God spread through Chamula and soon our first temple was not large enough. We built another measuring 50 by 80 feet. We did it with faith. We had no money, only the *diezmo* (tithes). Men worked as drivers, street cleaners, carpenters and so on and they all brought 10 percent of what they earned. With these offerings, we built this church, which measures 50 by 160 feet and has a roof of laminated metal.

We had only 10 acres of land, and soon there was not enough room for those who continued to be expelled. We founded the colony of Galilea in the municipality of Teopisca. Then we founded the colony of Betania. It is now very big, but, when we started it, there was just a congregation. We formed a congregation in the city of Santa Cruz and built a church on a hill and called it *El Paraiso* (Paradise). When a new colony named *Palestina* was founded here on the Ring Road we founded a small congregation called "Jesus Christ is the Resurrection." It is now a large church.

When the colony of Getsemani was formed on the Ring Road we founded three congregations named, "The Door of Heaven," "Emmanuel," and "Jehovah is My Witness." When many Brothers found jobs in the new Coca Cola factory on the other side of San Cristobal, we built a church for them there called "God is My Shepherd." When a colony of expelled settled in the selva near Guatemala, we built a church there called "New Nativity."

Jmol Miguel did not live to see all this. Many came here from Chamula to fast and pray. A man who said he was a believer came to see what was happening and went back to tell the caciques. They said: "If you kill Miguel Hernandez Kashlan we will give you money." They were losing business: no more liquor and candles. The more people were converted the more money they lost. So, for the love of money, they looked for a way to kill Miguel Hernandez Kashlan, the first leader of our people. Brother Miguel had been expelled many years earlier. He was working at a hotel in San Cristobal. The man who said he was a believer tricked him, and then he and others kidnaped him and dragged him into a car. This was July 24, 1981. They took him directly to a cacique's house in San Juan Chamula. There they cut his tongue, took out one of his eyes, shaved his head and tortured him and put an ice pick into his heart. Then they hanged him at a place called Mijitulal, 10 kilometers from Chamula. There was great sadness and pain for this deed. All the colonies gathered and a funeral was made here. Thousands of people came because our leader had died.

In 1982, we said, "Brothers, we have no leader. Let's name one. Let's pray to God to see who is approved by the will of God." Five persons were selected. From these, two were selected. I was chosen along with a Brother named Pascual. Then, it was decided that I should be sent to Tapachula to begin an extension course. I went every two months for studies and graduated on November 3, 1985 and was ordained pastor of this church.

That is how we organize our congregations and churches. It is all very democratic. Elders are responsible for spiritual affairs. They preach, administer baptisms and marriages and celebrate the Last Supper. When one is needed, we call a congregational meeting a month in advance. We invite everyone. Each Brother makes a special prayer to God because there is going to be an election. There may be five or six candidates. The people choose one by a majority of votes. He remains a candidate for six months and is told to prepare himself, and the congregation sees if he is capable of doing everything. If nothing goes wrong, he is invested and is sent to preach in different congregations. In this church, there are 13 elders, because there are many congregations and missions.

The same thing takes place with deacons. The task of a deacon is to administer the goods of the church, such as the offerings and church property. There are several deacons. Some give help, such as taking food to orphans, widows, and the sick. When one is needed, a meeting is called and the decision is by majority vote. We study a man, watching his knowledge and character to see that he is kind and respectful with the people. We see if he is good, because if he is rebellious or negative, the church does not want him.

Every Sunday, elders and deacons are sent to visit different congregations. They take turns. There is no set term for elders or deacons. A new election is called whenever there is a need because of sickness or death or someone moving to another place. The elders sit on the platform of the auditorium, and the deacons sit with the Brothers and Sisters in the front rows with the congregation. The deacons watch the Brothers and Sisters and the children to see there is good order in the church. They are organized in what we call the "Honorable Deacons Meeting," with a president, secretary and treasurer.

Pastors are selected from the ranks of the elders so everyone knows how he works, how he preaches and how he does the will of God. When there is a need to choose a pastor, everyone is given notice. They come and they pray. There may be two or three candidates. When the time for prayer is finished, the voting takes place. The one chosen by majority vote becomes a pastor candidate and is sent to a seminary to be prepared. After his studies, he is ordained.

Our church also has a Youth Society, an Intermediate Society and a Women's Society. These are under the elders, but the pastor must inspect the agenda of these societies and coordinate their work. The pastor must also instruct the elders and deacons, giving them classes, if necessary, so they can preach better.

We need many more Tzotzil pastors, so we have built another floor on this church as a seminary. It's just starting, but when it is ready, with all the teachers and books, we will call it the Miguel Gomez Hernandez Seminary. We will have a Tzotzil seminary of our own, named after our first martyr.

※ ※ ※ ※ ※

Later, with several visits, I explored Nueva Esperanza and asked how it was organized. When it was first founded, building lots were sold in the form of shares in a managing corporation. After 1988, they began to be sold to private owners so that the colony is now in private hands. With few exceptions, the residents are Presbyterians from Chamula families. No one is allowed to drink or sell alcoholic beverages or smoke.

Generally, the expelled give biblical names to the streets of their colonies, as if reflecting the zone of purity. There are two straight north-south avenues called *Getsemani* and *Belen* (Bethlehem) and five equally straight east-west streets called *Damasco, Galilea, Jerusalen, Rio Jordan* and *Nazaret*, so that the colony is divided into squares. Four of the seven streets are paved.

The colony has about 175 houses, with 8, 10 or as many as 12 families crowded into a house containing from two to four rooms. House plots vary in size: some have just a house, and others are large enough to grow vegetables for eating and for sale. Originally, the houses were built of wood but now almost all are of cement blocks with laminated tin roofs. All have drainage and drinking water.[1]

About 30 percent of the residents are merchants, which can mean anything from owning a store to organizing the groups of women and children who sit on the sidewalks or wander in the streets and parks selling handicrafts to tourists. Such commerce is not as casual as it might appear. Locations can only be established and protected through payments to officials or property owners. Furthermore, with competition becoming more keen and tourists more discriminating, the sellers must borrow money to buy quality goods made in small factories or imported from Guatemala and passed off as local.

About 20 percent of the resident males are masons or otherwise employed in the construction trades. About 15 percent are farmers. The rest are office workers, tailors, domestic servants and gardeners. A few are teachers. There are 10 stores. Most sell vegetables and fruit. One sells tortillas at a subsidized price. A state store sells corn, sugar and milk.

At the foot of Jerusalem Street is the Vincente Guerrero Primary School, with a row of six class rooms, a separate administration building and a basketball court separating the school rooms and the administration building. The school day is divided into two sessions, from 9 a.m. to 2 p.m. and from 4 p.m. to 8 p.m. There are 14 teachers, of whom nine are for the morning session and five for the afternoon session, plus two special teachers for physical and technological education.

When I visited the school, there were 299 students. The morning session had 101 boys and 80 girls. The afternoon session had 118 students, almost all boys. The first grade of the first session had 36 students. The principal said the average class size was 30. The two sessions were an effort to provide education for boys who had to work to help support their families. Although all the students spoke Tzotzil at home, the classes were entirely in Spanish. The fact that there were about eight girls for every 10 boys in the school's morning session is an almost revolutionary change from Chamula, where few girls were sent to school—providing there was

1 Details are drawn from Santiago Garcia (1993) and field interviews.

a school to send them to in the first place.

The community, like the church, elects its internal leaders. Samuel Lopez Hernandez, a merchant, was the head of the educational committee. He said he generally dropped by the school at the start of the day to ensure that all the teachers were present and to listen to any complaint against a student. He estimated that about 70 percent of adults could not read or write. He said the community does not want its children to suffer this fate but has not succeeded in persuading all parents to send their children to school, and only about 80 percent of the families cooperated in the educational efforts. He added that almost all the enrolled students completed primary education but not in the standard six years: some require eight or nine years. For almost all, that is the end of their education: few go on to a secondary school. There is also a governmentrun adult education class in the community, but it is poorly attended. Other committees look after the streets, drinking water, light and electricity. Finally, as a link with the real power, there is a committee of the ruling PRI.

In addition, there is an overall administrative committee headed, when I was there, by Manuel Gomez Gomez. There is also a secretary, a treasurer and first, second and third "*vocales*" (board members). These are members-at-large who fill in when the director is not present. Elections are held once a year, from a list of three candidates. Manuel Gomez was serving his second term and looked forward to the next election, when he would not be a candidate and thus could be relieved of the burden, not that the affairs of the community took up much of his time. There is only one scheduled meeting a year, to elect new officials. Other meetings are called when needed.

As closely knit as they are, sharing a history of oppression and the same Presbyterian denomination as well as addressing one another as Brother and Sister, there are still disagreements, jealousies and the clash of personalities. These came to a head in the election of 1991. The community was split. Since they could not divide the land, they divided the church. The minority imposed a *diezmo* on themselves and built another church two small streets away from El Divino Salvador. It is called *Cristo El Buen Pastor* (Christ the Good Shepherd). They meet at the same time and have the same services. The only difference, apparently, is a matter of some egos.

10
PENTECOSTAL CHURCHES

Although their numbers can only be approximated (because they see themselves as individual communities and resist merging into larger organizations, they are not easily counted) there is a consensus that Pentecostals make up somewhat more than half of the evangelicals in Chiapas. Once, I passed several times through the back streets of a refugee colony, searching for the home of a Presbyterian pastor. By daylight, there was no visible church, but, later at night, when I walked along the same street, I heard music and weeping. I followed the sound to a wooden shack packed with Pentecostals.

To some, Pentecostals may seem disordered and disorderly, but they are—as are all evangelicals in Chiapas—disciplined and ascetic. One Sunday, I went to a service in a lower middle-class Ladino neighborhood. It began, as usual, with about 20 minutes of standing, dancing in place, clapping hands and chanting the same phrases over and over again. Some cried aloud, others buried their faces in their hands and prayed silently, some knelt at their benches with their heads cradled in their arms while others stood in place and shook with tremors. Most, however, did nothing more than chant and clap.

Then all was quiet, except for an occasional "Hallelujah" during a 45 minute sermon by a young pastor. (He later said he was 33 years old.) His text concluded with a reading of the story of the Last Supper, after which the congregation came forward to receive ordinary bread and what seemed to be fruit juice. Finally, the congregation was called forward again for healing. As a choir of three women sang quietly, accompanied by a man with an electric guitar, the pastor and assistants moved among the worshipers standing before the podium, lightly laying hands on their heads. About a dozen fell in a faint almost as soon as they were touched. There was always someone ready to guide them gently to the floor.

When that ended, and all had returned to their places, the pastor made another appeal, asking if there was someone with a special need. For a few minutes there was no response, and then a woman walked forward with a child in her arms. As the pastor began to pray over her, another woman came and took the baby, and the woman sat on the floor with her head nestled in her arms on the platform. The pastor shouted his prayers, calling repeatedly on God to help her. The congregation watched in complete silence. Finally, his voice became lower and his words farther apart, and then he ended. There was no claim of miraculous healing. The woman simply sat up and other women came forward, one by one, to comfort her, taking her hands and lightly embracing her. She then returned to her place on a bench, looking a little dazed.

The entire service lasted almost two hours, so I had time to study the worshipers. All Mexican women wear earrings plus two, three, or more rings on their fingers, but not one of these women had an earring or a finger ring and all wore skirts falling below their knees. Trousers were also banned. In their asceticism, the Pentecostals recall the plain dress of American Puritans or Quakers.

They also resemble the "Separate Baptists" of the early American rural South, as described by Sidney Ahlstrom, who broke away from older Baptist churches and fiercely guarded their independence, "no more ready for a Presbytery than for a pope." They broke away for what they perceived as a laxity in manners and, like the Quakers, prescribed a plainness of dress and speech. Their meetings "were often tumultuous," and preachers "encouraged all the extreme forms of religious expression . . . More worthy of remark is the moral and spiritual discipline that the Separate Baptists brought to these uncharted areas . . . They compensated for their lack of education by close and serious searching of the scriptures."[1]

I have sat through hour-long sermons in Pentecostal churches with a pastor citing text after text and the worshipers listening intently. Many, including women, riffle through their Bibles to follow by chapter and verse. They do not have to look

1 (1972): 321–23

far for lessons on joyful healing:

"Shout for joy to the Lord, all the earth. Worship the Lord with gladness. Come before him with joyful songs" (Psalm 100:12).

"People brought the sick into the streets and laid them on beds and mats so that at least Peter's shadow might fall on some of them as he passed by. Crowds gathered also from the towns around Jerusalem bringing their sick and those tormented be evil spirits, and all of them were healed" (Acts 5:15–16).

"Then Peter and John placed their hands on them, and they received the Holy Spirit" (Acts 8:17).

"Do not get drunk on wine which, leads to debauchery. Instead be filled with the spirit" (Ephesians 5:18).

We have descriptions of early American meetings that closely resemble contemporary Pentecostal practices in Chiapas—that of Wesleyan Methodism. This is how a preacher named Jesse Lee described a 1787 service in Sussex County, Virginia:

> This meeting was favored with more of the divine presence than any other that had been known before. The sight of the mourners was enough to penetrate the most careless heart . . . [U]niting with other Christians in singing and praying, the heavenly fire had begun to kindle, and the flame of love and holy zeal was spreading among the people, which caused them to break out in loud praises to God. Some, when they met, would hang on each other or embrace each other in their arms and weep aloud and praise the Lord with all their might. The sight of those who were thus overwhelmed with love and the presence of God, would cause sinners to weep and tremble before the Lord . . . Some were on the ground crying for mercy and others in extacies (cq) of joy.[2]

However, in the last quarter of the nineteenth century, a change began within traditional Protestantism. An "outmoded theology" that emphasized individualism was attacked for its apparent neglect of pressing social problems. As this new "social gospel" became the creed preached from institutional pulpits, traditional worshipers, believing that these sermons were substituting social works for Saving Grace, retreated to new "holiness" congregations.

The concept of Saving Grace, rather than the Marxist borrowings of Bishop Ruiz and the Theology of Liberation, is at the root of the disagreement between Protestants and Catholics in Chiapas. Protestants, including the autonomous Mexican Presbyterian Church and certainly the many Pentecostal congregations, put the salvation of individuals ahead of all other concerns and have little direct interest in social problems, particularly elections and politics.

This is true throughout Latin America and the Caribbean. As the social scientist Samuel Escobar writes: "Although the Catholic Church took an option for the poor, the poor themselves have taken an option for the Pentecostal churches. It could be said that these popular Protestant churches have become alternative societies that create a closed world where people are accepted and become active, not on the basis of what gives them status . . . but of values that come from their vision of the kingdom of God."[3]

2 Ibid. 3 (1987) 169–70.

There are two 2,000-seat churches in the colonies along the northern Ring Road of San Cristobal. One is the Presbyterian Church of the Divine Savior in Nueva Esperanza. The other, which calls itself simply the Tzotzil Independent Church, is in the colony of El Paraiso. Its interior is plain cement-block, with not a single decoration. On the Sunday that I attended, the service began with chanting and clapping hands, but there was no loud weeping or even a summons to the altar for a mass laying-on of hands.

Each Pentecostal congregation has its own style. Yet, in all, spontaneity is kept within acceptable bounds. In a matter of minutes, a congregation can shift from loud emotional chanting and clapping to dignified silence.

Those who do not know Pentecostals, stereotype them as the refuge of the poor. In many cases, this may be true, but in Chiapas—and throughout Latin America—there are Pentecostal churches where a large proportion of the congregation is comparatively middle class. The Tzotzil Independent Church of Pastor Rafael Ruiz Jimenez is an example.

✳ ✳ ✳ ✳ ✳

I was about eight years old when my parents accepted Christ in the municipality of San Pedro Chenalho. My father was a member of the municipal government. He began to drink a lot and when he finished his term he continued drinking. He began to act crazy. He used to run without clothes and then come back and sit down and say, "What happened?" I used to go with him, crying. We went to curanderos and prayed. We went to spiritists and all sorts of persons but he was still sick. My father had cattle and horses but he sold everything and spent his money and never got well.

Pastor Ruiz' Tzotzil Independent Church: The false facade, echoing Catholic churches is typical of urban evangelical churches.

My brother-in-law was evangelical but we didn't want to accept it because people talked ill of it. I lived in the community of Las Limas and the evangelical idea was in Chimtic. My brother-in-law said, "I told you. My father-in-law is going to die." We didn't know what to do so we said, "All right. We put him in your hands." We took him to the Brothers and they began to pray and pray and pray. On the first day he felt better. A lot of time went by like this. At first, it was done once a week, then every 15 days. Finally we came to the church, and we were presented. Little by little, the sickness went away. That's how we came to know the Gospel.

I was at a boarding school in Chenalho. The teacher was from Veracruz and had married a woman from Chenalho. When the teacher's work came to an end, he went to Mexico City. His wife had come to like me and invited me to go with them, and my parents gave permission. For the first month in Mexico City, I was so homesick I cried and cried. However, I had to stay. The lady wasn't evangelical, and I got lost again, but gradually I knew the city better, and I found a Pentecostal church of the Assemblies of God. I met a woman from San Luis Potosi and we were married.

After I had been in Mexico City for twelve years, my mother died, and I had to return to Chenalho to help my father. I brought my wife, but, as there was no electricity, she could not adapt herself. After six months, we came to live in San Cristobal. There was no Pentecostal church here then, only a Presbyterian church. It was visited mostly by Tzotzils but there were also those who spoke Spanish. The message was very beautiful but painful. The Tzotzils didn't understand and were not really nourished, so I asked the Lord if it was His will that I could translate into Tzotzil. I was working in a hotel at that time. I was elected as an elder and translator, and they gave me the afternoon shift so I could attend the church on Sundays. I attended that church for three or four years.

We rented a house on National Army Street, where the church is. One day, my wife said she did not know how to pass the time and wanted to make something. She knew how to sew. We bought a sewing machine and went to look in the stores selling typical blouses from Chamula. She bought one as a sample and began to make them. She sold them to stores, and they sold like hot cakes. She worked a lot in this. One day, I asked her to teach me to sew so I could leave my job, work at home and go to the church in the afternoon to translate the services into Tzotzil. We bought another machine, and I worked in this and resigned my job.

Three years went by, and the Brothers began growing spiritually. They said, "When another person preaches in Spanish and has to stop for you to translate, it isn't the same. It's better to hear the message in our own tongue." They said, "Why don't we make a Tzotzil Pentecostal group. You can do it Brother."

We prayed and saw it was the will of God. We left the Presbyterian church and bought a piece of land in La Hormiga and inaugurated what we called an Independent Tzotzil Organization. There was a problem with that land. We had to move to the colony of Tlaxcala, but we had to meet in the street, and it was very hot. We leased land in the colony of Moreles and built a small house and kept praying to get a piece of land. I met a man who was the owner of *Colonia Paraiso*. I asked if he could sell us land. He said yes but not lots, only hectares [about two and a half acres]. We asked ourselves: "How are we going to buy a hectare?" But people began to come, more and more people. We prayed a lot, and we collected money, first to buy two hectares, then three hectares and finally 10 hectares. We divided it into lots with six lots assigned to the church. It took almost four years to build our church, because no one helped us except the believers with their offerings. We bought the land in down payments. God gave us this land.

Most of our worshipers are from Chamula, but there are others from Huixtan, Oxchuc and Mitontic who do not speak Tzotzil, so we also preach in Spanish. Still they are very happy, seeing what our doctrine is. I came from the Assemblies of God, who are very strict. They forbid women to curl their hair, to use lipstick and earrings, or to wear pants or short skirts. Men should not wear long hair. They are based on the Bible and believe that if there is a change on the inside there should be change on the outside. Since I came from that organization, the Brothers were happy here.

We believe in the Holy Spirit and in healing. We baptize by submerging in water. We permit those who want to sing or dance to feel the freedom of the Holy Spirit. That was the foundation of our church. From there on, things were harder. I had to gather a lot of papers and go to the Department of the Interior in Mexico City to be registered as a religious association. They told me that, since I was the founder, I should also be General Pastor and no one else. This is the mother church. I also administer eight churches in Oxchuc, Tenejapa, Chenalho, Teopisca, Zinacantan and the barrio San Antonio Monte here in San Cristobal.

About 800 worshipers come for Sunday services, from 9 o'clock in the morning and ending at noon, with Sunday afternoon services from 5 to 7 p.m. On weekdays there are services from 6 to 8 p.m. for different groups: a prayer meeting on Tuesdays, a general meeting on Wednesdays, a meeting for young people on Thursdays, and a general meeting on Fridays. We only rest Mondays and Saturdays. Just a few come to these weekday meetings because they live far away or finish work late, but on Sundays everyone comes.

We also have a Sunday School in two grades for about 150 children. We need more teachers. There are about 200 children who would attend if we had teachers. Actually, we need more than that. We need a full school for our children. That is in our prayers.

11

THE SEARCH FOR JUSTICE

International Human Rights organizations have protested abuses in China, Africa, Europe and the United States, but not one has heard the cries of persecuted evangelicals in Chiapas. They remained mute even after the Mexican National Commission for Human Rights, in 1995, issued a detailed report, complete with month-by-month and year-by-year citations of atrocities.[1] It was not as if Chiapas is on another planet. When Subcommander Marcos began a short-lived rebellion in January 1994, newspaper and television reporters flocked to San Cristobal, and a score of books were written. His Zapatistas were supposed to have started a Revolt of the Indians, and much was said about protecting indigenous rights but not a word about the expulsion from their lands and homes of 15,000

---

1 See Appendix I.

Abdias Tovilla Jaime

indigenous evangelicals. Except for minor funding from Presbyterian and other churches in the United States and Europe, they were left to save themselves, and they did. The courage and will to survive that Pascuala demonstrated was written large in the community as a whole.

Three men led the process of internal organization and external defense.

One, who formed and continues to lead a group known as the State Committee for Evangelical Defense in Chiapas (CEDECH), is Abdias Tovilla Jaime.

✳ ✳ ✳ ✳ ✳

My parents converted from Catholicism to Protestantism, so I was born in an evangelical family. I am a lawyer but, above all, I am a pastor. I completed my Presbyterian theological studies in Mexico City in 1979. In 1980 and '81, I worked in the Sierra Madre Mountains on the border with Guatemala. In February 1981, I came to San Cristobal to serve in the Presbyterian Church of the Divine Redeemer. The day I arrived, the caciques of Chamula, in a community called Piedracitas, destroyed a church that had recently been constructed with the help of my church, and no one said a word. To me, this seemed strange because on the coast of Chiapas, where I came from, nothing like this happened.

This was in January of 1981. In June of that year the first Tzotzil martyr, Miguel Gomez Hernandez Kashlan, a great man who converted more than 2,000 Chamulans, was assassinated. The caciques saw him as dangerous and expelled him from San Juan Chamula. He took advantage of this to evangelize families in and out of Chamula, preaching by day and by night. The caciques caught him in San Cristobal and carried him to the mountains where they cut out his eyes, his tongue, castrated him and cut the soles of his feet and made him run over a fire and then hanged him.

The destruction of that temple and the death of this martyr had a great impact on me. I continued to see many indigenous people beaten and robbed of their possessions. They came to the church where I was pastor and said to me: "Pastor, do something to defend us." I only knew how to pray. In my seminary, they did not teach us about the law. With this motivation, in September 1981, I enrolled in the university. Fortunately, the only law school in Chiapas was here in San Cristobal. I studied from 1981 to 1985, but I started to defend the community in 1981: while I was still a student I took their grievances to the authorities.

In 1988, I received a law degree. At the same time CEDECH was born, focusing on human rights, mostly of Protestants, but I have also given legal help to expelled Catholics. In 1992, the Presbyterian Church of Mexico recognized CEDECH as a ministry of human rights. The Presbytery and Synod of Chiapas allowed me to serve as a parttime pastor so I could devote almost all by time to this ministry. I am president of one of the Synods of the Mexican Presbyterian church and vice president of the National Presbyterian Church of Mexico.

CEDECH has both a legal and an educational function. When there is a violation of human rights, such as persecution and expulsion, CEDECH intervenes with the government, legally and politically. Here, we have had almost total failure in getting punishment for those who violate the most essential human rights. We were asked for proofs, and, if we presented witnesses who were expelled from the same community, we were told that the evangelicals who have been expelled could not testify because they are also affected by the case. Sometimes we were asked for photographs of damages, but the expelled could not return to their communities to take pictures. It was too risky, if not impossible. We were asked to present witnesses from the very places where the expulsions took place. This too was impossible because if someone was seen as taking the side of the expelled, that person too would face expulsion. Legal proceedings took so long that the aggrieved gave up hope. They thought their time could better be used in solving their immediate needs for work, housing and education for their children. With the passage of time, cases were given up for lost and forgotten.

Of course, the authorities deny they are dragging their feet. They always say, "Let us bring all sides to have a dialogue," but it is an indisputable fact that many of the dialogue committees that were set up at the suggestion of the federal and state governments have produced only talk. Some evangelicals, tired of waiting and finding life in exile too difficult, were allowed to return on certain conditions. For instance, in the community of San Miguel Mitontic the evangelicals had to sign an agreement that specified, in part, that they could not listen to Christian music on their tape recorders, could not have evangelical meetings, could not have Bibles, could not preach the gospel to their neighbors and could not receive visitors from outside the town.

Another so-called "voluntary" agreement that was signed in Chamula forced evangelicals to accept the traditional cargos and pay assessments for Catholic religious festivals, even though they already had another religion.

The caciques accused evangelicals of destroying culture and tradition because they have rejected alcoholic drinks, because they did not consult curanderos or brujos, because they did not burn candles or incense, because they did not worship idols or the image of San Juan, because they no longer displayed crosses in their houses and because they did not take part in religious festivals that, in reality, only serve to enrich the dominant and exploitative caciques. This, despite the fact that evangelicals use their mother tongues, wear their traditional dress, use regional herbal medicines, play their traditional musical instruments and conserve their traditional sayings and poems. Furthermore, their educational and religious material is completely in the indigenous languages.

In addition to its legal function, CEDECH has a social function. When a new evangelical barrio or community is born, it is necessary to fight for the most basic public services, such as schools, water and light. The expelled also use CEDECH as a nerve center. It acts as a mediator between evangelicals and the government to obtain many kinds of help. The expelled are poorly educated, so one of our main functions is education, principally Christian education. We have started, in the church of the Divine Savior in Nueva Esperanza, a united seminary where indigenous pastors and workers can receive theological education. Every now and then, we organize a three-day educational meeting in Tapachula for as many as 40 indigenous leaders. They study human rights, with teachers who are supplied by the National Commission on Human Rights. We have also translated human rights manuals into indigenous languages. This serves two purposes. One is so that indigenous evangelicals come to know their rights and begin to defend themselves. The other is so that the intolerant caciques can read in their own languages that the injustices, expulsions and violence they commit are punishable by law.

The caciques are rich people. They have exploited the poor villagers all their lives. The president of San Juan Chamula has used money received from the state government for the purpose of municipal improvements to buy arms. Municipal vehicles, some of them donated by the United Nations, have been used to transport hundreds of men to San Cristobal to attack the refugee colonies here. The problem is not only in Chamula. It has extended to other municipalities, such as Zinacantan, Mitontic, the zone of Amatenango and Huixtan. They too have learned this evil expulsion and robbery.

I should explain where our funds come from. CEDECH is primarily of Presbyterian origin, but it has received help from all evangelical congregations as well as some Catholic sources. Seven Presbyterian churches—four indigenous and three Mestizo—give monthly offerings for local expenses. In addition, the Presbyterian church of Mexico helps us to continue our ministry for the defense of human rights.

We are not anti-Catholic. We are all Christians under God. At every opportunity we have joined the Catholic Church in the struggle for social development and human rights, but we cannot ignore history. If the Catholic Church had done more to improve the lives of its parishioners, Chiapas would not have been such a fertile ground for conversion.

When evangelical churches in other countries learn of the problem of expulsions, they sometimes gather goods or other supplies, but they do not know where to send the aid. I was in Tucson, Arizona, and was told that a group called "Pastors for Peace" was coming to Chiapas with entire trailer loads of donated food. I asked where in Chiapas these things were going. They told me to Samuel Ruiz, the bishop of the diocese of San Cristobal. It happens that Bishop Ruiz already has a warehouse of goods. The Bishop is well known for his efforts on behalf of reconciliation with the Zapatista rebels in Chiapas. Half of the goods he receives are used for Roman Catholic works and the other half go to the Zapatistas, and yet goods that are sent by group like Pastors for Peace come from Presbyterian churches in the United States. The same thing happens with donations from the World Council of Churches or Protestant groups in Switzerland, Germany and England.

The expelled Brothers in the 36 communities in and around San Cristobal and Teopisca were agriculturists used to working with their fields and with the flocks from which they obtained wool for their clothes. When they were driven out to another world they asked: "Where are we going to live?" The government would not allow them to buy land for agriculture but they were able, sometimes with the help of small offerings from the evangelical churches of Mexico, to buy little plots where they put up, at first, mere wooden shacks. Even this was tightly controlled. Many were put in jail for having bought land from private parties without municipal permission. They asked: "How is it that persons born in Chiapas, who can not return to their native villages, could be treated as if we were foreigners in our own country?" We had to intervene legally on their behalf.

Another problem was their civil registry. Many were not registered because it was not the custom to register births in the records of San Juan Chamula. When parents tried to enroll their children in schools in San Cristobal or Teopisca, they were asked for birth certificates and, if they could not produce them, the doors were closed in their faces. If they went to Chamula to get some kind of paper, the authorities said: "You have gone to San Cristobal. We don't want you here." We went to the courts and the state government on their behalf. We are still fighting this campaign.

When the expelled indigenous people first came here, the hotel owners and other businesses liked what was happening. Women in colorful costumes selling handicraft items on the streets became a tourist attraction. They made San Cristobal different from many other cities so that those who made their livelihood from tourism benefited. Then, in about 1993, when the expulsions became more frequent and larger, the *Coletos*, as they call themselves—the "original inhabitants"—began to complain, although it was not a strong protest. They said the indigenous people were the cause of unemployment, crime, violence and traffic jams—all the problems that over-population brings.

Of course, the expelled have their own complaints. They are living on what was once farm land and scrub forest on the outskirts of the city. They are demanding many services: lights, water, schools, drainage, paved streets and clinics. Many were born here, registered here and vote here. They feel they have a right to an equal share of municipal revenues, but they face the opposition of powerful interests-people who have been long entrenched in power.

For example, the expelled have set up stalls to sell vegetables or handicrafts on the edges of markets or they have squeezed into odd spaces. Those who own established shops or spots say this makes it too difficult for shoppers to move and brings more garbage and crime, but the expelled can not afford established shops or spaces. That could cost as much as 50,000 new pesos. The municipality has suggested building a new market farther away, but the indigenous people say that would be a white elephant—no one would come to buy. The expelled say they are not against the concept of a special indigenous market, as long as it is centrally located and has all the services of light and water. But that again raises problems with the established interests. They think it would lure away customers. As a result, things are at a standstill and the huge market, with its small lanes, poor lighting and scarce water and sanitary facilities, keeps growing larger, with greater traffic jams and more social conflict.

Still, we are advancing, thanks to God. We now have an international profile. There is an organization based in Miami, known as "Open Doors," that helps persecuted evangelicals throughout the world. With its help, we received an invitation to appear before the International Court of Human Rights of the Organization of American States in Washington and also before the Congress of the United States. In 1996, we were privileged to explain the problem of expulsions to Congressmen who came here. Their arrival was important because, for many years, the state of Chiapas and the federal government covered up the problem of intolerance and expulsions. The government wanted to protect its world image and did not want this to come to the notice of international organizations. However, Christians in Switzerland and other European countries and in the United States wrote bulletins and articles for various magazines and newspapers. This is another way the problem became known at an international level.

In August of 1994, the last group that had been expelled—584 men, women and children—announced they would return without a guarantee of official protection. For almost a year, they had occupied, as a means of protest, part of the grounds of the Bureau of Indigenous Affairs in San Cristobal. On their own, they returned to 20 different communities. They showed tremendous bravery in retaking their lands. They told the caciques they would respect local customs and traditions but that they too must be shown respect.

On September 29, 1994, one of these families, who had returned to the community of Icalumtic, was attacked by a mob of 300 men. Miguel Mendez and his wife, Veronica, were stoned, clubbed, and then shot to death. Octavia, their fourteen-year-old daughter, was beaten and gang raped. Two next door neighbors, Miguel Lopez and Rosa Diaz, were also beaten with rocks and sticks. Miguel died but Rosa survived with a bullet still lodged in her body. She was left with 10 children to care for.

No one was punished, but the horror of the crime finally awakened the state and federal governments. Since then there has been just one brief, but violent, clash, in which four caciques and one evangelical were killed. Now, evangelical representatives are trying to work directly with the caciques—inviting them to work together for the progress and development of Chamula. Evangelicals have relationships, connections and channels to do this. The hope is to form one organization that will solicit help from government organizations. Here we already see results. In many communities there has been a return to friendship. We pray to God this will increase.

12
ORGANIZING FOR RESISTANCE

In September 1984, evangelists of several denominations formed the Regional Council of the Indigenous Peoples of the Highlands of Chiapas (CRIACH). A year later, the Presbyterians withdrew and CRIACH thereafter lost its religious hue, becoming another part of a broader group called the Regional Organization of Indigenous Peoples of the Highlands of Chiapas (ORIACH). In July 1985, in its publication *Indio*, ORIACH reprised what had been tried to that point:

Six meetings with Governor Absalon Castellanos.
Three meetings with the leaders of the Chiapas Congress.
Six joint meetings with federal, state and municipal officials.
Three meetings with the secretary-general of Chiapas.
A complaint presented to a meeting of national and foreign historians.
A complaint to Latin American bishops when they met on the 25th anniversary of Bishop Ruiz.

A complaint to the Senate Committee investigating migratory labor.
Dozens of meetings with the under-secretary of Indigenous Affairs.
Three large demonstrations in front of the municipal palace in San Cristobal.
An assembly of 4,000 expelled when the governor visited the colony of Nueva
    Esperanza.
One thousand involved in a sit-in at the Bureau of Indian Affairs.

In the same month, ORIACH sent a delegation to Mexico City. Over a period of
10 days, wearing traditional costumes and playing traditional instruments, they
demonstrated in front of the National Palace, the Juarez monument, the National
Museum of Anthropology, the Attorney General's office, the INI and the Ministry
of Internal Affairs and there were press and radio interviews. Then they went
home, and their plight was again forgotten. In November 1988, when then-presi-
dential candidate Cuauhtemoc Cardenas came to San Cristobal, ORIACH handed
him an appeal:

> We, the Indians, are fighting against the mistreatment, privation,
> humiliation, exploitation, lies, expulsions, threats, tortures, imposi-
> tions, jailings and death beginning with the Spanish conquest and
> lasting until the governments of today. The Indians are tossed like
> balls between different government institutions and are treated like
> animals in a zoo for the entertainment of tourists. No government has
> lived up to its word. Their promises are pure demagoguery and lies.
> They only want to ease our pain with words. For the caciques, justice
> is bought for money, or chickens; for drink and for women. Political
> parties only appear at election time. They hear our complaints but
> never act.[1]

Obviously, petitioning and complaining was fruitless. The crucial problems
were where to live and how to earn a living. Was sweeping the streets or being day
laborers—the mules of Mexican agriculture and the construction trades—their
Indio destiny? Before the expelled came in vast numbers, San Cristobal was a
Ladino city. They owned the stores, the construction companies, the stalls in the
market places, the taxis and buses—everything—and would not release any part
of it without a struggle.

In 1990, CRIACH withdrew from ORIACH to fight and not just to petition. Its
leader was (and is) Domingo Angel Lopez. Pacifism does not rank large in Mexican
popular culture. To be Mexican is to be macho—a strong man quick to strike when
insulted or hurt and never accepting second place. Domingo Angel acts macho and
looks macho. Like many indigenous people, he is short, perhaps 5 feet 4 inches,
but he has a large chest and shoulders and a grand mustache. For a few years he
served in the Chiapas legislature and still favors the impersonal "we" of a states-
man and answers questions as if making a speech. Although he rose from the ranks
of the expelled he is, essentially, a politician who casts his net widely. He once
said: "When we had problems . . . I told those who were evangelical to pray to God
and those who were traditionalists to pray to their gods, who would listen and give
them strength. For others, I said they should ask their political chiefs for help."[2]

1 Morquecho (1992): 34–35, 66–67. 2 Ibid., p. 82.

Under Domingo Angel, CRIACH organized fleets of taxis, small van/buses and trucks. It allied itself with indigenous peoples who made their living by gathering wood from the forests, and when government and forestry officials tried to seize their trucks CRIACH blockaded the highways, cutting the all-important tourist routes. The authorities quickly accepted a compromise solution.

When the Ladino merchants tried to monopolize vital spaces around Santo Domingo and Caridad churches, CRIACH filed a suit. The Catholic Church, embarrassed at appearing anti-Indio, ordered space to be found for them. Now the wide terraces around the two churches are carpeted with several hundred costumed women—their textiles and other handcrafts spread out around them. This and the neighboring streets have become one of the principal tourist attractions of San Cristobal.

Domingo Angel lives in a small house in the colony of La Hormiga (the Ant, a name given to the area when it was vacant and privately owned). The colony, founded in 1984, was the second to be organized after Nueva Esperanza. It is on the mountain side of the Ring Road, so that the streets angle sharply up, with the roof of one house at about the level of the foundation of the house above it. It has a primary school, complete with a basketball court, and two Presbyterian churches, but, unlike Nueva Esperanza, the streets are named after patriotic days (such as May 5, September 16 and November 20) or national heroes (like Villa, Zapata, Carranza and Obregon). The streets are mostly unpaved, but, thanks to the pressure of Domingo Angel, residents have electricity and piped water all the way to the houses high on the slope.

In May, the judicial authorities of San Cristobal called a meeting of representatives of the expelled and the caciques of San Juan Chamula to negotiate the return of 60 persons who had recently been expelled from the community of Yalhichin. The reply of the caciques was blunt: "If they try to return, the people will kill them, and there will be a little war. The people are ready. If they want to live in peace they should remain in San Cristobal or go to Betania because, if they come to Chamula, they will be met with machetes and ropes for hanging."[3]

The following August, another 50 were expelled from Yalhichin, after first being forced to sign a document saying they were leaving voluntarily. With that, the Bureau of Indigenous Affairs issued a statement: "The government will not permit any expulsion for whatever reason. We will arrange a dialogue to settle the problems, and, if the expulsions continue, we will apply the full force of the law."

It was mere words. The expulsions continued and no one was punished. In March 30, 1992, a group calling itself the Cooperative Society for the Betterment of Our Race sent a letter to Governor Patrocinio Gonzalez Garrido saying the caciques were preparing to arrest, fine and then expel evangelicals from Yalhichin and Chiotic. On the same day, 62 believers were taken to the Chamula jail and then expelled.

Domingo Angel Lopez decided to strike back. On the last day of March, two officials of the Chamula municipal government and 25 other Chamulans were picked up from the streets of San Cristobal and hidden in a Seventh-Day Adventist church. As soon as the news spread, an estimated 3,000 Chamulans rushed by car and truck to their rescue. One wing climbed to the slopes above La Hormiga and

---

3 Lopez Meza (1992): 153 69–70.

fired shots and threw down stones. The expelled fired back and threw rocks down on the people and vehicles parked along the Ring Road below them. The governor mobilized heavy police contingents to restore order, and the captives were soon released, although by then they had been beaten and their heads shaved.

The official report later said 23 persons had been wounded, five by bullets. One had been hit in the face by a stone and lost an eye. The expelled said two assailants had been killed. "We won," they shouted. "They had two dead." Although there was no direct evidence of his complicity, Domingo Angel was taken to jail. He made the most of it and came out more of a hero than ever.

❊ ❊ ❊ ❊ ❊

I was born in 1954. My mother and father died in 1966. In 1968, I went to Tapachula to work for a gringo on a finca, and there I went to a Catholic church and began to read the Bible in Spanish. The Catholics read the Bible in the mass. I began to talk with people and to study the Bible. I found good advice in it. It guides us and gives us light. Then I met some Pentecostal people. I always asked why are there two persons and two ideas. I studied some more. I learned that until Martin Luther took the Bible into the open no one could read it except Catholic priests. I kept studying the history of Chiapas, of the country and of religions. What do religions come to do? What is their purpose? I decided the Bible is not bad. The Word of God is good. Man is bad according to how he uses the Bible.

I studied alone from 1968 to 1970. Then I received a visit from gringos from the United States. They were Seventh-Day Adventists. They talked to me and other companions and taught us that Saturday was a day of rest. I looked in a dictionary and found that Sunday was instituted by the Emperor Constantine on March 7, 321. It was an imposition. I saw their idea was good.

I was expelled in 1974 and was in that church until 1983, but then they took a piece of land from me. Out of my own good will, I gave the land to build a church. According to the Constitution a church belongs to the federal government [under the nationalization of church property in 1917] but they forged my signature to say I gave it to them. When I claimed it was mine, I was accused of stealing and was put in jail. But when I presented my title and showed there was no crime, I was released.

We are not in the Seventh-Day Adventist Church any more. We are the Church of God because we can't put another name on God. We have studied the Bible and we don't find an Adventist church there. The Church of God was founded in the year 30 after the death of Christ. That is our church. We don't need *diezmo*. We don't need anything more. God doesn't need anything more. He just needs that we behave well with each other. We know that Christ died for us. We respect Christ, the teacher.

We have religious standards but we don't force them on people. With the help of God, I don't smoke. I don't drink. I don't have several women. I respect my wife but not because of religion; it was in the teachings of our forefathers. We don't have cantinas or stores that sell alcohol in La Hormiga but some people smoke and we respect their rights. We say, "Let's have an end to all that machismo." We are finishing with it. We study human rights. All of us have the same rights. We also respect our children. They should be educated, including girls. For example, my daughter is 16 and she is in high school. I only completed the second year of grammar school but my daughter can keep on learning and can become anything she wants—an accountant, a lawyer—anything she wants.

We were farmers before. We worked the land. We planted potatoes and cauliflower but when we came to San Cristobal we became small merchants, buying and reselling. I am a photographer. My companions are electricians, drivers, construction workers and carpenters. Others sell fruit in the market. Here we had another problem. The central market was full, so we organized ourselves and bought 30 hectares [about 75 acres] of land. Each one paid 1,000 or 2,000 pesos. The government said they would help us, but it wasn't true. We bought the land and organized our own market.

CRIACH grows. It raises children. It is called *Chantasel Yuntotimei*, which means "The Teachings of our Ancestors." We have a cooperative of artisans, with Maria Lopez Hernandez, my wife, as president. We sell in Mexico City, in Cancun, in Tijuana and other places. We also have more than 100 taxi drivers. We registered a cooperative and asked for 20 permits. They gave us eight, but we understand how the Mexican Constitution works. It says nobody can take away your right to work. We went through all the legal process. We did everything right. We bought our cars and went to work, and then they gave us the permits. I have always taught men and women to work like ants. Some work in transportation, others in the market. We are dealers. We buy fruit and sell it again. We not only sell in San Cristobal. We also take merchandise to Comitan, Tuxtla, Villaflores and Villahermosa.

When the city police or the highway patrol bother us, we defend ourselves. How? We do not go to beg on our knees or with tears in our eyes. We have a legal representative to claim our rights under the Constitution of our country and our state. We are united, without consideration of religion or political parties. Anyone who wants our help and protection can join us. We give an identification card that costs 55 pesos. The money is for an office we are building. We are growing fast because we protect the people. People from the PRI and other parties are joining us because they find protection.

The fight began due to all the injustices in San Juan Chamula. The problem is not religious. The government wants us to be ignorant, to be manipulated any way they want. The government has great power and a large bank of votes in San Juan Chamula. It isn't true that we are fighting with the Catholics. The evangelicals are fighting for justice, liberty and democracy. The government stages a pantomime to make people feel that there is a dialogue going on, that they are trying to solve the problem of the Indian people. To that we say they are making it worse. We are more than 35,000 expelled from San Juan Chamula. We were sent to San Cristobal, Teopisca, Cintalapa, Selva Lacandona and Las Margaritas but we hope to go back to our land. We are not going to leave our Mother Earth. Here, we don't have land. Here, our lots are 10 by 20 meters [about 30 by 60 feet]. We can't sow anything. We thank our Mother Earth who feeds us. We cannot forget our Mother Earth. Chamula is our traditional home. We will still live and work here. We will have two houses. We will keep our traditions. The land they took from us belonged to our ancestors. We think we must get back what is ours. How? Only by unity! There are so many political parties and so many religions. Religion is dividing us in the same way as parties. [A play on words. In Spanish, *Partido* means "party" and also "to divide."] The only way is to work together. It has taken us 500 years to open our eyes. A little puppy opens its eyes after 15 days, but human beings? Five hundred years have gone by and men still couldn't see. They didn't know their enemy. Now our eyes are open. We say *Ya Basta* [That's enough] to so much injustice. CRIACH is a social organization. It looks for justice, equality, and housing for everyone in the interest of all society. We are not fighting for creeds or political parties. All have the same rights, Indian and Mestizo. We are the same human beings. We think we should learn from ants. Ants don't fight. They are united in their work.

On April 1, 1992, when the caciques of Chamula came to expel us from La Hormiga, we defended ourselves. There were 53 persons hurt and two caciques were killed. We did not have guns. We were armed only with reason and justice. As St Paul said, we were "dressed in the armor of God." We did not have arms so the two caciques must have been killed by their own people in the confusion. Still, they took me and some companions to prison. They accused me of kidnaping but I called Amnesty International and the national and international newspapers, and they took up my case. When we were in jail, the other prisoners asked me: "What is your problem, Domingo?" I told them I was a political prisoner. I told my companions we must go on a hunger strike to the death. We prepared for 12 days. I called the bishops of San Cristobal, Tuxtla Gutierrez and Tapachula, and they came to visit us and pray for us. National and international newspapermen came too. I tried every way to get my freedom and the freedom of my companions. I was 28 days on hunger strike. I only drank water. How did I feel? I was weak in the flesh but strong in spirit.

Finally we said if there is no progress, we are going to burn ourselves—five comrades and myself. We wrote letters saying we would burn ourselves on April 29. "But how are we going to burn ourselves?" the comrades asked. "There is no gasoline here."

"Don't worry," I said. "At the right moment we'll get it." There was a man in the jail named Xochitl Velasquez who was a human rights fighter. He told me we could use paint thinner. There was a carpentry shop in the prison. We went there and got it. Thinner is more flammable than gasoline. We had a lighter. We set fire to the can and we got burned but Xochitl Velasquez quickly covered us with his jacket and put out the fire. We caused so much trouble they let us go free.

13

THE POLITICS OF EXPULSION

The third man who played a pivotal role in rallying the defenses of the expelled evangelicals is Esdras Alonso Gonzalez. In the context of Mexican ethnicity he, like Abdias Tovilla, would be classified as a Ladino. In Mexico, not being an Indio has advantages, as being White does in the United States. A Ladino does not suffer the conscious or subconscious feeling of inferiority bred by a lifetime of slights. If he comes from a middle class family, he may be college-educated and is sure of himself in manners and dress. He can claim an equal place at the bargaining table

Esdras Alonso Gonzalez

and thus might serve as a link between the worlds of the oppressed and the oppressors. Among evangelicals, it is not a superficial relationship, like a lawyer and client: it is the spiritual bond of those who call one another Brother and Sister.

✽ ✽ ✽ ✽ ✽

I was born into a Roman Catholic family on July 13, 1962, in the district of Tehuantepec in the state of Oaxaca. I was converted to the evangelical belief when I was 18 years old, on November 15, 1981. I was very sick, with a tumor in my lung and needed an operation, but it was very expensive. An evangelical preacher visited us and prayed for me. The Bible says that we must pray for the sick so they can heal. When he prayed for me, I got well. With this, I got to know the Word of God, and all my family followed. In 1985, after I finished secular high school, I began my pastoral studies. In 1991, I obtained a degree in theology from the Mexican Nazarene Seminary in the Mexico City. Actually, my pastoral work with the Nazarene Church began in 1985.

The roots of the Nazarene church go back to a Pentecostal church founded, in 1908, in Pilot Point, Texas. In 1919, it became the Church of the Nazarene. With the passage of time it has become more formal—more like the Methodist Church—but here in Chiapas and in Oaxaca it remains strongly Pentecostal.

As Pentecostals, we have always preached the doctrine of the Spirit but we also place great importance on the practical teachings of the Bible. There are many sick people. When the Gospel comes, it is a healing Gospel. It forgives sins and also heals the body. It is an integral Gospel because it changes the lives of people. Before they drank very much, but, now that they are Christians, they don't drink any more. All their money is for their family to feed, dress and educate their children. The Gospel we preach is a Gospel with signs, like the Book of Acts of the Apostles. God is keeping His word. Faith is part of what we live every day.

God manifests himself in a powerful biblical way. When we pray that people receive the Holy Spirit, they speak in tongues. Some even prophesy. We have in this church two Sisters who prophesy. This isn't a theoretical church, a formalist church enclosed in its traditions, but a church that is experimenting with the power of God. This is what gives the Gospel life. Even if evangelical believers are threatened with persecution and death, they still believe in the Word of God. They are convinced by the testimony of believers. The Bible is practical. It changes lives but does not change the ethnicity of a people. They read the Bible and pray in their own tongues. Then, when they pray to God, He makes miracles. Thus the people believe in the Word and it keeps growing more and more.

I was the pastor of a big church in Oaxaca, with many believers. I knew people from Chiapas, and through them I knew of the persecution of evangelicals. At the end of 1993, God sent me to Chiapas. After we prayed, fasted and read the Word of God, we were certain it was God's will. I also knew of the work of Abdias Tovilla. I came here to cooperate with him—to help stop the expulsions—and to find a way for believers to return to Chamula to live in peace. Abdias is Presbyterian, more formal and organized, while I come from the Pentecostal movement, more open, more liberal in thought, and more spiritualistic. Still we got together and have never had a problem. I became the leader of an organization called the Ministerial Alliance of the Highlands of Chiapas, consisting of 25 Presbyterian, Independent Presbyterian and Pentecostal churches, which was formed by Abdias in 1981.

The expelled need their own defense system. They face not only the caciques but also political corruption. There is no doubt that one of the causes of the expulsions was the economic power and corruption of state and local officials. For many decades the government of Chiapas has been married to the cacique system, especially in Chamula, where the only party was the Institutional Revolutionary Party. PRI deputies defended the caciques with cape and sword while the caciques, for their part, did not permit any other party to exist in Chamula. The caciques were untouchable. If the expelled managed to obtain arrest orders, the caciques warned they would stop delivering votes, and, with that threat, the orders were canceled.

Evangelicals must also contend with Mexican anthropologists who have argued that Protestantism or, as they say, the Protestant "sects," are causing division among the indigenous people and that "gringos" in the sects are "denationalizing" the indigenous people. Priista [PRI] deputies have repeated this argument in defending the caciques. They cite Article Four of the Chiapas Constitution: "The law protects and supports the growth of languages cultures, usages, costumes and other forms of social organization." This, however, refers to the agrarian social system. It does not refer to such Chamula customs as drinking posh or a man having as many women as he desires. They ignore Article 24 of the Federal Constitution, which says we are free to practice whatever religion we choose as long as our practices do not violate specific provisions of the law.

What were these customs that the evangelicals defied or ignored? They refused to get drunk, which deprived the caciques of one of the main sources of income. The caciques manufactured and distributed posh and were the only ones allowed to sell it at the traditional festivals. Posh was a way to enslave the indigenous population. The witchcraft of the traditional healing ceremonies was bathed in alcohol. Posh was wiped on the lips of newly born children as a form of medicine. The sale of sodas like Coca Cola was also a cacique monopoly, along with the manufacture and sale of ritual candles. Traditional cargos were another form of control and exploitation. They were imposed on the indigenous people, and, if they could not pay the costs, they were forced to borrow the money from the caciques at a high interest. Most Chamulans did not know how to read and or write. Their ignorance was deliberate—another method of keeping them in slavery from their earliest childhood. With all this, they could never free themselves from poverty.

Although we still hope the expelled will be free to return, we no longer demand that the government force their return. Let those who want to return do so without fearing for their lives, but most will not want to return. They work here and have their houses here. Their children go to school here. Their lands in Chamula have been used by others for 10 or 20 years. It would be almost impossible to dislodge them. What we work for is peace so that evangelical belief can grow, not only to Chamula—the most intolerant of all places—but throughout Chiapas.

That has been one of our aims for the past few years. We have been using the cell method developed by the immensely successful South Korean Pentecostal leader Paul Yonggi Cho. He teaches a more integral evangelization—not only spiritually but also socially. His cells consist of small groups of laymen or laywomen with related interests—professionals, educators, merchants or farmers—who meet in houses to testify and share. The first cells were started by another Nazarene pastor here in San Cristobal. I am using this method with the indigenous people as well as Ladinos. The object is to share the Word of God, a message of hope, love and unity. The biblical message is not a theoretical message but a very practical message. Believers can share this practical message with others who don't know Christ.

I wrote a little book about the method. I call it a "Guide for Leaders of Family Groups or Cells." [Showing a palm-size pamphlet.] The book answers such questions as, "Who is a cell leader?", "What is a family group?", "How does the method work?" and so on. When we began there were few, but now this method is being used by many pastors. Each works with it in his church, dividing his congregation into cells. The numbers of cells keep growing. In my congregation there are 18 cells.

As evangelical belief grows, there will be a need for more men like Abdias Tovilla, who combines evangelism with the struggle for human rights. For this reason, for the past three years I have been studying for a law degree. God put this in my heart. The indigenous people have suffered since the Conquest. They are victims of race discrimination as well as exploitation by the caciques. The rights of the indigenous people must be respected. There must be equal treatment without discrimination. They have been exploited, marginalized and forgotten. They, and all of us, are part of a suffering church.

We need to know Mexican laws because the problem here in the Highlands is not one of Catholics against evangelicals. It is an economic, social and, especially, a political problem disguised as a religious problem. Our relations with the Catholic Church are good. We are not angry with the bishops of San Cristobal, Tuxtla Gutierrez, or Tapachula. We have good relations with all of them. We have theological differences, but, like Brothers and religious ministers, we have good relations. We respect Roman Catholics, and we are sure they also respect us.

However, I must add that there is a particular disagreement with some in the diocese of San Cristobal. They have a Marxist line. Some might not use that word—just calling it a "liberal" line—but just the same they are willing to ask if it is necessary to struggle with guns to obtain a just and equal society. We are pacifists working for reconciliation, not for conflict. We look for unity, not for separation. We call our fellow men Brothers. We don't say, "Over there is one kind of people and here there are the indigenous people." No. We are not dividing. The Catholic Church in this diocese has another method. It tries to justify its belief in the possible use of arms to settle disagreements. Evangelicals do not agree.

14
THE RELATIONSHIP BETWEEN EVANGELICALS AND ZAPATISTAS

When Marcos and his small band entered San Cristobal on January 1, 1994:

> their Declaration of War was an emotional appeal to the conscience and frustrated electoral desires of the nation, and it was broadcast on the radio, read on national television and faxed to the Mexican and international press . . . On the day that the official ceasefire was declared, there was a large demonstration in Mexico City. Over 100,000 people marched together, shouting, "The First World Ha Ha Ha!" in open defiance of the ruling class and its economic allies in the "developed" countries to the North.

So writes Elaine Katzenberger in the introduction to *The First World Ha Ha Ha! The Zapatista Challenge*, one of a score of book-length panegyrics that have heralded the uprising. Ms Katzenberger, the book's editor, bills it as "a direct attack on the New World Order."[1]

In their "Declaration of the Lacandon Jungle," faxed (they were soon labeled as the world's first revolutionaries with fax) to the outside world, the Zapatistas demanded "work, land, housing, bread, health, education, democracy, liberty, peace, independence and justice," plus the dismissal of a president who had only six months left in his term and scrapping the North American Free Trade Association (NAFTA), which came into force on that very day. Rights for women and homosexuals and renegotiation of the "external debt, exchange rates, the patent system, etc." would be added later.

Aside from the scrapping of NAFTA, there was nothing here that could be construed as a direct attack on the New World Order, but there was much—including the ouster of Carlos Salinas de Gortari, a hugely unpopular president—to appeal to a populace with the pentup frustrations arising from impunity for a favored few and a political system that seemed to reward corruption, inflation, unemployment and economic failure.

There are questions: Was the cheering for the Zapatista revolutionary or for the purport of their demands? Did all but a few of those who celebrated even know of NAFTA and the First World? In the summer of 1994, Lynn Stephen did a reality check in the neighboring state of Oaxaca, where she went to observe the national presidential elections and to find out what, if anything, people thought about the Zapatista rebellion. Specifically, she wanted to assess if the Zapatistas had influenced villagers' opinions of the government and its agrarian reform and farm-subsidy programs.

"What emerged from this period of fieldwork was intriguing," she wrote. "Many men and women whom I interviewed supported and even identified with the Zapatistas and their demands, yet a majority still voted for the PRI. Even in a community named for Zapata—*Union Zapata*—the PRI got 175 votes, while both the

---

1 (1995).

center-left PRD and the rightwing PAN received a combined total of 13 presidential votes. The voters plunked themselves squarely in the middle and, when interviewed, said they hoped to continue to receive the PRIs largesse of farm subsidy checks along with other parts of the government's long-term rural-development strategy."[2]

A strategic city where it is possible to assess evangelical opinion of the Zapatistas is Ocosingo. It was occupied (along with San Cristobal, Las Margaritas, Altamirano, Oxchuc, Huixtan and Chanal), and there was serious fighting, with about a dozen casualties in its main market place. For about two years after the Zapatista withdrawal, the Mexican army maintained a base on the outskirts of the city, looking down on the green plain of Lacandon selva.

Gaspar Hernandez Lopez is pastor of the Presbyterian Prince of Peace Church in the village of Tzajalja, about ten miles west of Yajalon.

✳ ✳ ✳ ✳ ✳

I am now 42 years old. As a child I was sick and dying when two women [referring to Marianna Slocum and Florence Gerdel] came and said if we accepted Christ, He would cure me. It was very difficult for my father to accept the Gospel but my mother accepted immediately because she saw my suffering. After three or four days my father also accepted. They prayed very much for my health and God healed me. That was in 1962. When my parents saw the marvels of the Lord they accepted the Lord and so did other families.

I first went to church because I liked to sing and pray. When I was older, I went because there was no school where we lived. Finally, the families in our community paid a teacher so I learned to read and write. That was in the community of Basiviltik in Bachajon in the municipality of Chilon. I studied only up to the fourth grade. Later I saw how preachers worked and wanted to learn the things of the Lord. I began looking for a biblical school when I was 14, but they would not accept me until I was 16. I went to the *Escuela Cultural Berea* in the city of Oaxaca and studied for two years. They were going to send me to a mission, but I didn't feel ready to face the problems of preaching so I went to Chihuahua.

While I was in Oaxaca, I finished grammar school and in Chihuahua I finished high school. After three years there, I studied in the Department of Theological Education in a school called *Vida y Verdad* (Life and Truth). When I graduated, I saw the great need in Chiapas and returned to join the Presbyterian church. They sent me to study at the Theological Seminary in Mexico City. I was there for three more years. I was named as a candidate for the ministry and was ordained on January 13, 1973, and, at the age of 22, I was made pastor of the Presbyterian Church of *La Nueva Jeruselen* in Batsiviltik.

When I graduated, they were going to send me to work in the Tarahumara Mountains of the north, but I felt that, if God called me to begin my ministry in Chiapas, He would bless me with growth of the church in size and knowledge, and so it was. In the first three years, the congregations and missions began to grow. The growth was because we had special monthly courses for elders and deacons. They are the ones who carry the message of the Gospel. We were a team—another pastor, two elders and myself.

It then happened that I had to leave the first church where I worked to join my present church, *Principe de Paz* (Prince of Peace). There were four congregations

2 (1997).

when I began in 1983. Now there are 24. In numbers, there are about 3,000 new believers. We are thinking of forming a new church and dividing the congregations, so that each church will have 12 congregations. Each congregation is run by elders and deacons. Preaching is done by young men who want to practice the Gospel. They preach the Word and don't concern themselves with administration.

Preachers are chosen by call—through the message of the Word. Those who are interested can come and take special courses. Then, in monthly meetings of this church, the elders select who will be sent to cover different congregations, or, if there are places where there are no evangelicals, they will be sent in pairs to declare the Word of God.

We hear of such places, but we don't go immediately. We must look for contacts—a family for example—because when a family accepts the Gospel, the Word passes to another family by testimony. Only then will preachers be sent. We do not just go knocking on doors. We introduce ourselves to local authorities. We must be given permission before the Good News can be preached in a town or community.

If there are no contacts, the preachers may ask someone if he or she would like an explanation or if they would like a visit. If they say yes, the preachers go to the authorities and ask permission to begin. In the beginning—maybe 20 years ago— literature was distributed but no longer. The initial acceptance is with someone in a family, usually a younger member, and then the parents come to the Gospel little by little.

The principal reasons are moral and spiritual needs. Sometimes a father is not responsible. He may drink or have two or three women. He is deep in misery. Then there is sickness. People look for healing because they have heard of cures through testimonies. They come to know that God has power. Especially among Indians, it is difficult to believe without seeing changes in another person's life.

The Gospel is explained to them in their own language, like mine, which is Tzeltal. Spanish is a foreign language to us. [Showing a Bible.] Here is the fifth edition of the New Testament in Tzeltal, published in 1985. The first edition was published in 1964. [Showing a larger Bible] Now here is Tzeltal translation of the Old Testament published in 1993 in an edition of 700 copies. It is a great joy. We waited so long for this.

We think our preoccupation with education will bring a great change. This is more important than just numbers. We need more seminaries for Tzeltals. Now we have just one, in Villahermosa, in Tabasco. It has 15 Tzeltal students. Ten have graduated and have joined churches as pastors and five are still studying. There is another seminary in Tapachula, in Chiapas.

Author: You are near the Zapatista zone. Ocosingo was briefly captured in 1994. What is your opinion of their movement?

GHL: Maybe they are the fruit of some of the injustices in our state. People have asked for help many times, and the government has never heard. By and large, our congregations have not been threatened. There are persons who tell us they were expelled. Some people who did not follow the Zapatistas felt they had to leave, but this may be caused by a lack of communication.

There are many churches in the selva. Maybe two, or three or five persons have left because of rumors or because they felt threatened, and maybe people who follow the Zapatista leader sometimes have acted harshly, but we do not find any general opposition or threats to believers in the selva.

Those who follow the Zapatistas say they believe in democracy and justice. Well, we also believe the church has the responsibility to take an active part in the search for democracy, justice and general social well-being. We are agents of peace. We believe in going near our Brothers—in living together and listening to their complaints. I have always had in mind, ever since I began as a pastor, that we must help all people, not only Christians. I was a child who suffered, and, when I see children suffering, I want to teach them so they can live better. The church says there must be an integral answer. That is the most important thing for me. It is my duty not only to take the message of the Word to people but also to see that their standard of living is improving.

※ ※ ※ ※ ※

Luis Sanchez Rodriguez is pastor of a group that left the selva to escape the Zapatista occupation of many of its villages. They have built a church called Peniel and also a long log dining hall, in which Pastor Sanchez served a lunch of tree snails. Later, with about 20 members of his congregation listening, he told his history.

※ ※ ※ ※ ※

My parents accepted the Lord in 1948 when my mother was sick. They were not believers, but the Sisters Marianna and Florencia came to preach, and my mother was the first to accept the Word. This was in Corralito, in the municipality of Oxchuc. In 1971, I was a believer, but then I went to other places, dedicated myself to things of the world and forgot the Gospel. When I returned home in 1978, a Sister who knew me said I should come back to the church. I went to Tuxtla Gutierrez to work, and there I joined a church called *Getsemani* and joined the choir.

A few years later I met my wife, may her soul rest in peace. Her name was Aurora Reyes de Leon. We were married in Tuxtla. Some years later, I went back to live with my mother and father, may their souls rest in peace. It was a place called Cueja. I lived there for a long time and attended a church named Damascus in the village of Abasolo, where they named me as a candidate to be an elder. Less than a year after that, they sent me to study at a biblical school at Buenos Aires Ranch near Altamirano. It was occupied by land invaders when the Zapatista revolt began, and the church is still trying to get at least the school and administration buildings back.

There I met some Brothers from a new church called *Maravilla* (Marvelous). They knew me and were looking for a director. An application was made to the Tzeltal Presbytery of Chiapas, and, in about 1985, I was named pastor of that church. At that time, there was a land invasion at a place called Carrizal near Buenos Aires. They attacked some people who had only two or three hectares, and drove them out. They killed about five persons. Some Catholics have told me—even some catechists—that they were instructed by a priest.

The Maravilla church, where I was pastor, began to get confused. They thought they saw people who were shooting everywhere. They were afraid, and they decided to transfer the church to some other place. Around 1989, they considered moving it to Cushulja, but, because the Zapatistas were organizing, we couldn't do anything there, so some Brothers sought refuge in Ocosingo.

At first nothing could be done there. Even a small lot—10 by 20 meters—cost about 18,000 pesos. Then a Brother said, "Why don't we look for a piece of land, like an hectare, and use part for a church and divide the rest for our houses." After a time of discussion we all agreed to accept that idea. We made a list, and went to look for people to join in buying the land and found this place. Then the Presbyterian Consistory agreed we could build a church here in the barrio of Jerusalen. We call it the Peniel Church.

Some people want to go back now that things are getting quiet, but we have an agreement with the Consistory to settle here. Ocosingo is a short distance away and there are good communications. There's a lot to do, but the Brothers are working hard, and our Peniel Church will remain, growing little by little if God permits. We are still a congregation under the charter of the Maravilla Church. Five years ago, it had seven congregations and one mission. Now it has 10 congregations and eight missions.

Last year and the year before, many families went back to their homes in Cueja, but felt they could survive only if there were other houses near. They felt they could be easily bothered. When the war started in 1994, one of our churches was occupied by the Zapatistas and mines were planted in some places. We have a congregation called Ujkumilja where some Brothers were forced to take part in the Zapatista activities. In 1992, while they were still getting their army ready, they told people they would be killed if they did not join them. But now Brothers who have gone back have not reported such things. The church that was occupied is still there and some Brothers now use it. Brothers who go back say they sometimes meet men with guns, but when they say they are going to their church they are not bothered. I don't speak badly of the Zapatistas, because the Bible says a man is known by his deeds. I think they were planning good things, but something went bad. They said they were planning to help the Indians. This would have been good if it was true, but they also said they were against the *kashlanes* and against the rich. As a believer I can't pass judgments on people. I can't say this man is a kashlan. That is where things went wrong. There were conflicts, so we looked for refuge in Ocosingo. We think it isn't good for Indians to fight against Indians. God does not want this and so we left.

15
THE MITONTIC EXPULSIONS

The people of Mitontic, a municipality bordering Chamula on the north, speak a subdialect of the Tzotzil dialect of Chenalho. They are also separate in their traditional dress, customs and leadership structures. The growth of evangelism in Mitontic was slow, but when their numbers had grown to about 600 in several communities, the municipal authorities decided to crush them. In July 1987, more than 300 men from various communities—armed with rifles, pistols and poles—surrounded the houses of believers in the community of Suyalo. Seventy-seven men, 120 women and 35 children were herded outside. The men's hands were tied and they were herded on a three-hour march to the Mitontic community center. Since they could not fit in the municipal jail, they were jammed inside a warehouse used for storing construction material, where they sweltered, with a hot sun beating down on the roof, for three days without food or water, listening to shouts of men milling around outside, threatening to rape the women and drown the children. At midnight on the third night, their leaders were taken out and forced to acknowledge that they did not take part in religious festivals and did not accept cargos and so had voluntarily accepted expulsion from traditional society. The next morning, the door of the warehouse was opened and they were told they could return to their homes, but only after being forced to clean the overburdened latrines of the warehouse.

At the end of the long walk back to Suyalo, they found their homes had been stripped of clothing, food, work tools and ransacked for hidden money. State authorities quickly intervened. On July 15, 1987, at a meeting in Tuxtla Gutierrez with representatives of the governor and the municipal president of Mitontic, an agreement was signed to allow the believers to remain in Mitontic if they would, from then on, take part in the traditional cargos.

Two years later, in June 1989, the Mitontic caciques called 30 evangelical men to a meeting in the municipal center, where they were accused of not living up to the 1987 agreement. The municipal president said there were "too many evangelicals" in Mitontic. When the men left the city hall, they were seized and tied by a mob. Others were sent to round up their families and they were all then loaded into UN-supplied trucks and dumped at the Indian Affairs Bureau in San Cristobal. The next day mobs were sent to Suyalo and another community to destroy a Presbyterian church and several homes. Once again, there was the farce of a government-sponsored dialogue. The Mitontic officials presented a list of 15 stipulations, including a ban on building a church, a ban on visits or contacts with Presbyterian pastors or evangelical leaders from other communities, a ban on services in their houses, even a ban on reading evangelical literature. All of this was rejected by Chiapas authorities as a blatant violation of the Constitutional guarantees of freedom of belief. A bland agreement to keep the peace was substituted. With that, the believers were told they could return home.

Within two days, a mob almost beat to death one of the first of the returned evangelicals, charging that someone had heard a tape recording of Tzotzil gospel music coming from his house. Although there was no such prohibition in the agreement, the caciques said the terms had been violated and ordered the few believers who remained in Mitontic to leave. Since it was obvious that INI and state authorities would not back up their talk of peace with police force, Presbyterian leaders in San Cristobal advised the Mitontic believers to abandon their lands and homes and settle among the earlier expellees but, with their distinct dialect and internal structures, they could not blend with the predominately Chamulan refugees.

They were settled far away, at the edge of the wide, low-lying plain west of the Highlands. I discovered their exile community by accident. I was driving to the city of Ixtapa, about 20 miles from Tuxtla Gutierrez, and saw a sign pointing to "New San Miguel Mitontic." I returned a few weeks later. If one knew what to look for,

New Mitontic could be seen about five miles away on the slope of a mountain, but the narrow rocky road went up and down interlacing gullies so that it took half an hour to reach what had been a cattle ranch. The old sheds were useless for the exiles. Instead, they had built about 20 small cement-block houses and named their streets Damascus, Sinai and Palestine. The men were away working when I arrived. A boy jumped on a bare-backed horse and galloped off to find Agustin Perez Perez, their leader, who came back on the same horse and told a little of the community's history.

※ ※ ※ ※ ※

Evangelical belief began in Mitontic about 32 years ago. The first to believe in God were two brothers, Miguel and Mariano Mendez Gomez. I was four or five years old then. I am now 36. There was one church in the community of Suyalo, built about 30 years ago. The caciques never accepted us. They came to our houses and yelled at us, saying we did not believe in God. The trouble began when Domingo Perez Lopez was municipal president. Before him, there were some problems, but not so big. They put all the Brothers in jail for three days with no food and no water—nothing. Some children almost died it was so hot. One child was only one month old. Then we went back to our lands, but we were rounded up again and expelled. We were separated in the colonies of Getsemani, La Hormiga, and Palestina. We suffered very much. We had to buy wood and food. If we didn't work, we didn't live.

The government brought us here three years ago. There were no houses. We built them with our own hands. The government gave us the land, and there was electricity because of the old ranch. We did the work to supply water. We are 81 men here, in addition to women and children. We all have some land. We work on it and we have food for our children. They all go to school from 9 a.m. to 2 p.m., through the third grade. There are three teachers and all the children can read and write.

In the beginning, all the Brothers went to the coffee plantations to earn money to pay for our houses. Now, if a family does not have enough land, some men still go to work in the lowlands. Before, when we lived in Mitontic, we used to go to Tapachula but now we go near here, to San Juan del Bosque, Jaltenango, and Simojovel. We take a bus or a car. A man might return to visit his family every month. It depends on how the work is. Sometimes it's only a three-week job. The problem is that if they go far away, they don't know how their children and wives are. If they get sick, the men don't know. If we work here, it is much better. We go by walking. We leave at around seven in the morning and finish at about two in the afternoon, but most still go far away because they need money for their children.

They don't want us back in Mitontic and we don't want to go back. We have a house here, and the land is much better, and we have work. When we first came here we had nothing. It's different now. We have wood and corn, and, thank God, we have peace.

※ ※ ※ ※ ※

My interest in Mitontic had been stirred some months earlier by an old leaflet demanding justice for the expelled. It had been issued in the names of former Mitontic officials, including several former municipal presidents. It said some were living in La Hormiga, but, when I asked, some said they remembered the men whose names were on the list, but they had all gone away. Then someone remembered a professor who did not live in La Hormiga, but who was director of the community's primary school. His name was Felipe Lopez Vasquez.

I called on him and he confirmed he had once served for a year as president of the Mitontic municipality. When I showed him the pamphlet and asked about the expulsions, he said he needed time to review his notes to refresh his memory and asked me to return a week later. Before I left, I outlined some of the things I hoped he would talk about. First, there was his school: how many students were there; what was the language of teaching; how many of the students were girls and, most of all, what was the difference between education in Mitontic and now among the expelled in San Cristobal.

My purpose was to explore a seeming paradox. Why were almost all indigenous adults illiterate despite the mandate of the INI to build and staff bilingual schools? They were certainly built. An old progress report, dated 1981, showed 86 schools in San Juan Chamula, of which 40 were under the direction of the Department of Indigenous Education. They were supposed to be bilingual primary schools. Why did they not educate? A facile assumption might be that indigenous people were not interested in education, but this is the same "blaming the victim" conclusion offered by some in the United States to explain the failures of education among African Americans. When we met again, I asked Professor Lopez to begin with the school and adult illiteracy and then discuss the expulsions.

* * * * *

Our registry shows 138 students in two sessions, from 9 to 11:30 a.m. and from 12 to 2 p.m., with most students attending the morning session. The policy is to teach first in Tzotzil, with Spanish as a second language, but in this colony there are Tzotzils, Tzeltals, Chols, Tojolabals, Zoques, Mames and Kaqchikels. We can't teach in only one of these languages so we teach in Spanish.

We have 80 boys and 58 girls in the morning session. Parents think women are not as valuable as men. Men must finish grammar school, because they go out to work and need more education. Girls stay at home to prepare meals, look after animals and do other things. That's why there are fewer girls. Still, whatever the deficiencies, education here is much better than in Mitontic. There, though the teachers were Indian too, they were *maleados* [corrupt]. They were partners of the caciques. They didn't help the people look for a better life. The teachers sometimes worked two or three or maybe four days a week. They never worked a whole week and the government was happy with this. That was what they wanted—to keep the people ignorant and powerless. You must understand this if you seek the cause of the expulsions.

There are two aspects: the politics of the government of Mexico and the politics of religion. The people are divided into communities—*parajes* we call them. Each community has its representatives and takes care of itself. The religious problem began in 1964 and 1965, when four or five families in the community of Suyalo accepted the Presbyterian doctrine. Since it was forbidden to practice this doctrine in Mitontic, they went to the Tzotzil community of Chimtic, where they gathered in a house to practice their prayers and organize themselves better.

In this way, they antagonized traditional Catholics. But what is practiced in

Mitontic is not Catholicism. They don't believe with all their hearts in God. It is a name and nothing more. They don't have faith; they only know that God exists. They have their saints in the church but they don't go every day to pray, to sing or to worship. They go only once in a while, when they get sick. There are among them people with a stronger mind who know how to *pulsar* [to take pulse readings] the blood. The people go to ask them a favor. They ask them to pray for them so they may be healed. They pray in houses, and they pray in the church, but just that. The person who asks for the favor doesn't have the faith himself. He doesn't cure himself by his faith. He asks the favor from another. The one who asks the favor does not think of God. He doesn't ask for forgiveness for all the bad things he has done. He just wants to be cured. The problem is these curanderos used liquor in their healing. On many occasions, the sick person doesn't get better because there is only drunkenness. Sometimes they begin to fight and the sick man lies there. That's why the people can't heal. The liquor affects their brain, their senses, their hearts and their thoughts. In Mitontic you could find children and women drinking liquor. All goes wrong because of the liquor.

I say it is the fault of the governments of Mexico and Chiapas. They permit liquor to be sold. Mestizos, as well as Indians, are allowed to produce all kinds of drink. They gave liquor to poor Indians—all the liquor they could take. If they didn't have money they gave them liquor on credit until the debt grew to 100 or 200 pesos. They lent this money with a lot of interest. The poor Indians then went to the coffee plantations to work for several months so they could pay their debts. When they came back they drank again, so they were lost, always in debt. The governments of Mexico and Chiapas were quietly watching and were even glad as the people were sinking into ignorance and moral decay. They thought, "All right, that's fine. The Indians are quiet because they are on the floor, drunk." For the rulers, this was perfect. They could do anything they like without opposition.

Well, then the Presbyterian religion came to Suyalo. It was this religion that took them out of the darkness in which they were living. Many people left off drinking liquor and stopped saying bad things. They dedicated themselves to working, to believing in God, to having fear of God. But the people in the communities didn't like this. They said this religion ruins everything. That's how it began in 1965. The believers could not pray in Mitontic and went to another community. One night the *pistoleros* of the caciques hid by the side of the road and shot the believers as they passed. Four people died. The believers did not stop what they were doing. Their religion continued to grow until 1981 and 1982. Some caciques got together again, thinking and planning what to do. They didn't want to do anything themselves. They wanted the state government to send the police and soldiers to drive them out. They went to Tuxtla Gutierrez several times to ask the governor to drive the evangelicals out of Mitontic. The government said, "No. It can't be. The law protects them. It authorizes man to be free."

In each of the different municipalities there are caciques. The government did not stop or punish those caciques who harmed the evangelicals. This made them bold. Finally, the caciques of Mitontic said to the evangelicals, "Keep quiet, once and for all. If you want to live in peace, then keep quiet and be calm. If you want problems you will have them. We will put you in jail." In June 1989, they expelled all of them. They were brought from Mitontic to San Cristobal and were dropped there. The caciques who organized this are today walking happily on the streets. The government likes it when the Indians fight among themselves and are divided. The government wants to live well, to eat well, to steal well. They are friends of those with huge land holdings. If there is a cacique, the government will buy him so it can do anything it wants. In return, the caciques are protected by the government. Ordinary people have suffered from them for many, many years, but now things are changing. The Priistas are losing support and no longer back the caciques because they're afraid of losing votes. In 1994, the evangelists started to return to Mitontic, and now Catholic catechists, Pentecostals and Presbyterians are meeting quietly in houses. The caciques are just watching. They are without government support and are afraid to begin new expulsions.

16
PUNISHMENT FOR PERSECUTION

The authorities had the power to stop the expulsions but refused to use it. Yet there is ample evidence that when the authorities chose to act, the persecutions ended. When local caciques threatened the Tzeltals of Cancuc and Bachajon and the Tzotzils of Chenalho, Manuel Castellanos Cancino of the INI warned the offenders to stop and put some of them in jail, and the harassment ended. He was even able to halt the expulsions in Chamula from 1967 to 1974, but, when he was replaced by two pro-PRI lawyers, the massive expulsions began.

In 1967, when 12 families were expelled and their houses burned in the municipality of Chanal, a governor ordered the caciques to pay for the damages. After that, there were no further expulsions. In July 1968, when an itinerant evangelist was shot and seriously wounded in the municipality of Huixtan, the assailant was arrested and jailed. There were no major incidents in Huixtan for almost 20 years. In 1989, a municipal official was arrested and put in jail after 154 persons were expelled from the Chenalho communities of Santa Martha and Aldama. After some bargaining, the expelled were allowed to return in exchange for freedom for the jailed official.

In the same year, in the Lacandon selva near the Guatemalan border, when 18 Tojolabal families were expelled from the ejido of Saltillo in Las Margaritas, Governor Patrocinio Gonzalez Garrido put those responsible in the local center of prevention and social reform. When the expelled later pardoned their oppressors, the men were set free. Later, when there was another expulsion, the governor arrested three men and said they would not be freed until the believers returned to their homes or at least were allowed to establish a separate community nearby. This was accepted. In 1990, Governor Gonzalez again came to the defense of beleaguered evangelicals—this time in the community of Amatenango del Valle, on the Pan American Highway south of San Cristobal.

Their community began in 1984, when the Reformed Church in America (in conjunction with the Presbyterian Church of Mexico), sent Steve and Susan Van

Bronkhorst (with their three children) to learn the Amatenango dialect and to begin evangelization there. After 18 months they left on a four-month home leave. When they returned, the town president told them they were no longer welcome. The Van Bronkhorsts moved to Teopisca, about five miles to the north, and tried to maintain contact with Amatenango from there. Four evangelical families, who had also been expelled, settled in Betania.

In early 1989, to help revive the Amatenango mission, Tzeltal missionaries, Pedro Dias Gutierrez and his wife, joined the Van Bronkhorsts in Teopisca. When, in August, Pedro was called to be a teacher at the Buenos Aires Ranch Tzeltal Cultural Center, he was replaced by a church elder from the Oxchuc area of the Highlands—Roberto Gomez Santiz, with his wife, Micael and children. To witness the Gospel in Amatenango, Roberto walked the streets selling handwoven bags that he and his family produced. A small congregation then began to form, meeting secretly in Van Bronkhorsts' home in Teopisca. In 1990, due to Steve's illness, the Van Bronkhorsts returned to the United States and Roberto continued the work alone.

In 1990, when the houses of the few believers were destroyed, Governor Gonzalez Garrido had the Amatenango president arrested and said he would remain in jail until he paid a fine equivalent to 6,000 American dollars for ordering the destruction. The president tried to impose an assessment on each family in town to pay his fine, but they told him, in effect, "You ordered us to tear down the houses. You pay the fine." He had no funds. The evangelicals offered a compromise: "You allow us to remain and hold services and we will forgive you the debt." The municipal president had no choice but to accept.

A year later, the believers' houses were again burned. This time, state authorities arrested three leaders who had instigated the mob. They were told they would remain in prison until a fine of about 8,000 American dollars was paid. Under pressure from the families of the jailed men, the community agreed to pay the fine.

One of the expelled, Santos Gomez Bautista, recalled the events.

✳ ✳ ✳ ✳ ✳

The president of the municipal committee called us to the plaza of the Municipal Palace, and began to ask us if it was correct that we had changed our religion. We replied that it was true. Of our own free will we had accepted the new faith of Jesus Christ. The crowd shouted: "Beat them." They told us that, if we were disposed to renounce our faith, we could stay in our community. We replied that we had freedom of religion, guaranteed by the law, and we did not want to lose our patrimony. Then the municipal officers, with the agreement of Roman Catholic traditionalists, began to beat us in the presence of our wives. In my case, I was brutally struck in the head with a soda bottle. I began to bleed and lost a lot of blood, and then they struck me in the mouth. Later they kicked me and broke my ribs. After most of the men had tortured us, the police were told to put all the men in the jail, allowing the women to return to their houses.

Inside the jail, we could hear their shouts and lamentations, and we thought they were beating our wives. After several hours, we were taken out of the prison. We then discovered that our houses had been burned along, with all of our possessions. Our wives and children had to watch as the mob took out what would not burn and threw it on the streets and on the international highway that passes through the side of our community.

The persecution took place twice. After the first time, we reached an agreement with the authorities, and they allowed us to continue in the community. The next year, the same thing happened. They would not allow us to receive irrigation water for our crops, and so we could not have any harvest of corn that year. After this second persecution, we filed a complaint with the authorities, and the caciques were sent to jail, and the state government forced all the Catholics to pay for the houses and possessions that we lost.

In this community, we see that, when the authorities apply the law, the persecution stops. Now Catholics and evangelicals can live together and respect each other. We have suffered and been persecuted for our Christian faith, and none of us has returned to the old ways. Just the opposite, it has made our faith stronger. We know our God will sustain us with His grace. Because of this demonstration of His power, many of those who persecuted us have repented and live with us in our new congregation. Together, we serve the one God and Father of our lives.

✻ ✻ ✻ ✻ ✻

There was even further progress. In May 1992, by which time a formal Presbyterian church had been established, an agreement was signed in Tuxtla Gutierrez that provided a legal means for the congregation to grow. It stipulated that the believers would make a contribution for municipal affairs but would not be obliged to assume religious cargos. In turn, the believers would receive irrigation water and, most important of all, would be allowed to build a chapel, although not in the community center.

A list of evangelicals was begun at the municipal office. A man need only ask that his name be added to the list to be freed from the obligation to serve cargos. By 1997, when the congregation had grown to about 200 adults, walls had been raised for a large permanent church. However, they could not afford material for the roof and, a year later, they were waiting patiently for promised help.

Amatenango is evidence that, if political rivalry can fuel violence, it might also serve the purpose of peace. In recent years, the PRD has gained strength in the Amatenango area as a rival to the entrenched PRI. The political division and conflict have distracted attention from the evangelicals. As a result, the Presbyterian congregation is growing in relative peace.

17
WE WILL NOT BE STOPPED

A vivid illustration of how the new believers of Chiapas are reexperiencing the early lessons of American evangelical history is the story of Juan Lopez Gomez, whose life in Chiapas parallels that of the Baptist "farmer-preachers" of the rural American south in the final decades of the eighteenth century, as recalled by Sidney Ahlstrom:

This immensely effective servant of God was usually of humble agrarian origin, from a family on the move, living in a region where schools were non-existent and hopes for a "higher education" unheard of. He had in all likelihood been shaken out of his dreary agricultural routine by one or more visits from some itinerant evangelist. Under the force of an "awakening" sermon or a new convert's testimony, he had been "born again" and baptized. Recognizing gifts of preaching in himself and feeling a "call" to exercise them in the locality where he lived . . . he would gather a congregation and be ordained as its minister. Since the preacher did not leave his farm, the question of support did not arise—indeed, paying a minister might be frowned upon—and since a home, barn, or shaded clearing would suffice for a meeting place, the poverty of his people scarcely hindered the work of his church.[1]

Farmer-preachers were responsible for the surge of Baptist growth in the early American rural south. Their modern equivalents—men like Juan Lopez Gomez—are similarly responsible for the surge of Pentecostal churches in rural Chiapas.

In 1988, when Juan Lopez was 28, he picked up and read a leaflet tossed onto the Pan American Highway by an itinerant American missionary named Aaron Testa. Juan was then living in the barrio of La Grandeza in Amantenango del Valle. He invited Testa to his house to teach him about his new religion. Then, inspired, he became a teacher himself and formed a small group in the barrio, separate from the earlier Presbyterian believers in Amatenango. When the Presbyterians were expelled in 1990, the La Grandeza believers moved to Teopisca, where Juan Lopez founded and became the pastor of the independent Pentecostal Church of the Good Shepherd.

There were perhaps a dozen churches of various denominations in Teopisca, while the surrounding small communities were an untouched mission field. In 1992, Pastor Lopez sought new believers in Aquacatenango, a town of about 700 Tzeltals on a road that branches off from Pan American Highway a little south of Teopisca. Soon a congregation of about 20 people was formed, meeting at each others' houses for worship.

Although they no longer took part in the frequent festivals of various saints, they were willing to contribute money to avoid problems with their neighbors. Then, community leaders no longer came to their houses to collect the donations and leveled the familiar accusation of a failure to respect customs and traditions. The evangelicals were threatened with death if they did not renounce their faith. When this had no effect, gangs broke into their houses, smashing doors and windows and brandishing machetes and sticks, and, in 1992, they were forced to flee to Teopisca.

However, one of the families soon returned, and a new congregation grew to 22 families, or about 150 men, women and children, still meeting in peoples' houses. Again there was harassment and threats until, in February 1995, they were forced a second time from their homes and sought refuge in Teopisca. The first small group had been welcomed in 1992, but it was difficult for those families, who were themselves poor and barely able to survive, to succor another 122 people.

1 (1972): 323.

All along, Abdias Tovilla and CEDECH had denounced the authorities of Aquacatenango and sought redress and justice from local, state and federal authorities. The evangelicals joined in the legal actions and attended regular workshops in San Cristobal given jointly by CEDECH and the human rights organization "Open Doors."

Unlike the expulsions from San Juan Chamula, the authorities tried to be helpful. Two of the most active caciques involved in the February expulsions were arrested and remained in jail without trial until they promised to keep the peace. In addition, in attempts to establish a peaceful dialogue, several meetings were scheduled between evangelicals and Aquacatenango leaders, with state officials to serve as mediators. Nothing happened because the caciques simply refused to attend.

Eventually, an alternative site was found for the evangelicals on a hillside across a low valley from Aquacatenango. They promptly named it *Monte de los Olivos* (Mount of Olives). Police and state officials accompanied them to the site to see that they were established without problems, but soon the threats and harassment resumed, and the evangelicals returned to Teopisca.

In August 1996, they were sent back to Monte de los Olivos, accompanied by a truckload of armed police and observers from Open Doors and another organization, Christian Solidarity International. This time the original 22 families were joined by others who had been expelled from San Juan Chamula, Amatenango and the nearby village of El Puerto, so that the community now numbered about 325 men, women and children.

Not long after the officials and observers left, the threats resumed. It was said the evangelicals had no right to the land because it belonged to the Virgin Mary, and it was rumored that a water tank, supplied by the organization "Helping Hands," would be poisoned. The evangelicals refused to be cowed. They had been given building materials by the state government and Helping Hands, and, by mid-November 1996, they had completed the foundations and walls of a church as well as 20 of 27 proposed houses.

Toward the end of November, about 350 men from Aquacatenango and other villages arrived with pickaxes, poles, axes, machetes and several pistols and rifles. It was a Sunday so there was no construction work. About 100 evangelicals came out of their incomplete houses and asked what they wanted. They were told: "You had better go because this land and these houses now belong to us and our children."

The evangelicals replied that if more land was needed they could take an area next to Monte de los Olivos. A leader of the mob shouted, "We're in charge around here. You must leave." Some of the crowd shouted, "Throw them out, throw them out," and began throwing stones. The evangelicals were determined never to be driven away again. They rushed toward the mob and tried to snatch away their weapons. There was a general melee and shots were fired. Pastor Juan Lopez Gomez had come to Monte de los Olivos for the Sunday service and was standing back from the crowd. He later said: "I could hear the bullets passing by my ears."

One of the attackers was killed by five bullets from the assailant's own guns. With that, the fighting stopped, and the mob melted away. By then, 15 other assailants had suffered cuts and bruises as did two evangelicals.

About a month later, on the Sunday feast day San Sebastian, when the men of

Aquacatenango were drunk, they mulled over their defeat. Shortly after noon, about 100 men gathered guns and machetes and went across the valley to Monte de los Olivos. They stopped short of the settlement, however, and simply shouted threats and fired shots at the houses of the evangelicals who, by now, were prepared for defense. Using a car radio, they called Pastor Juan Lopez in Teopisca, who notified the local police. Meanwhile, the evangelicals had managed to seize one of the attackers and handed him over to the police when they arrived. They promptly beat him and said they would take him, and anyone else who kept making trouble, to prison.

Monte de los Olivos is now a growing well-ordered, cinder-block village with a packed church. No other evangelical community in Chiapas has demonstrated such courage and resolution. The following is the testimony of Pastor Lopez, who started it all, and three of those involved in the expulsions.

The first is Juan Baptisa Gomez, one of the earliest of those touched by Pastor Lopez.

✳ ✳ ✳ ✳ ✳

I am from the barrio of La Grandeza in Amatenango. I was suffering very much due to the sickness of alcohol, the sickness of the devil. Brother Juan came to us, and, together with my wife and about 10 others, I accepted the Word of God. After the persecution of believers began in Amatenango, we bought a piece of land in Teopisca to be with Brother Juan. We enlarged the group and went to preach in Aquacatenango. Brother Jesus Vasquez was the first to accept Christ there. After he was tortured, he left Aquacatenango to live with us in Teopisca. The people thought evangelical belief was finished there, but, with time, another group was formed. Then, what happened to brother Jesus they did again. One night, around 11 p.m., they expelled the believers. They stole everything in the houses of the Brothers and burned their houses. With the Sisters, the Brothers walked to Teopisca and arrived at sunrise with empty hands. They came crying. The people thought evangelical belief was finished but God formed another group.

✳ ✳ ✳ ✳ ✳

Jesus Vazquez Mendez, who is mentioned above, suffered the most. Here is his story of the expulsion in 1992:

✳ ✳ ✳ ✳ ✳

I did not know God, but Brother Juan came to talk with me, and I accepted the Holy Word in 1992. In a little while, people began asking if I was an evangelical, and I answered yes. Later, people from the town center came to tell me to leave. I told them I would never give up the Word of God, and they dragged me out of my house. I said I didn't do anything, and they said: "So, you are never going to give it up?"

They left, but they came again and asked me if I was going to give it up, and I said no. Then they came and threw stones at my house. Every time they had a fiesta and got drunk, they threw stones at my house. At midnight or two in the morning, when they were drunk, they threw stones. We were sleeping and we were scared. The roof was so damaged the rain came through.

One day, the Brothers came to my house for a prayer meeting. I told them, "Brothers, I had a dream last night, and I wonder what it means. I dreamt my two little children told me, 'Father, don't be afraid of the people that are coming to destroy our house.'"

Brother Juan told me, "Don't be afraid. Just call on the Lord and pray to Him." When the service was over, I decided to go to Comitan [a major city about 25 miles to the south]. I asked my son, "Do you want to go with me to Comitan?" He asked, "But why so late?" I answered, "I don't know. I just want to go to Comitan."

"All right," he said. "I'll go with you." My wife also said she would go with us, but my daughter did not come. When I was in Comitan, I began to think, as if a spirit had awakened me. I asked myself, "Why did I come here?" I had forgotten about my dream, and I was thinking about my daughter, whom I had left back home, and began to pray. I kept on praying. I was not happy. [Here he began to cry. After about a minute, he got control of himself, but haltingly.]

My heart jumped. I don't know why I felt uneasy. I felt sad, and my heart was sad, and, at about nine in the morning, I told my family we had better return home. We got down from the bus at a stop just before Aquacatenango. A man from the town asked me, "Where did you go?"

"To Comitan," I said.

He told me that all the houses of evangelicals were burned. He said the caciques and other people came at night with torches and gasoline when the children were asleep so everyone would be killed. He said the families were able to take out the children. Everything else was burned. I told my wife and son, "We better go to our house." I wasn't afraid. We went to our community, and I saw many people gathered, and I wondered what they were doing. We walked a little, and I saw they were coming toward us with sticks and stones in their hands. They wanted to kill us, but I told them, "Look Gentiles. Are you going to kill a snake or are you going to kill me because I stole something?"

"Why did you change your religion?" they asked. "That's your crime."

I answered, "I didn't steal anything. I just began studying the Holy Word, and that's what you don't want." When I told them this, they threw stones at me. They hurt me, and I fell to the ground. They grabbed me by the hand, and dragged me about 10 meters. When they left me, I turned and saw my son and wife thrown to the ground as well.

My wife called out, "Are we going to run away?"

I said, "No, we are not going to escape because, if our God still loves us, we are going to live." Then we began to pray to our Lord. We were praying when they came again. They hurt us. They threw us on the ground, and one said, "Watch them because they're going to run away. See that they don't. If they try, throw stones at them."

Some rural police and caciques came and tied my hands and took me to the presidency. They tied me to a post with ropes around my neck, arms and legs and left me in the strong sun. All the people laughed at me and insulted me. They called me a thief and a witch. Someone brought gasoline and poured it on my legs.

"Burn him," they shouted. A drunken man came and asked, "Why are you doing this to that man? He has committed no crime." They told him my crime was that I studied the Holy Scripture. This drunken man was an unbeliever. Someone shouted, "Tie him up." They tied the drunken man to a light post and began beating him, and lots of blood came out. They beat him because he defended me, but they didn't beat me. I was tied to the column until about five o'clock. Then they untied me and took me to the jail. They threw a paper bag on the ground for me to sleep on. They put the other man in the jail too. The next day, they took me out of jail and asked if I was going to give up my religion. I told them I was never going to leave it because it was the Word of God. When I told them this, they said, "He's a witch. That's why he's not afraid. He's a witch. He's a thief. Beat him."

People were laughing and screaming at me, "Throw him into jail again until he tells us he's going to leave his religion." They released me because the Brothers had used a radio to call San Cristobal, and the authorities called the municipal office and told them to set me free. I went to my house. It was burned and everything was gone except a shirt. My family was gone and I was alone. As I was leaving, they fired two shots at me but they missed. They threw stones too but again they missed.

I had no information where my family and the Brothers were. I had to walk eight miles to Teopisca, where, by the grace of God, at the entrance to the town, all the Brothers and my family were waiting. They said they had walked all night, carrying the little children to where other Brothers, who had been expelled from their homes some time ago, now lived. These Brothers gave us clothes and places to rest and live until we recovered from our wounds and could look for work and find new homes.

✳ ✳ ✳ ✳ ✳

Juan Mendez Juarez was involved in the expulsion from Aquacatenango and the building of the community at Monte de los Olivos.

✳ ✳ ✳ ✳ ✳

In February 1995, we decided to have a prayer meeting with our brothers in Teopisca, and we spent the night in a church there. The people of Aquacatenango were watching, and they knew our houses would be empty, and they burned all of them. When we came back the next day, a woman said to Brother Pedro Perez Giron, "So you are here. Look at how your houses are—just ashes." She said, "I know who did it. It was so and so. They came by night, and they called my son to go with them, but he didn't go."

Brother Pedro denounced this in the presidency. The municipal agent called the person who was accused. He also called all the people. He said, "Now we are going to fix this problem because they are blaming this man for burning the houses of the evangelicals."

Brother Pedro was asked to present the witness. He called the woman but she denied everything. "I didn't see anything," she said. They were going to put the woman in jail, but the people called out, "Better put that evangelical in jail." They acted as with Barabbas and Jesus. They put Brother Pedro in jail and freed the one who burned the houses. We went to Venustiano Carranza because the Aquacatenango colony belongs to that municipality. We complained to the authorities, and they sent a summons to let Brother Pedro go free. They decided it wasn't right to have him in jail, because he was the one who was damaged.

The next day, a message arrived telling the Aquacatenango municipal agent to free the Brother, but he refused to accept it. I was there, talking with the Brothers, watching everything. The agent said to the man who brought the message, "You don't give orders here. We are the people." Then he called all the people on the public address system, men, women and children. "We are going to see what we shall do with the evangelicals. The people came, and they said, "Let's go for the others. Let's put all of them all in jail. Let's burn all their belongings and put an end to it, once and for all."

The municipal agent organized a group who came and put six Brothers in jail. I was there, waiting to be put into jail, but they didn't touch me. I saw how they took the Brothers and locked them in jail. They were released after about 10 days. Then the municipal agent decided to catch all the Brothers and burn them or their houses. He formed groups with someone in charge of each group. That was around 10 o'clock at night. With God's blessing they did not find us. We knew what was going to happen, and we took our families to a hiding place. We left our houses, and they burned or stole everything they could put their hands on. We slept in the hiding place until three in the morning, and then we walked to Teopisca. We were 122 men, women, and children.

Two of the caciques were arrested for doing this. After three months they said, "Let us out of jail, and we will let the evangelicals go back to their houses. We are not against them. We did this because the people demanded it from us." So they were freed after paying bail. After many months of talk, there was an agreement that we could return if we built a new community on the other side of the road, completely separate from the town.

We went there on December 16, 1995. An assistant attorney general and people from the Bureau of Indian Affairs and public security came with us. Still, the people gathered again and blocked the road. They put stones, nails and other things so no truck could pass by. The assistant attorney general talked to them. He said we were of the same blood—the same people—and Article 24 of the Constitution says everyone is free. He began to explain, but the people didn't want to hear. They began yelling. When the assistant attorney general saw how the people were, he said he would apply the law, and the police seized one of the caciques. They took him to prison in Tuxtla Gutierrez, but he was soon set free on bail.

We had returned to our new community across the highway from Aquacatenango, but still there was no peace. They whispered, "After the authorities leave, we will kill you one by one." We decided it was too dangerous, and we returned to Teopisca to continue our exile. Then, there was another agreement, and they said we could return. That was August 9, 1996. They still want to get rid of us. They do not let us go to other places to pick up wood for cooking or to plant corn. In November 1996, they came in many trucks, thinking to seize us. They had bars, axes, machetes, sticks and guns. We threw the stones back at them and they ran away. Six evangelicals were hurt. We don't know how many of them were hurt.

We will never leave. We have divided the land into lots and are building houses with cement blocks that we buy in San Cristobal. The government has supported us with 50 percent. The other 50 percent comes with the blessing of God. Some Brothers have helped us. They come and give us offerings so we are able to buy more material. When the government brought us here to this new place on the other side of the road, the people said we could not live here because the land belonged to the Virgin. They want to get hold of the houses we are building, but we are not going to leave. This is God's land. This is our Monte de los Olivos and God will protect us.

✳ ✳ ✳ ✳ ✳

Finally, Juan Lopez Gomez, whose life began anew when he picked up the pamphlet thrown by Aaron Testa.

✳ ✳ ✳ ✳ ✳

I am from Amatenango del Valle. I was lost in my community, without knowing the living God, and suddenly a friend came along who taught me the Bible and God's things, and I was converted with all my family and with other persons—a group of about 16 people. I was a Catholic, but I didn't go to church on Sunday. The priest didn't teach the Bible. He preached about other things. The man who taught me about God was an American missionary who worked in Veracruz for three years and then came to Chiapas. His name was Aaron Testa. I was at home when he came by in his car throwing leaflets. They were in Spanish. I speak Tzeltal but I had learned a little Spanish. I went near and began talking to him. He talked to me about God. He said, "If you want, I can go to your home to teach you something." I said, "I invite you," and so we began to talk about the things of God. Brother Ron lived in San Cristobal and came to my house every week. He said his practice had no name—that he was just a Christian. But, in Mexico, the government wants to know which is your group, so we call ourselves Pentecostal.

I called him because I was worn out. I used to make liquor, and I drank, and my sons were very sick, so I wanted another life—to change everything. I am now 39 years old. I was born in 1957. When I was converted to Christ in 1988 I was 28.

When we were expelled from Amatenango in 1990, I went to Teopisca. Then I went to Aquacatenango to preach. Brother Jesus and eight other persons were converted. In 1992, the people put Brother Jesus in jail. They tied him to a column, and people were yelling, "Why aren't you afraid? We think you are a witch because you are not afraid. Let's burn him! Let's burn him!"

We are not afraid because God gives us strength. We are not alone any more. His Spirit is living within us. He never leaves us. We are not afraid of death or of anything or anyone who threatens us. We know we have life everlasting in Jesus our Lord. The Bible says to live in Christ and to die in Christ is of great worth. Christ said, "Do not fear those who kill the body because they can not kill the soul." This and other Bible texts have encouraged us. We have seen the power of God. When people tell us they are going to kill and burn us, God does not abandon us. They were going to burn Brother Jesus but they didn't, because God did not will it. It was not His will. We always wait for the will of God because we are in His hands. When Brother Jesus and the others were expelled they never defended themselves. They came to my house in Teopisca. In December 1995, the government said the people could go back but they would have to live outside the town—on the other side of the highway—to avoid further trouble.

We said, "All right, if you will support us." We accepted that, and began to build a community on a little hill that we call Monte de los Olivos. But then the people attacked us and we left again. The government said we could return. They asked, "When are you going back?" We answered, "On August 9, 1996," and, thank God, the government helped us. They sent public security and officials from the Bureau of Indigenous Affairs to protect us. Then we began to work, and again the people came to kill us. They came with a group of about 300 men and women. They brought machetes, sticks, stones and guns too. I told my Brothers not to use anything like sticks or machetes—nothing—and that we would talk in a peaceful manner.

The municipal agent was with them. I went to talk to him, and he said, "You have no right to live here because I was not here when you arrived to give you permission." I said, "No, we are staying here because we worked here, and this is our community." He said, "But you are invaders."

"No, we are not invaders," I said. "You are the invaders because you invaded our lots. We are not invaders because we don't have a place to live." So they began to beat us with sticks and stones, and then they began to shoot, and we took the same sticks they threw at us and defended ourselves with them. We defended our wives and children, so there was a confrontation, and six of the Brothers were injured.

We will not be stopped. I make my living with faith and the help of my Brothers. They give us corn and beans and a little offering for my bus fare. I have two children and my wife embroiders blouses. With this, and the help of God, we have a meal every day. That is now my life. There are places where there are no evangelicals. I visit about 10 towns. I pray to God to give me time to go to teach them. There is some opposition from Catholics, so it is necessary to make several visits. I just go to different towns and give leaflets to people on the street. These leaflets talk about Christ, and some who read them come to believe in Christ. I know God wants to save more lost people, because Christ said, "Go throughout the world and preach the Gospel to all men. Those who believe and are baptized will be saved." I think the Gospel is going to keep growing. It is not going to stop, because the Word of God is the power of God. Some men want to end evangelical belief, but they cannot do that. God has put us here to keep on preaching His Word.

18

THE PERSECUTION ENDS

The evangelicals of the Highlands of Chiapas called for justice from 14 state governors and five national presidents. Every time, they were assured something would be done, but all that happened was another "peace" dialogue and the appointment of another committee to investigate. The pattern was demonstrated in 1982, when Governor Juan Sabines, instead of insisting that the expelled Tzotzils of San Juan Chamula had as much right to the lands of their ancestors as did their cacique persecutors, merely offered them other lands far away. The state thus became a partner in the expulsions. In September 1982, a Chamula municipal secretary gave a list of what was wrong with the evangelicals: "They destroy our culture because they do not drink, or fight, or use curanderos, or burn candles or incense, or respect the saints, or use crosses in their houses and they pray a lot. If they do not stop these practices we will expel them and burn their houses, kill their children with machetes and shoot the adults."

In September 1984, Governor Absalon Castellanos signed what was called a "compromise" that called for an immediate end to expulsions, the return of those already expelled and a guarantee of freedom of religion. He also proposed the creation of a federal-state commission to oversee security, along with a vast new social and economic development plan. It was forgotten almost as soon as the ink was dry.

In July 1985, a group of expelled began a sit-in in front of the National Palace in Mexico City to ask President Miguel de la Madrid to intervene. It was the first time they had come to the heart of the country to publicize their grievances. They said 10,000 people had lost their homes and asked for justice. What they said was written in the newspapers, and they were interviewed for radio reports. When they left they were forgotten.

In May 1989, Governor Gonzalez Garrido told reporters he was obliged to recognize traditional authority and brushed aside their questions with a statement that there was no easy solution. He drew an analogy with the ouster of the Roman Catholic Church from Chamula and its replacement by the self-proclaimed Bishop of the Orthodox Church of St Pascualito. "Look, I have been governor of Chiapas for six months," he said. "Samuel Ruiz has been bishop for 25 years, but with a kick in the ass they threw him out. Chamula is the only place in the history of humanity where the people changed their religion in one day. If, after 25 years, Samuel Ruiz can be displaced from one day to another and the people converted to Orthodox, a word that they can not even pronounce, there are obviously no easy answers."

He said if he tried to impose his will it would "provoke a massacre." He added: "I could avoid it if I sent a detachment of police to live with each family, but for how long could I do that?"[1]

While the politicians claimed to be merely respecting indigenous rights, no one doubted that they were, in fact, guarding their vote bank. This was never more obvious than on July 4, 1988, when the Chamula caciques refused to allow local elections until 21 arrest orders had been canceled. The arrest orders were canceled, and, when the voting took place three days later, all of the votes were in favor of the PRI.

Sometimes the expulsions coincided with national elections. In 1991, with simultaneous municipal, state and federal elections, increased expulsions ensured there would be no opposition, and once again the PRI received 100 percent of the ballots.

The Evangelists Begin to Fight Back

In 1993, the leaders of the expelled began a process of confrontation that would bring an end to their persecution. On September 8, recently expelled men, women and children began a sit-in in the sprawling compound of the Bureau of Indigenous Affairs in San Cristobal. Others joined in the following weeks until their numbers increased to 584. To break their resolve, they were left without food or medical care. On October 16, a recently-born boy died. There was a hospital nearby, and the authorities said the mother should have gone there, but no one would leave the grounds. There was a suggestion that the government might at least pay for the child's coffin, but it did not. On November 25, a second newborn child died, and there was a protest march, led by Domingo Angel Lopez, through the streets of San Cristobal. Now, food was sent by Bishop Ruiz and the evangelical churches.

The sit-in did nothing to halt the expulsions. On October 8, Pedro Hernandez Diaz, of the community of Chiotic, was called to the Chamula community center with his wife and three children. They were told that, if they did not leave volun-

---

1 Rojas (1993): 113.

tarily within three days, they would be killed. This had become the form of expulsion. Rather than rounding up groups of believers for a mass expulsion, and thus attracting unfavorable newspaper publicity, individuals were selected and told to leave "voluntarily"or else. The Hernandez family complied. In this way, they could at least take a few possessions with them.

Two days later, 12-year-old Juan Heredia Perez, whose family, a month earlier, had been forced to "voluntarily" leave the community of Arvenza II, returned to harvest the corn in his family's fields. He was captured, accused of being an evangelical, beaten until the blood poured down his face and sent away with a warning that he would be killed if he returned "to preach and give a bad example to the people."

During the sit-in, the government, as usual, made appeasing gestures. In early December, the state assembly appointed a "conciliation" committee headed by a PRI deputy. He proposed that they all move to an empty government warehouse outside the city during a "dialogue" to reach a solution. It was an obvious trick to get them out of sight and was rejected out of hand.

In turn, the representatives of the expelled said they at least should be allowed to return, with guarantees for their safety, to harvest their crops and recover possessions they had left behind. The authorities of Chamula were consulted. Only two of the 20 communities affected agreed. It was then learned that the caciques in the other communities had already harvested the crops and had sold them on the markets of San Cristobal. With that, the "conciliation" committee never returned to talk to the expelled.

Suddenly, there was what seemed to be a revolutionary change. On New Year's Day 1994, Subcommander Marcos and his Zapatistas occupied San Cristobal and proclaimed what was called a "Revolt of the Indians." The 584 actual Indians occupying the grounds of the Bureau of Indigenous Affairs could no longer be ignored. On January 5, by which time the Zapatistas had retreated from San Cristobal, representatives of the Office of Social Development (SEDESOL) met with representatives of the expelled and agreed to form two committees to examine the history of expulsions and to review the existing situation. More down-to-earth, SEDESOL realized it had to do something about the unhealthy conditions of the families taking part in the sit-in. It established a dispensary and installed a kitchen, including a mill to grind corn, and also installed latrines. Furthermore, SEDESOL said it would ensure that outside help sent to the sit-in would arrive promptly and safely.

On January 11, President Carlos Salines de Gortari appointed a special committee of three highly regarded Chiapanecos, including the scholar Andres Fabregas Puig, with a large agenda: end the expulsions, punish the authorities and caciques, arrange for the return of the expelled, ensure respect for all religious beliefs and draw up a plan for services for the expelled colonies in San Cristobal, including the creation of an indigenous market. When commission members visited the sit-in, they were given a large package of documents, including correspondence with various governmental organizations to that date. A commission spokesman later said the problem was very complicated and "a difficult matter to resolve." The commission was never heard of again.

Meanwhile, an official of the state attorney general's office announced that, during the Zapatista occupation of City Hall, when the rebels tossed files out of a window, all previous complaints against the caciques of Chamula had been lost. He said that there were no copies of the documents in the state capital and that, to get justice, it would be necessary to file new complaints.

Before the Zapatista uprising, Governor Elmar Setzer Marseille had refused to accept the complaints of the expelled. He was dismissed for having failed to anticipate the revolt and was replaced by Javier Lopez Moreno, who then formed a "Special Commission for the Investigation of the Expulsions." It evaporated when the Chamula authorities simply refused to meet with it.

In February, when peace talks began at the cathedral of San Cristobal between Marcos and a government team led by Manuel Camacho Solis, with Bishop Ruiz acting as go-between, representatives of the expelled tried to find a place at the table. Outsiders were not permitted, but a Tzotzil who had been expelled and was part of the Red Cross guard slipped a note to the Zapatistas asking for help. Marcos replied that he would demand their "unconditional return" along with punishment "for those of the same race and blood who have committed this injustice." Through another note, Marcos was asked to meet leaders of the expelled. On February 26, 30 Tzotzils, led by Domingo Lopez Angel and Esdras Alonso Gonzalez, entered the cathedral and met him. Marcos said he had discussed their problems with Camacho Solis: "I told that bastard (*pinche*) Camacho that the PRI was dipping its hands in Chamula and that it protected the caciques. He told me that the government in the future would pass a law to prohibit expulsion and penalize those responsible. I asked him what had happened in the 20 past years when the rights of the expelled had been violated ... The government is asking me to put down our arms. It would be better that I give them to the expelled to defend themselves against the caciques who are exploiting them."

The Zapatistas did put an additional demand on the negotiating table: "We ask for an end to the expulsions of the indigenous peoples by the caciques aided by the government. We demand a guarantee for the free and voluntary return of all the expelled to their lands and indemnification for their losses."[2] It was lost in the mass of other demands and simply forgotten.

The Mexican government's concern about the political aftershocks of the Zapatista uprising did not soften its attitude toward the expulsions of evangelicals. On March 29, 1994, the most massive expulsion in recent years, involving 228 persons, was carried out from the Chamula community of Pugchen Mumuntic. A letter was sent to President Salinas asking him to intervene. He replied that the matter had been referred to the government of Chiapas.

This expulsion posed a problem among leaders of the long-established evangelical colonies. The expelled were Jehovah's Witnesses, who had long been resented because of their aggressive evangelization of other denominations. No one wanted them as neighbors. The government found a place for them far away in the mountaintop community of La Traya in the municipality of Ixtapa. (I can testify to its remoteness. I once tried to reach it with a friend driving a small car. We struggled for two hours up a steep road strewn with rocks and then turned back, fearing the car would disintegrate.)

Since the peaceful sit-in had drawn no response, the evangelicals decided on more forceful action. In May of 1994, eight months of empty promises after the

2 Alonzo (1995): 46–51.

start of the sit-in, they kidnaped Enrique Lunes Patishtan, the elder statesmen of the Chamula caciques. He was regarded as the intellectual author of the expulsions. He was also, oddly enough, a member of the State Commission of Human Rights. He was seized on a street in San Cristobal and handed over to the authorities, ostensibly to stand trial for dozens of complaints previously filed against him. About 500 Chamulans, led by municipal president Domingo Lopez Ruiz, piled into cars and trucks and raced to San Cristobal, where they blocked the main streets and began a sit-in in front of court offices. Patishtan was freed two hours later, under a bond of 3,000 pesos. (The Chamula authorities maintained a cash reserve fund for such emergencies.)

The government responded with two gestures. One was positive: a promise that the families taking part in the sit-in would be recompensed for the land and possessions they had lost and would also be paid an allowance, while continuing the sit-in, to buy food and clothing. The other was the appointment of a committee to survey the refugee colonies in San Cristobal and Teopisca to find out what they needed and what damages they had suffered, with monthly meetings with the expelled for progress reports. As with all earlier committees, it vanished without a trace.

Then came another kidnaping—and this would prove decisive. At 10 o'clock on the morning of July 5, 1994, Chamula municipal president Professor Domingo Lopez Ruiz was seized, despite his bodyguards, as he walked in the center of San Cristobal. One pistol was pointed at his head and another at his testicles and he was bundled into a car and rushed away. Immediately, the caciques kidnaped Andres Gomez Lopez, the head of the Emiliano Zapata Transport Agency (OTEZ) and four others of the expelled. OTEZ was the main support of Domingo Angel Lopez's CRIACH. They were beaten and taken to the municipal jail in San Juan Chamula. The Chamulans announced they would burn Andres Gomez alive if Lopez Ruiz was not set free. A message was sent back: "If at 12 you burn Andres, at one we will burn Lopez Ruiz."

By now, the new governor, Javier Lopez Moreno, had returned to the old policy of refusing to have any dealings with the spokesmen for the expelled. The kidnaping forced him to change his mind. That same night, he met representatives of the sides in the government palace in Tuxtla Gutierrez, from about midnight to three in the morning. It was agreed that there would be a simultaneous liberation of prisoners under official supervision, and that the governor would meet in San Cristobal with a group of the expelled to quantify their damages and to arrange for later peace talks.

However, when the leaders of the expelled returned to San Cristobal, they found that a PRI assemblyman, in their absence, had gone to the sit-in to say it would never be possible for the expelled to return to their homes. They were furious, and, when their leaders now tried to carry out the simultaneous prisoner exchange, the expelled refused to give up the Chamula municipal president, who, it developed, was hidden among them.

When this news circulated via two-way car radios, the Chamulans mounted about 3,000 men in a convoy of 89 cars and trucks and raced to San Cristobal. They were armed with rifles and sticks and carried cans of gasoline. They announced that they would burn down the buildings of the Indigenous Affairs compound. As the caravan moved slowly up a hill on the southern side, a Tzotzil mounted a wall surrounding the compound and pulled an Uzi submachine gun from beneath his *chuj* (the black wool jacket of a traditional costume). He fired separate shots and then a burst, killing two of the attackers and wounding four others. Although this was not the first armed encounter, it was the first time either side had used arms of such high power. The assault force retreated and in the afternoon the prisoner exchange took place in the municipal palace of San Cristobal.

Two days later, Governor Javier Lopez proposed still another commission for peace and reconciliation. Now, with the escalation of violence—especially with the expelled bearing modern arms—the Chamula authorities were persuaded to agree to meet evangelical leaders on July 18. In return, the government paid damages to the families of the Chamulans killed in the attack. The meeting, at a large hall in Tuxtla Gutierrez, included agents of 92 communities as well as state and federal authorities and officials of human rights and religious organizations. This time the focus was not on rectifying wrong but on establishing the parameters of permanent peace. It was an historic step forward—seeking a way out of the morass. A subcommittee labored for 10 days and produced a blueprint for good will and mutual understanding.

On one hand, the traditionalists agreed that the cargos were not obligatory. On the other, representatives of the evangelicals said they would respect San Juan, and would recognize him as a representative of the people, and would take part in offices that did not require great expenses but would not, however, participate in ceremonies that required them to drink alcohol, use tobacco or buy candles. They would also recognize that curanderos, using natural medicines and herbs, had a tradition in the communities and said they would respect them and not oppose them. The Chamulan authorities said they had customs: that they did not want them to die and become a part of history. The evangelicals said they would respect this culture, customs and traditions because they too were from Chamula. The Chamula authorities said they did not want to be criticized because their saints were of stone and wood and the evangelicals said they would respect these beliefs too, but, at the same time, they said their religion should not be called a sect. They felt they should have respect too. Both sides said they were concerned about the division between friends and families, criticized aggression and hoped to resolve their differences through dialogue.

However, peace is not achieved so easily. When the traditionalists returned on July 30 to ratify the draft, they did not wear their costumes. It was a sign of disrespect. They said the people of Chamula were special and did not take orders from outsiders, that they had their own governmental structure, that they were Catholic and Priistas, that they had adopted Priismo as part of their culture and that they would never permit the entry of another religion or political party from outside. These were the claims heard in the early 1970s when the massive expulsions began.

Rather than go through another round of pointless talks, the expelled decided to take the greatest risk of all—to return to their homes without a guarantee for their safety. It was announced that, on August 11, the first 10 families would return to the community of El Pozo. A day later, 10 would return to the community of Cuchulumtic. On the next day, 13 would return to Botameste and, on August 15, three would return to Cruxho. By September 7, 27 days short of the first anniversary of their ordeal in the compound of the Bureau of Indigenous Affairs, the return was completed.

They were brave indeed. Only four months earlier, the car of a believer who drove with his family to Cruxho, was strafed by 26 bullets. Fortunately, the passengers suffered just minor injuries. Journalists who accompanied the first to return to El Pozo reported there were hidden arms in the long official caravan but there was no trouble, since the returnees were accompanied by officials.

In early September, however, a report surfaced that the caciques were preparing to strike. The report was so exact that Abdias Tovilla was able to send a warning to the national secretary of state and the National Human Rights Commission that the blow would fall on the community of Icalumtic. His warning was ignored. In Icalumtic on September 29, 300 men attacked the houses of returned families. Two men and a woman were killed, and a girl of 14 was raped. Another woman was shot and wounded but managed to save her children. The dead left nine minor orphans. Not content with bloodshed, the assailants stole money that the Bureau of Indigenous Affairs had given as compensation for the damages suffered by those taking part in the sit-in. State officials came to recover the dead and wounded. An estimated 5,000 persons, some carrying placards of three of the men responsible for the massacre, walked silently through the main streets of San Cristobal following the coffins. The governor later distributed 35,000 pesos for the orphans and the families of the victims, but there was no effort to arrest and punish the guilty.

The persecutions had never stifled evangelical growth in Chamula. One area where the flame flickered was in the twin communities of Arvenza I and Arvenza II. On September 20, nine days before the killings at Icalumtic, Agustin Perez Lopez, a man of great courage who had inspired the spread of evangelical belief, was kidnaped from Arvenza I. On the demand of the evangelical community, about 80 special and judicial police descended on the community of Cuchulumtic where, according to rumors, he had been taken. Two men identified as his kidnappers were arrested but Perez, or his body, could not be found.

Then came the massacre at Icalumtic. Even the caciques realized the spiral of violence was becoming uncontrollable. They agreed to send representatives to a newly appointed Commission of Reconciliation. However, now the evangelicals refused to take part until the disappearance of Augustin Perez Lopez was solved. On December 15, one of the detained men led police to the place where his body was found. On the same day, representatives of both sides signed a truce and a pact of non-aggression, putting into effect the agreement of mutual understanding formulated the previous July.

There were no public celebrations—no rockets and speeches to imply a winner or loser—just a verbal agreement. Still, there were a few who refused to accept peace, and, for this, they would pay with their lives.

19
FINAL BLOODSHED AND NEW BELIEVERS

Once there was a single community of Arvenza but the population grew and it was split into Arvenza I and Arvenza II. They still consist of the interlocking families that typically form indigenous communities so they are twins and share a similar fate. Arvenza I, the older twin, is on a ridge. Looking down toward the north, there is the valley containing the Chamula ceremonial center. Looking down toward the west, is the separate municipality of Zinacantan.

When evangelism took root in the two communities, persecution soon followed. On July 11, 1995, Ernesto Ruiz Perez was seized by a group of men, beaten and taken off toward another mountain—probably so the men could kill him. Fortunately, he escaped and fled to San Cristobal. On August 2, a mob entered the house of Domingo Gomez Pachulel in Arvenza II and took him to the jail in the Chamula community center. They beat him and let him go the next day. On August 6, 11 men and women were rounded up in Arvenza I and expelled to San Cristobal where, a few days later Abdias Tovilla took a statement from one of them, Ciriolo Cruz Patishtan, to be used as evidence for a formal complaint against the Chamula authorities.

✳ ✳ ✳ ✳ ✳

We are only five evangelical families. We were called to the rural authorities where we were asked if we were evangelicals and if we would refuse to deny Jesus Christ. We said yes. Then, in the presence of hundreds of people, they told us it would be better to renounce our religion and leave the community peacefully, and if not we would be beaten by all the community. We said we would not leave because it was not just and that we are not robbers or killers, but we are learning to live well. They seized us and carried us to the municipal jail of Chamula, and there the municipal president and judge asked us the same questions. When we again said that we believed in Jesus Christ, and would not give up the evangelical life and would also not give up our lands because we were not doing anything bad, they ordered us to be put in the jail from noon until 8:30 at night. Then they put us in a municipal vehicle, and the president, Domingo Lopez Ruiz, took us to the state attorney's office in San Cristobal. There, they took our declaration at 11:30 at night on August 6. We were set free because we had not done anything wrong, and were told that we could return to our community if we wished. To avoid major problems, we did not return and we are now refugees. On August 19, we wanted to return to harvest the radishes that we had grown, but the caciques called many people, and they began to beat us with sticks and stones and took us again to the municipal jail. The municipal president and judge asked us why we had returned. They said the president had the authority of the governor of Chiapas to expel all evangelicals and that, if we returned again, they would take us through all the communities of Chamula, and if they killed us, it would not be their fault. Then, in the presence of these officials, the caciques began to beat us, and my shirt was soaked in blood. They said they would give us three days to take our belongings from our houses and leave. Now we are refugees and do not have clothing, food or money, and our families are sick.

* * * * *

On September 2, Augustin Perez Lopez, who had earlier been expelled from Arvenza I, returned to Chamula to see if it was possible to return to his home and lands if he agreed to accept a traditional cargo. As soon as he arrived and announced his wish, he was seized, beaten, put into a white truck and taken away. The evangelicals obtained arrest orders for the men they believed were responsible. When the orders were not carried out, the evangelicals tried to enforce justice themselves. On November 18, at about 10 in the morning, a group of eight evangelicals tried to seize the two men. It turned out the men were armed. One of the evangelicals, Domingo Lopez Mendez, was shot and killed. The others ran away to hide, but their whereabouts was soon known. They were in the house of a new believer, Hilario Shilon Jimenez.

The caciques called for reinforcements. One hundred men responded with guns and bottles of gasoline, shouting they would burn down all the houses of Arvenza I and kill the evangelicals as they emerged. But when they began to shoot, their fire was returned and a battle raged for the remainder of the 18th and far into the next day. Calls were made to the police, but none came until the shooting had ended. They found, according to later official accounts, one evangelical killed and four of the cacique attackers dead. In addition, there were four wounded, and 12 houses were burned. Unofficial accounts put the death toll as high as 28.

That was the last battle of Chamula. Not that the caciques were reconciled to evangelism; they had no other choice. In the battle of Arvenza I, the evangelicals had demonstrated they were no longer willing to accept their fate as "God's will." A reporter for the Mexico City newspaper *La Jornada* captured this militancy in an interview with a man identified as an evangelical leader: "The speeches of Brothers and pastors say it is the will of God that someone is killed. I say, 'Amen, but if you are raping my daughter and wife, or if you are burning my house, should I do nothing?' It is here that our faith is in question, and we wonder in which God we believe? We say: 'I will not go to find you, but, if you put a foot in my house, I will kill you.'"[1]

One reason for the militancy was the conversion of Manuel San Juan who was once among the caciques who persecuted the evangelicals. His home in Arvenza I is now used for church services. Evangelicals call him a Saul turned into a Paul.

* * * * *

When we had our meetings, the municipal chief incited us saying the evangelicals were burning Catholic churches and all kinds of things like that. We could not stand for that. In private, the president told us that we could no longer sell beer to the evangelicals and that was proof of their bad influence. For a year, a Brother talked to me about the Gospel. He was always willing to talk and answer questions. Then I had a dream. I was traveling in a three-quarter-ton Ford truck when I came to where the road was divided into three parts. The most tortuous road was that of the Gospel. The Brother had talked to me about this road. He said, "You have to decide." I decided to become a Christian.

Since then, many old friends have asked me about the transformation of my life.

1 June 30, 1996.

I try to answer them in a comprehensible way. I tell them I am still their friend. Not all have asked questions or tried to understand. One time, when I was driving a truck on the road to my house, some men had camouflaged themselves with branches and leaves. I heard a shot and thought the leaders wanted to see me dead, but it missed.

I will not let them intimidate me, and I will not disobey God. If they want to do anything to me, here I am. It is obvious that God wants me here. My life is in his hands. My wife and son used to get sick. We bought candles, and they were cured by the curandero, but they charged money for this—20, 50 or 100 pesos. If a fever comes, you buy candles and they kill chickens for the healing. They say the Word of God doesn't do any good.

I accepted the Word of God in 1995. When I accepted, we went to San Cristobal but we came back in '96. I was here when that fight started, and there was shooting with high-powered rifles. We don't know who killed the caciques who attacked us. Maybe, with all that shooting, they killed themselves. Thank God, my family was not here then, and I was not killed. Now it is calm. In my family, my wife and son have not been sick for one year. We are happy. In Chamula, there is liquor and beer and some of them steal chickens and beat their wives. They go to jail and the municipal president fines them. Religion is good. We don't drink liquor, we don't beat our wives and we don't go to jail. Thank God, I have my house and I don't drink so I have enough money for a cement floor in my house.

✳ ✳ ✳ ✳ ✳

The peace agreement is having its effect. For four years, the caciques tried to force evangelicals to emigrate by refusing to accept their children in primary schools. The governmental complicity in the expulsions was never more evident than in this: the closing of the schools to evangelicals was condoned. However, with the truce agreement of 1996, hundreds of children were admitted to schools, and there are efforts to make up for the teaching they had missed.

By the fall of 1998, the known evangelical community in Chamula had grown from the 584 who had returned in 1994 after the sit-in at the INI compound to more than 2,000. There are probably many more who cautiouly keep a low profile, since cacique tolerance remains marginal. In August 1998, 30 adults, with 40 children, were forced to flee from Icalumtic, the same community where three men and a woman, members of two families who had returned after the sit-in, were killed by a mob and a 14-year-old girl was gang-raped. The authorities quickly intervened and the new refugees were able to return to their homes a week later.

The evangelicals are determined not to cowed or defeated. On December 4, 1998, about 600 Tzotzils held a worship service at a church in Arvenza 1, where cinder block walls were raised four years earlier but still without a roof. State officials were present to insure the peace. Abdias Tovilla insisted the prayer and song gathering was not a challenge or active defiance. "We didn't come here to provoke our Catholic brothers," he said. "We came to invite the mayor and Catholic residents to unite with us in a search for peace. We just can't keep fighting between brothers of the same race."

With the growth of numbers, there are new preachers. As always, the principal attraction is healing. One Sunday, I visited the house of Manuel San Juan as 24-year-old Mario Perez Hernandez, was conducting a Pentecostal service.

❊ ❊ ❊ ❊ ❊

One day, when I was lost, yes I was lost, I didn't know the Gospel nor did I know the way to be saved, a bus hit me. I didn't want to accept the Word of God because people said it was no good, that it was a plague, and so I believed that. Before the bus hit me, a Brother told me to get near the Gospel, but I didn't know what to do. The Brother said the Word of God is life eternal if we accept it. With this, a message entered my heart. I wanted to accept the Word, but my father used to drink very much, and he didn't want to go to accept the Word.

Then, one day I went to San Cristobal and the bus hit me and I couldn't be healed. I went to look for that Brother who said the coming of Christ is near. I told him, "Oh, what can I do?" He said, "This happened because it was God's will to make you come to church. If the bus hadn't hit you, you wouldn't have come to the church. It is God's will that you accept his Word."

So my brother (I have an 18-year-old brother) took me to a church because I could only walk with a stick. They began to pray so I might get my strength, and I began to walk well. I saw, thank God, how God is alive and His Word has power, just like the preachers tell us. They prayed for me, and it was then, on January 20, 1993, that I accepted the Word. A Brother said I should be a preacher. He took me to [the state of] Mexico to study the Bible at a Pentecostal church called "The King is Coming" in the municipality of Netzahualcoyotl. I studied the Word for 50 days. Now I'm taking courses in how to preach at the Divine Redeemer church in San Cristobal. I preach to three groups. One is this group that meets in the house of Brother Manuel. A second, with about 20 believers, meets at a place called Cruxho in the hills of San Cristobal. A third, also of about 20 believers, meets at my house here in Chamula.

The numbers are growing. People come for healing. There was a woman in Arvenza I who had a terrible infection in her ear. Even her face was swollen. No one could cure it. Her ear was aching and pus was coming out, running down to her blouse. Her husband, Mateo, was very sad, and they said to him, "Why don't you accept the Word of God?" The Word heals. God saves us. The Word of God says He is with us only if we believe. If you accept it, you can be healed. So Mateo and his wife accepted, and they fasted for three days. As soon as the fast ended, the pus dried, the pain was gone and she got well. Thank God they continue to accept the Word of God and are in good health. We have seen these miracles many times.

❊ ❊ ❊ ❊ ❊

After the service, we drove Pastor Perez to his home. It had a metal plaque above the door, easily seen from the road. It read, in Spanish: "This is an evangelical house." He was one who did not believe in keeping his head down.

Vernon Jay Sterk, who has been a Reformed Church translator and missionary in Chiapas for more than 20 years, titled his 1992 doctoral thesis, *The Dynamics of Persecution*.[2] He believes, contrary to the assumption summed up in the phrase "The Church Advances Over the Bodies of its Martyrs," that growth is hindered by persecution, so that even greater evangelical growth can be anticipated with an end to persecution.

There appear to be two major reasons why persecution ended. The first is a combination of the willingness of state authorities to punish offenders and the

2 (1992).

weakening of support at the community and town level. In Amatenango, persecution stopped when there was a rivalry between the PRI and PDR for votes. The second reason is that indigenous people have learned to live with a plurality of opinion. I asked Sterk about this and also about something that, so far, has not been touched on: How has evangelical growth affected the status of women?

❊ ❊ ❊ ❊ ❊

The main reason why persecution has stopped is that the people within their cultural communities have met with their enemies. They have seen they are not their enemies, although it took 30 years to develop. We have one example in our experience in the Bible translation project in Chenalho. When we started, there were all kinds of conflict, but we got the Catholic catechists and the Presbyterian pastors together to work on the translations. After 10 years they treat each other as Brothers in Christ. They see differences in their church structures and organization but they felt they have one Bible and worship the same God. They feel: "We are all Chenalho people. Why can't I go to this man's house and have dinner with them?" They invite each other. They work on projects together. Long ago, in the municipality of Zinacantan, people said, "Why are we doing this to our own people? Why do we expel our own people?" It was a power issue, not a religious struggle. Now we're seeing a breakdown of the political power structure. The PRI is not willing to allow the caciques to do pretty much as they want, and to control all the political and financial structure in the tribal areas.

The end of persecution makes for greater growth as people are less afraid. The Catholic Church will also find it is able to reach its goals in the tribal areas— opening them up for the catechists and the diaconates. All of a sudden, the Catholics are feeling this autonomy. The catechists we work with in Chenalho are proud that they are building a Catholic Church now and that it's going to be the Chenalho Catholic Church. It may be connected with the Roman Catholic Church, but they're finding a new identity, a new autonomy. That will cause growth.

As for women, go back to the beginning. Women were nothing, only someone to bear children and cook food. As the evangelical church develops, women are taking leadership roles, even though the indigenous culture does not give women formal leadership positions. Informally the women run a lot of things in the church. You can go into a church where a woman is running everything. There are no men at all, but, if you asked who the leader is, no one would identify a woman as such. I think there will be further changes. As women take leadership roles, they'll get leadership respect. That's a big change and it's coming from inside their churches. They've found a kind of autonomy. They're free to make those changes in their culture.

In Pentecostal churches, women are standing up. They never had that right before. That's what some people call "contextualization" of culture or acculturation—allowing people to develop their own forms and structures, whether it is dancing or playing drums. The cultural forms are not, in themselves, something that Christianity has to change. Christianity can use any cultural form, just as Jesus used the form of Baptism in Christianity to become recognized as a Christian form but it wasn't. Jesus used it. That same thing happens when people are allowed to use their cultural forms, whether it is dancing or drums or all kinds of good forms that have cultural meaning.

20
"THE BIBLE IS THE BEST UNIVERSITY"

A social benefit of evangelical growth is that it erodes the barrier between the indigenous people and middle class Ladinos. Furthermore, as evangelism spreads, the ghettoization of believers is eroding, so that a multicultural Mexican society, both social and religious, is becoming the norm. Chiapas is also becoming multi-denominational. The predominance of Presbyterians in Chiapas results from a decision taken by American missionary societies in the early part of this century to divide Mexico and avoid a duplication of expenses. The south fell to the Presbyterians. When Mexican revolutionaries in the 1920s closed the door to foreign missionaries, it was left to Mexicans to decide who should be evangelized and by whom. That was the start of an indigenous evangelical church.

Cusberto Perez Perez is the Pastor of the Bethel Baptist Church in San Cristobal.

✳ ✳ ✳ ✳ ✳

I am 43 years old. My family is from Chiapas. I was born 12 kilometers from San Cristobal. I grew up in a Christian environment, knowing part of the things of God, but I had no personal knowledge of God until I was 17 when I met a missionary from Georgia named Richard Komer. He gave me a Bible, and I saw I had to have a personal encounter with Christ, not just inherited belief. I asked God to forgive my sins, and all the guilt I had felt for years disappeared, just like that. Two years after I accepted Jesus Christ, I decided to dedicate my life to the ministry. That meant I had to go to a biblical school for four years. After that, I worked in Reynosa and Matamoros, in the state of Tamaulipas.

In 1984, I began working in San Cristobal. We began the Bethel Baptist Church because Catholicism was not meeting the needs of the people. There were believers but the Christian movement wasn't strong. Christians of those days were much more persecuted. They were constantly asked to help with traditional Catholic rites with work and cash. Because they did not participate they were attacked. We have two families in our church who left Chamula years ago. They say they listened to the Word of God, and they believed it, but, when other people learned they were not Catholic anymore, they told the father of the family that, if he did not return to the Catholic religion, they would burn his house and kill him. The family was firm in their belief. One night, people came and killed him and burned their house They killed three other people too. They cut a girl severely and left her on the floor thinking she was dead and then ran away. Only the mother and two sons could escape. On the next day, they went to look for the girl and she was found alive, so they took her away and saved her.

Things were difficult too for us in the beginning. We couldn't even put a spot on the radio. Now we can use television and have services on the street. As people saw how the lives of others who had accepted the Gospel were changing—spiritually, morally and socially—it became easier. We have gone knocking on doors, talking about the Word of God. Maybe these people don't take part in our services, but they have some knowledge. Thirty percent get together in a truly Christian church, reading the Bible. Forty-five percent have heard about God but do not know about God's message. In the beginning, many did not want to accept because of social or family pressure, but when they clearly saw that the Word of God was the divine truth, they accepted Christ as their Savior.

We are working with five indigenous communities. They have greater prosperity because, as the men stopped drinking alcohol, they saw things differently. They began growing economically and getting better, thanks to God. The Bible is the best university. It teaches you in your material life as well as in your spiritual life.

People live widely separated, so we have established four churches in different parts of the Ring Road where the expelled have established colonies. The church where I am working is in Colonia Morelia, behind the central market. Last year, we had—in round numbers—200 adults and children in our church. Now we have about 250. Of these, only 180 are baptized. Our Sunday attendance ranges from 120 to 150. The way we work is to have every member of a family feel the responsibility to share Christ's message. We don't impose it on them. It is just the knowledge and responsibility that they have. If I know the Gospel I must give testimony to others. It says in Acts, 1:8, "You will receive power when the Holy Spirit comes on you; and you will be my witness in Jerusalem, and in all Judea and Samaria, and to the ends of the earth."

According to this, we have prayer groups in different parts of the city. We are winning more people who were Catholic. We go to those who don't know anything about the Bible, those who live only on tradition, on what they heard. We are not interested in other Christians who already have knowledge.

In July 1996, we felt in our hearts the need to work with children. We also began to work with children in two other towns, San Felipe and El Sabinal, near the border with Guatemala. We have 80 children every Sunday in these schools and 40 every Tuesday. In the Bible we find a complete teaching of how a child should behave with his parents, his teachers, with grown-ups and with God himself. The Bible says Jesus was obedient to his parents and helped them. Proverbs 22:6 says, "Train a child in the way he should go and when he is old he will not turn from it."

The Bible is a great influence in the home because the family and marriage are divine institutions, established by God. In Ephesians, Chapter 5, we have the way in which a man should love his wife. He should love his wife as his own body, and the wife should respect her husband as Christ gave Himself to the church. This gives us much satisfaction because we can forget about the word "machismo." As Christians, we are not macho anymore. The Bible says the man is the head and the woman his perfect helper. They should be a team. If parents have a good relationship, the children will have that teaching. Let's take Sarah's example. She addressed her husband as "Sir." That shows the respect she had for him. The same with Abraham: he loved his wife very much. We emphasize such examples because nowadays there is no respect. Women do whatever they want and so do men.

Many times people come to us for advice. If the problem is big, we talk to the couple or to the children and tell them about their responsibilities as a mother, a father, a son, or a daughter. We must see that they solve problems before they get bigger. When people come from the pagan world, with certain vices and attitudes, they don't know how to solve their problems. We try to educate them in their way of talking, thinking, behaving and making decisions, but, more than anything, to show them how to live their lives before God. That's our goal—to show people there is another way of feeling happiness without drugs or alcohol or nightclubs. The only way to feel really satisfied is in Jesus Christ.

21

INDIVIDUAL CHOICE

Sociologists tend to present religious conversion as the result of economic change and historic movement—a response to the anomie of modern times. This is the functionalist view, as if those who convert are victims of a world they have not made. It is also part of the Marxist inheritance, which sees religion as an opiate, so that, if we solve the contradiction between the base and superstructure, religion will disappear along with economic and social oppression. Something is missing in this functionalism: the values, aspirations and voices of those who have assumed a new religious identity. Why does seeking God need to be a form of political struggle? Why can it not be seen as the individual decisions of a man and woman reshaping their lives?

Pastor Teodoro Vera Cortez is the founder and pastor of a Baptist congregation that he has named the Peniel Fundamental Independent Church. Peniel is a variant of Penuel, where Jacob wrestled with the angel. That nicely sums up his own experience, not as a toy of destiny but as a Jacob: "It is because I saw God face to face, and yet my life was spared" (Genesis 32:30).

✳ ✳ ✳ ✳ ✳

I am from a little town in the state of Zacatecas. There were 14 members in my family. I went to Texas when I was 15 to look for my life, but instead I found bad things, sin and vices. I first went on vacation, but then I got some false papers, because I was a minor, and found a job and stayed. I worked in a good enterprise where I earned well, but, because of the vices, what I earned was not enough, so I decided to go to Chicago. There, a friend invited me to the First Baptist Church in Hammond, Indiana. Many talked to me about receiving Christ as my Savior, but I didn't understand because I was born a Catholic, and I had not read the Bible. Until I was 20, nobody talked to me about the Gospel that saves.

I felt someone was calling me but I resisted. I thought I was betraying the religion of my parents, but I could not resist any more. A Brother told me how I should pray. That was in January 1983. I went to the altar and I was baptized in water. I received Christ as my savior. I went on a youth campaign in St Louis, Missouri, where God touched my heart. He told me of the need to prepare myself for the ministry. I felt every Christian should be prepared to testify for Christ, full time. By that, I mean leaving work, family and all other things. I knew it wouldn't be easy. I went to the company where I worked and told them I was resigning to serve God and preach his Word.

Furthermore, I read an article in a newspaper, *La Espada*, edited in Mission,

Texas by Dr Elmer Fernandez. It said there were North American missionaries in Cuernavaca, in Monterrey and many other parts of the Mexican Republic, and asked why were there no Mexicans winning the hearts of their own people. That was like a sword in my heart. I prayed, "Lord, if you are going to use me, I am here. I will give my life to you." That sealed my decision. I went to Monterrey and studied in the Baptist Biblical Institute from 1986 to 1989. In 1988, I came for a visit in Chiapas. I always felt an attraction for the south of Mexico and, more than anything, the need to preach here. God put the desire in my heart and also an incentive. While I was studying in the Biblical Institute, I met a lady who was from Chiapas. We began to see each other and then we got married.

The beginning of the Peniel Church came out of nothing. I am talking about 1989. A family here helped us in this ministry and my father-in-law helped too. For 35 years he knew the Gospel in a Presbyterian church, and then he changed to Baptist. I worked in secular society, in the Coca Cola company, at the same time that I began knocking on doors to get people to come to church. God has blessed us. We now have a congregation of 130 to 150 people, on special occasions even up to 280 people. Maybe half are indigenous families, but I don't like to talk about race or color. We are all souls for whom Christ died.

We have not suffered persecution here because we are concentrated in the city, but we are menaced when we go to other places. In one place they threw stones at us. In another we were completely rejected. We have some Brothers who live here, who can't go back to their places and fields because they have been converted. We had a mission for some time in a town called Yauteclum on the way to Chenalho, but it is closed. The traditional authorities would not let us go back.

We have a goal—to erect a big, strong church in San Cristobal. We go out to evangelize, knocking on doors to win souls, every Tuesday, Wednesday, Friday and Saturday. Without an organization to support us, it isn't easy. For almost two years, I worked at night from 9 p.m. to 6 a.m. Then, when the group grew to about 25, they decided I should not work, but I should study more so as to concentrate on the work of God. They decided to give me some money and sometimes they paid my rent. God blessed us. We live well. God doesn't abandon us. We used to meet in a private house. Later, we met a man near here who sold land. He gave us a piece of land and said we could pay for it or not, as we wished. With time, he regretted this and took half the land. He said that if we didn't pay by a certain date he would take the rest. We paid him even before that date, so we don't owe a penny. I designed the church and we built it ourselves, even though I know nothing about construction. God is worthy of a better place, but He is happy with what we have here. Most of the money for the material was a sacrifice offering from the Brothers here. Some Brothers from the northern part of the Republic also helped us.

Now we are developing a school, starting with a kindergarten. We think the state education department should not take charge of educating our children. We think this is a job for a family. If there are children who are not wanted somewhere else, we want them to be in a school that loves Christian children. We want it to be independent of the state but incorporated in the Department of Education so that the certificates have value. We are affiliated with a kindergarten in San Luis Potosi in the north. They offered to help us and are going to arrange for the school certificates. We already have a teacher who has a teaching certificate. I have a little girl who is six and who knows how to read and write. We are beginning with kindergarten and will continue through primary school. We have other members of the church with certificates to teach the necessary subjects. We want the school to grow for the glory of our Lord.

22
SEVENTH-DAY ADVENTISTS

Itinerant Seventh-Day Adventists were among the earliest evangelical missionaries in Chiapas. For instance, as a young man, Domingo Angel Lopez was an Adventist leader. He was expelled, along with 28 others, from Chamula in October 1974. Although it apparently was not their early policy, Adventists now insist on an educated, well-trained clergy, which inhibits bottom-up growth among the indigenous population. Furthermore, it uses a Spanish-language Bible and other literature in Spanish, which confines its appeal mainly to Ladinos. Still, the number of Adventists in San Cristobal has grown in recent years as the result of a stronger effort to evangelize Tzotzils and Tzeltals.

I had often passed what seemed to be a small Adventist church on the Ring Road near La Hormiga. The frontage was barely 15 feet wide and so I assumed there was a small congregation, but, when I attended a Saturday service, I found the small entrance led to a still wider building that extended about 100 feet back toward the base of the hill. I found it packed wall-to-wall and front-to-back with about 400 worshipers, many of them indigenous women. The sermon was in Spanish, but with a Tzotzil translation. The believers listened intently with many, including some women who apparently could read Spanish, leafing through their Bibles to follow the citations.

I asked Pastor Villaney Vasquez Alegria, who is head of the church's central association, with an office in Tuxtla Gutierrez, to summarize the present situation of the Adventist Church.

✳ ✳ ✳ ✳ ✳

The Seventh-Day Adventists arrived in the Isthmus of Tehuantepec of Oaxaca in 1892, when a man named Aurelio Jimenez went to buy some bread. The clerk handed it to him wrapped in a page from a magazine called *La Verdad Presente* (The Present Truth). He took it home, and, when the family read about the second coming of Christ, they were so interested they wrote to the Mexico City address of the people who published the magazine—*The Adventists*—asking for more information. To skip over other details, two years later, Aurelio and his family were baptized as the first Adventists in southeastern Mexico. Aurelio also became the first Adventist pastor and later traveled throughout Chiapas and Tabasco, preaching the Gospel.

The church has grown so large that we have divided the state into three associations and sub-divided these into districts. The Central Association, of which I am president, has 28 districts with 38,000 members. The Soconosco District, on the Pacific Coast, also has 28 districts and 40,000 members. The North District, which is mostly along the Gulf of Mexico, has 30 districts and about the same number of members. The members, of course, are in different churches, so that each district has from 20 to 40 congregations.

In addition to our churches, we have extensive health and education programs. Our schools extend through high school, college preparatory and the university level. There are two levels, external and internal. External schools are where a student comes for half an hour of study on morality. The teachers are baptized Adventists who are known for their good principles so they can set an example. The internal schools have boarding facilities where students pay their tuition by working on farms, growing vegetables for sale, or in factories or by selling religious books and other literature. They work four or five hours no matter what social class they come from. Work is part of their physical and mental formation. There are also rules they must obey: when to go to bed, when to wake up, when to work and when to study the Bible. Parents entrust their children to these schools because they are safe, and they know the teachers have high moral principles.

We have two hospitals in Chiapas and one in Tabasco and others in northern Mexico. They are supported by donations from the United States and have very low fees and are open to everyone. We don't discriminate on the basis of creed. There is also a medical brigade here in Tuxtla Gutierrez. This includes doctors of other churches as well as Adventist.

As for myself, I was born in a place called Tecpatan in the Zoque [an indigenous people] area of Tabasco, an area that was evangelized by Adventists in the 1920s and that now has only two religions—Catholic and Adventist. My family was not one of them, however. I came to know the Gospel through a worldwide extension course called "The Voice of Hope" that was, a long time ago, administered through an office in San Cristobal. When I was 14, someone signed me up. I studied it and was baptized when I was 15. I immediately began to preach to my parents. My father was an addict of alcohol and tobacco and I imitated him. Thanks to God, when I knew the Gospel, I transformed myself through the Spirit of the Lord and my parents were baptized too. When I was 16, I left home and became a Colporteur, supporting myself as a missionary by selling the Bible and other religious books. After this, the Church gave me administrative charge of a group of young male Colporteurs. Then I went to the Theological School at the University of Montemorelos in Nuevo Leon in northern Mexico and graduated with a B.A. in Theology. I served as a pastor for four years in various places in the North and then was ordained in the ministry by the laying on of hands. After that, I was elected as a member of what the Adventist Church calls its Department of Evangelization, which promotes the preaching of the Gospel in places where it has not been heard—for instance the inner cities of large metropolitan areas and among different ethnic groups such as the selva of Chiapas. After 10 years, I was made secretary of that department. Three years later, I was named to the position I now hold.

That was just about the time the Zapatista revolt began. Five of our districts, with about 100 churches, were affected by the conflict. Some Brothers were expelled from their communities and others were pressured to join the Zapatista army, but not one of them deviated from the faith. When the conflict started, and people had to run away from their homes, we supplied them with sugar, salt, oil, and bacon.

There is also the problem of expulsions from Chamula, but that seems to be easing. Some of our Brothers have returned to Chamula and other municipalities to reclaim their lands and homes. We remain firm in our belief that God will keep His promise to protect His children. That there can be persecution and expulsion in Mexico is why we need the Gospel. Before being Christian, a person without principles has no respect for society, for the laws, or even for his own life, but, when he accepts Jesus, there is a total change. A family lives better socially, children are educated and there is more respect for the laws of the country and for civil and human rights.

23

GROWTH AND PRAYER

The largest church in Chiapas is the *Templo Auditorio Cristiano* in Tuxtla Gutierrez. From a distance it looks more like a skating rink than a church, with a roof of colored vanes—green, brown, yellow, blue and orange. It is, as its name says, an auditorium, with a high ceiling, banked rows of pews and a balcony over a third of the interior space. It can seat 6,000 worshipers. Light streams through windows the same colors as the roof, except on one side where there is a huge painting of a snow covered mountain and stream, of no obvious religious significance. While I was waiting for the service to begin, I glanced at the notices on a bulletin board in the vestibule. This was known as a Pentecostal church, but the notice read:

Not permitted:
1. Plays of any kind.
2. Clowns to illustrate the Bible to children of the church.
3. Mimes of any kind.
4. Modern or popular music concerts of any kind.
5. Disorderly services.
6. Preachers who put their hands on worshipers so that they faint.
   (The apostles never did this.)
7. Applause or singing preachers.
8. The sale of articles within the church.
9. This church does not shout Jesus, Jesus.

As the congregation entered, they appeared to be almost entirely middle class, with the men in business suits and women in modest, mostly black, dresses. As they reached their places, they took handkerchief-size black or white lace cloths from their purses and covered the tops of their heads. Unlike the usual plain platform and podium of evangelical churches, there was a high altar of fine polished wood and on the wall behind it, a red neon sign: "Christ the same yesterday, today, and for the centuries." The first four rows of center pews had been removed to make room for a four-piece band, including a young woman on a full set of traps. To the side, four other young women sang with individual hand-held microphones.

The service lasted an hour and a half beginning with 15 minutes of clapping hands and standing in place, a long prayer during which the worshipers wept and cried, a fairly short sermon and then the customary call for curing. However, instead of walking forward and standing before the altar, the worshipers went to either side, where there was a long, red-velvet covered railing and a similarly covered kneeling bench. Assistant pastors walked along an aisle behind the railing, placing their hands on the heads of worshipers who knelt at the railing—their heads on their folded arms. The prayers were silent and there was no weeping or fainting.

After the service, Pastor Jesus Castelazo Sanchez showed me to a small conference room with a wall-size map of Chiapas marked with red or white-topped stickpins. He said the red marked churches and the white marked congregations. He said there were 14 churches or congregations in Tuxtla and another 155 in the Highlands and the selva. Then we went to a small, book-lined office, where I asked him about the sign on the notice board.

✳ ✳ ✳ ✳ ✳

People think of this as a Pentecostal church, perhaps because of our music and enthusiasm and sincere prayers, but I am neither a Pentecostal nor a Baptist nor a Presbyterian. I am only a Christian, just like that. As I didn't have any instruction or biblical school or anything, I preach what the Bible says. God does these marvels. How was this temple constructed? Just by faith! The Bible says that when we are not Christians we are like beasts, closed to understanding. The Gospel makes us intelligent. It teaches us many things. I am grateful that God gave me life. I serve Him and have dedicated my life to Him. My wife and my children all serve God. I didn't even know how to read but God gave me the ability to write six books. I am grateful for his favors. I never went to biblical school, but I have taken part in conferences in Guatemala and in Colombia in South America. I was preaching in Tijuana, and a Brother heard me and said I just must go to California. He sent me tickets to preach in Los Angeles. I have preached in Texas and in Baltimore and will go to San Francisco. I have other invitations. I think it's necessary for pastors from here to go over there, but I don't have time. I prefer to work here. I must go to the selva here in Chiapas. There are many people there—many Indians—who have not heard the Gospel.

I am 74 years old. I first knew the Lord in 1947 when I was living in the state of Hidalgo. My parents were Catholic. I had no education—not even grammar school—because I went to work in the gold mines when I was very young. When I was 25, I went to a Christian church and was converted. I think the Bible is truth. I believe in it literally. Since the Bible says we must serve God, I went to serve Him immediately after I was converted. I began preaching in cantinas. Drink destroys the soul. It destroys a family. My first church in Hidalgo used to be a cantina. I also began to work for the most oppressed people of Mexico—the Indians. I have worked all over the country with many different people: Totonacas, Zapotecas, Otomis. I did not know any of those languages and spoke through a translator. I think that way the message can be better adapted. People say the Indians are losing their culture because of conversion, but that's not true. They only lose their vices. They keep their own way of living but without sin. They stop having several women. They keep their language and their dress. The only thing God changes is the heart. The rest remains the same.

One morning, when I was in Hidalgo, God told me to go to Chiapas, here to Tuxtla. He said, "You must go." God gives orders without explanations. I came immediately with my wife and five children. I didn't know this city or anyone here. I found the zone where there are many clubs and bad houses, and it was there that I began to preach. We started in a cantina and within seven months built our first church. The drunks helped me. Some continued to drink and others stopped, but together we built our first church. It was a miracle. [Showing a picture of a small, narrow storefront.] This was it, a night club called *Sala Bremen*. It was a prostitution house. I began to preach and people came. Soon it was too small. We built this one [showing a photograph of a small church]. It could hold about 700 believers. Then that became too small, and we built this one [showing another, wider church]. It could hold 1,500 people. That too became too small, and we built this church. Six thousand people can fit inside. We have more than 300 children in our Sunday School. We did this ourselves. Not a cent came from outside. We built the benches and I painted the picture. In November 1996 we had a celebration and more than 7,000 came. We gave them three meals a day for three days and we didn't charge one cent. It all came from believers. We don't have money from outside. We now have 14 churches in Tuxtla. Some are two-story buildings. We built them all over the city because there are so many believers. Some cannot afford even bus fare. We need churches to which they can walk. In all of Chiapas we have 160 congregations. We can build two churches a month. We have 10 in the planning stage. This week I went to inaugurate two near Comitan, where the selva begins.

The only reason for this growth is God. I don't know any other reason. God always gives a better life than what anyone is living, so men go where things are better, where there is more peace, and, best of all, where their sins are forgiven. When we raise one church, the next year that one raises three more. This happens because it is good for men and women to follow God. We have seen many miracles. Once some Brothers were preaching the Gospel and came to a house where there was a funeral. A man had died that morning. When they finished praying, the dead man opened his eyes. There was a woman with cancer of her vagina. She was cured. In our kitchen there is a Sister who had leprosy, her hair had even fallen out. She has been cured for 20 years. Many of the people in the night clubs were saved. The owner of some night clubs came one day. Her legs were rotten with syphilis. We prayed and she was cured. She closed her night clubs and was saved. There have been murderers who have been saved by the Lord. That man who was resurrected came here to work for two years. Then he fell in love, and I performed his marriage, and he had already been dead.

Beside curing, there are two reasons why this growth is taking place. First, there are more preachers. Several Brothers convert, and soon there are more preachers. When people have found the Word of God, they recommend it to others. The second is the Catholic Church. History tells us the Catholic Church grows for two reasons: because of the ignorance of the people and because it is given power. Now the law has diminished its authority and people can read books. They have awakened. They know the Catholic Church is just fiestas, firecrackers and drink. They then see that this is not good and that evangelical belief is better. If the

Catholic Church still had power, this church here would not exist. They would have cut my throat. The people who suffered the most, the Indians, are no longer trapped. They have awakened.

* * * * *

During the service, as I listened to Pastor Castelazo's sermon, I was struck by how quietly he spoke, without emotionalism, as if reasoning with his listeners. To ensure accuracy, I taped a portion where he preached of prayer and thanksgiving.

* * * * *

When we pray, we need wisdom. As Santiago said in his letter, "If you ask and you don't receive, it's because you are asking wrongly." We sometimes ask out of vanity and greed but men and women who believe in God and truly adore the Lord, who are living in God, don't ask a lot from the Lord. If you need anything, even if you don't ask for it, it will be given to you. When a Christian asks, he asks for all; he asks a little for himself and much for others. Make others' problems your own. There is a popular saying: "What you ask for others, you are asking for yourself."

There are some who keep asking for something, repeating and repeating, as if insisting that the Lord listen to them. No, Brothers, it isn't like that. Then how can we solve our problems? I will explain. First, to pray is to adore God. Even if you don't have anything to ask for, you must spend at least 15 minutes worshiping God. Secondly, the nearer we are to God, the more we must think of our fellow men before our own necessities. If you are sick and in pain, there could be another person who has cancer. He is crying. He needs more of your prayer than you. Isn't it so, Brothers? I'm asking you: yes or no?

If I have a debt of 1,000 pesos and have no money, I must ask God. However, if a Brother owes only 20 pesos and they threaten to put him in jail, he needs more of my prayer than I do. Alleluia. Please Brothers. Let's understand what it means to be a Christian. If we don't live our Christianity, sooner or later we will abandon the Bible, we will abandon the Church and we will leave the Lord.

Then there is thanksgiving—giving thanks because God is going to give us what we are asking for. Alleluia. Giving thanks by faith. As Saint Luke says, "All that you ask for in prayer it will be done." Anything that you want, if you believe, you will receive. When I was converted I had negative prayers. "Lord, help me. I need money. I don't have anything. Help me even if I am not worthy of receiving anything." Then why are you praying if you know you are not worthy of receiving anything? Christ said everything we ask for in the Lord's name will be given to us, but it will not be according to our merits. It will be according to our faith. Brothers, it is not for our merits that we present ourselves to the Lord, it is for our faith, and for what we receive in prayer we give our thanks.

Worshiping God, you will spend a good time in petition, not only for yourself but for all the Brothers who suffer. That will take a good while—15 minutes of prayer at least. Then, if you have faith, you will end by giving thanks to God. All that will easily take half an hour. Yes or no, Brothers? When one knows what prayer is, when one loves God and is grateful, we can be on our knees and lose all sense of time and even of space. Is it not so Brothers? Yes or no?

24
EVANGELISM MADE IN MEXICO

Evangelism has permeated all of Mexican society, not just the indigenous people. We have already seen this with Baptists and Seventh-Day Adventists. Another is the Nazarene Church, which has 105 congregations in Chiapas, 15 missions and more than 7,000 members. The Nazarenes were originally Wesleyan Methodists but never developed as a Methodist denomination. Perhaps one reason was that they clung to the early Wesleyan style that would now be called Pentecostal. Esdras Alonso Gonzalez, one of the three leaders of the expelled communities in San Cristobal, is both a Nazarene and a Pentecostal, but he is in a distinct minority: almost all Mexican Nazarenes are virtually indistinguishable from mainline Mexican Methodists. Rene Jimenez Guzman, is the church's administrator for southern Chiapas.

✳ ✳ ✳ ✳ ✳

The Nazarene Church was born in England. When John Wesley moved to the United States, the doctrine of sanctity passed to America. Then it passed to Mexico in 1908. Later, when the Mexican Revolution broke out, missionaries went away, and the Church of the Nazarene had to support itself, so this church has grown along with Mexican national resources—financial resources and human resources. My call was given when I was a child. I was born in Ixtepec, Oaxaca on November 29, 1948. When I was six years old, I discovered the Church of the Nazarene through the grammar school that I attended. I had a chance to go to a Sunday School where I heard the Gospel. When I was about seven, I received Christ as my Savior. Little by little, God prepared me to serve. I wasn't sure I was going to be a Pastor, but I was sure that God needed me. At 15, instead of going to Junior College, I went to the Nazarene Hispano-American Seminary in San Antonio, Texas. The Brothers of the congregation saw my gifts and talents to serve the Lord and supported me in going to the seminary. God confirmed it. After four years of theological studies, I established a new work in the colony of Rancho Nuevo in the municipality of Huixtan, here in Chiapas. That was 1968.

In 1969, I went to the city of Hidalgo, in Chiapas, to restore work that had been started earlier. I remained there for 11 years, until the work was restored completely. We began with 30 believers. When I left, the church had 250 members. From there I went to a church in the town of Villa Flores. In 1985, the Assembly of the Southern District called me to be District Superintendent. I have attended to this work for 11 years.

When I say that I was confirmed in the calling, it wasn't a call provoked by great deeds or events as sometimes happens. It was step-by-step, ever since my conversion as a child. Part of that confirmation is the growth in believers. When I received this district in 1985, there were 52 churches. We cannot say that our growth has been explosive, yet we have grown to 93 churches in 11 years. This is only in my district, here in the South, with only 20 of the municipalities of Chiapas. We don't cover the North.

Ours is not a region with many indigenous people, except for those who were expelled from the Highlands and have been resettled here by the government. We have established three works for them. The Nazarene Church has identified with them. Though they have come from different denominations, they have asked for our help, and we have been teaching them our doctrine. Our evangelical method is to go from house to house, distributing literature. We also have campaigns in local churches and in public places, where we can bring large numbers of people together. On January 1, 1997, we began an "impact project." It lasted for three months and covered all of Ibero-America—from Argentina northwards. It was a prayer program for 10 persons. After praying for them for three months, we invited them to listen to the evangelical message. By the end of the project we had prayed for more than two million people in all of Ibero-America.

To meet such growth, we develop leadership from within the congregations. We have lay ministers who have grown in knowledge and with a capacity of leadership. They are selected by a congregation and assigned by the district superintendent to serve where there is no pastor. However, this is an acting position—to meet the need of the moment. For a lay leader to advance to the position of pastor, two conditions must be met: he must have a call to the ministry and he must be theologically prepared. Candidates selected by local congregations, based on their knowledge of a man, can enroll in something like an "open school," with ministerial studies by mail. We also have different places where students go to study for a few hours, and we give them credits as they advance.

We are totally linked to the Bible. We do not recognize any other norm of truth. We educate children from the crib. We say education begins in the "Home Department," the Crib Department. In kindergarten, children begin to practice through drawing and education from the age of three.

Our doctrine is practical sanctity. The Holy Ghost is within us. When someone accepts Jesus Christ as his Savior, and has faith that the redemption of the Cross is sufficient and effective for his transformation, that person receives the promise and experiences a total transformation. The Word of God is complete, but each person has to discover it in his own character, in his own personality, through development acquired by education and discipline, and through brotherly communication within the Church. As a result, the person who is converted abandons his or her former practices. They leave any vice that they had and are thoroughly changed. They don't live for themselves alone, they live for God and for others. There is always an interest in others. In that way, believers have better values, better health in their bodies and better resources in their work or profession. Everything has a new value for them. Not just the down-and-out or the depressed come. Families come. People who are well-educated and disciplined come. They find the Gospel can transform their lives. They find a "becoming beautiful."

We have in Mexico a "macho" man who, by his nature, acts in a certain way. If he comes to us, through development and growth, he begins to understand. There is a transformation in his life: no longer does a man impose himself on his family. We seldom find it necessary to give marriage counseling. With our doctrines and teachings our members don't get involved in extreme things. We teach from the pulpit, but, if something does arise, a pastor may counsel in his office. All pastors are told to pay attention to family problems. The Bible teaches us this. Ephesians 5 and 6 give us the essence of the rules that govern a Christian family. The Book of Proverbs, almost in its totality, calls us to wisdom and reasoning. Jesus Christ is an example for children. "Jesus grew in wisdom and stature, and in favor with God and men" (Luke 2:52). This summarizes intellectual growth from childhood to adulthood. My favorite text is Psalm 27:4, "One thing I ask of the Lord, this is what I seek, that I may dwell in the house of the Lord all the days of my life, to gaze upon the beauty of the Lord and to seek him in his temple." I learned that as a teenager and it has been an inspiration for the development of my Christian life.

25
CATECHISTS

There is a movement within the Catholic Church in Latin America to distance itself from Rome and to form autochthonous (self-ruled) churches. The reasoning is that just as the Apostles did not found a church at the start of evangelization, but, by their missions, caused a particular church to come into existence, so the Catholic Church in the Americas should favor the birth of indigenous churches, each with its own hierarchy and organization, and with a theology and liturgy adapted to its own culture and religious expression, but still in communion with other particular churches and basically with the church of Peter in Rome.

As explained by a pastoral agent among the Aymaras of the highlands of Bolivia, the goal would be to constitute Christianity as "a form of living Aymara culture, to present to the Aymaras a way of being Aymaran in the way that Jesus would have been, had he been Aymaran."[1]

This is what evangelists have always been doing. They create what William Dyrness has called a "faith framework" out of the material and experiences of lives and cultures. He writes: "In various settings in which Christianity has emerged, there are widely different attitudes and practices that spring from a common tradition and scripture. In addition to any normative judgment that might be appropriate, and certainly well before any such judgment, it is required that we give each expression of faith its own voice and allow it to appear as a unique local theology."[2]

Evangelists in Chiapas have formed church structures that reflect the customs, traditions and, most important of all, the demands and aspirations of specific peoples. Missionaries of the Summer Institute of Linguistics worked to make themselves unneeded. Once the Bible had been translated, and a relative handful of believers had been instructed on how to understand its message, it was they who evangelized relatives and friends. They formed a new congregation and a new church and selected their own deacons, elders and pastors.

Perhaps the most enthusiastic proponent of an autochthonous church for the indigenous people of Mexico is Bishop Ruiz. Thus, as much as Roman Catholics and evangelists in Chiapas might disagree on political activism, they agree on the need to evangelize indigenous people from within their own communities.

In 1996, Ruiz was a featured speaker at a symposium in Cleveland honoring the

---

1 Orta (1995): 100–101. **2** (1996): 268.

late Cardinal Leo Jozef Suenens, a major architect of the Second Vatican Council, who was remembered as a leader who urged members of the church "to behave as non-infallible seekers after truth." San Francisco's Archbishop William Levada spoke of Suenen's almost reckless optimism and his conviction that "where caution is everywhere, courage cannot be found."

Renowned both for his incaution and courage, Ruiz was right at home. He put two questions to an audience of more than 500 church leaders and laymen: Does God know how to save bodies or only souls? And, since the Word of God is seed, does only the bishop have seeds or do the people have seeds too? He said he had attempted to respond to these questions by encouraging analysis and activism among the indigenous members of his parish and by training catechists and ordaining deacons.[3]

Ruiz is far in advance of the Roman Catholic hierarchy in Mexico. An autochthonous church runs counter to centuries of teachings that the Church of Rome is the only true Church of Christ and that it continues, by virtue of an uninterrupted Apostolic succession, the primitive community of Jerusalem.

The disagreement between evangelists and Catholics can be found in the word "church." For Catholics, the Church is an institution and a hierarchy. For evangelicals, reaching back to the Reformation, the church is a group of people. Puritans constructed plain, unadorned buildings as a shelter from the weather and as a community meeting and teaching hall. The evangelicals of Chiapas do the same thing. A Chol in Bachajon once derided the evangelicals for their "empty" buildings. "All you have is a table with a Victrola on it," he said.

There has been a softening of attitudes among Mexican Catholic leaders. While not going as far as Bishop Ruiz, they realize there are bishoprics with as few as one priest for 30,000 or even 50,000 nominal believers. They know there are fewer and fewer vocations for a celibate, poorly paid, priesthood. As a matter of sheer survival, the Catholic Church must train lay catechists to take up the burden.

I met Felipe Toussaint Loera, the Vicar-General of the San Cristobal diocese, in his office next to the cathedral to discuss efforts to form a cadre of catechists and deacons as the beginning toward the formation of an autochthonous church.

✻ ✻ ✻ ✻ ✻

Before Samuel Ruiz came here, Bishop Lucio Torreblanca worked on the formation of catechists who would go to the communities to teach. According to the idea of that era, the teaching was the standard catechism, with questions and answer such as, "Who is God?" and, "What are the Ten Commandments?" When Don Samuel came, there was a growing interest in Latin America to catechize communities in a more complete manner. Then there was a movement to catechize in a people's own language so they could better understand the doctrine.

However, when this was done by taking people from their communities for instruction, it was discovered that this generated conflict. When a student returned to his community, he brought a different mentality. There was a positive and negative transformation. Students learned many things, but, in many cases, when they returned home, they worked against their culture. They disregarded traditions, the force of their ancestors and the force of the elders in their community. After watching this process, the idea of closing the outside training cen-

3 *National Catholic Reporter*, June 14, 1996.

ters began to form. Instead, it was decided to travel to the communities to give instruction. Now, in each parish, there is a training center for catechists. The courses move from one community to another, so one year instruction may be in one community and the next year in another.

When a catechist is a teacher who goes to a community to read and discuss the Bible, he discovers how communities work, how they reach decisions, discussing a matter until an agreement is reached so they speak in one voice. When the topic is announced all the people begin talking, so it is like the sound of a beehive. After much discussion, the voices of different groups begin to unify. Then the different groups finally come to an agreement. There can not be a communitarian agreement when a catechist says: "This is how you should understand the Bible," or, "This is how you should act." That would be a mistake; a pedagogic failure.

In the Tzeltal zone we call this the *Tijwanej* method. The word means to agitate, like a spoon stirring sugar in cup of coffee. The object is to agitate or motivate a community to discuss something and come to an agreement. A dialogue has seven steps: First, an introduction and then a Bible reading. Here a catechist has a certain training to help a student focus on outstanding biblical passages. After motivation by the catechists, there are questions and then the people begin to dialogue in small groups. There may be a group of women or a group of children. When they come to an agreement, they give their response to the assembly and the catechist, or a member of the community, takes all this in as a harvest. Finally, the community tries to make a summary and reach an agreement. This method of Bible study and reaching community decisions creates great dynamism, great force and greater consistency.

Since 1975, we have seen a good evolution of catechists. In the 1980s, indigenous deacons first appeared. They have three years of training, after which they are evaluated. This has generated a ministry that was never known before. We have divided this diocese into 226 zones. Our last census was in 1993, when there were 2,608 communities. They were assisted by 7,822 catechists for adults and 1,575 for children. This included 951 female catechists. We also had 1,812 men and women who perform other services, like health promoters. In addition, we had 422 deacons and predeacons and 208 Eucharistic priests.

A predeacon is a candidate for the diaconate. He has similar work but only for three years. At the end of that term, the community and the bishop evaluate him. If they agree, he goes on to complete his studies for the full diaconate. The diaconate is permanent. It is a ministry. In the theology of the church, the diaconate is the first step to the priesthood. There are three steps: diaconate, presbyterate and episcopate.

Everything begins from the bottom up. The community presents a candidate and not only the community, but the entire zone must support him. The candidate is generally a farmer who offers this service voluntarily. He and his family will continue to live in their home and work their fields. This is a service of honor, not of reward. The priest who receives the nomination of the community generally agrees with the selection, but, if he knows of an objection, he has a dialogue with the community. He may object if the candidate is not married or is divorced—which automatically bars him—or if his wife does not agree. When everyone agrees, the candidate is presented to the Bishop for an interview and final approval.

There have been many questions about the difference between deacons and priests. In the 1980s, when deacons first appeared, the communities began to ask themselves: "Why do we have to depend on missionaries who come from far places to receive the sacraments?" We then had a dialogue between the communities and the missionaries of the church, and it was agreed that the only thing the Church could offer at that time was the diaconate, but we still discuss it. We say an indigenous church, according to Vatican Council II, should be a local church and should have local ministers even up to the episcopacy. Now, the indigenous church is still part of the Roman Church, with the same norms and cultural values. It is not a local church.

There are a number of criteria to get to the ministerial priesthood. The first is the requirement of celibacy. The second is academic instruction. Celibacy in our indigenous cultures is a problem because the Indian communities in Chiapas consider it a trait of immaturity. A person is not thought capable of governing a community if he can not govern a home. As for the academic obstacle, our communities are a long way from high educational degrees. We must demonstrate to other Catholic churches that the indigenous church here is different from the Roman Church. It requires norms and treatment of its own. It is not the same to be an Indian in Chiapas as it is to be an Italian. The priesthood must necessarily be different in one place than it is in the other.

However, there has been work done since 1993 on the theological fundamentals, including an uxorial [married] priesthood. The Roman Catholic Church is a very old structure. If a change is to take place, there must be many efforts. But other bishops in Latin America face the same problems and are also taking part in the search for a solution. In North America and Europe, there are others working hard to open the priesthood to women, so change is in the air. Unfortunately, a priest needs many years of instruction, and, for this reason, our sacramental life is not complete; however, even without further changes, we think what has already taken place represents great strides ahead. A permanent married diaconate is a very big step. Catechists and deacons are the pastors of their communities, although we don't call them pastors. A deacon can administer the sacraments of baptism and marriage, assist the sick, pray with the community for the sick, bless houses and direct the community assembly. What he cannot do is confess, celebrate mass or give the last Sacraments.

We have no doubt that we are building an indigenous church. We don't talk any more of *Indigenismo* in the Mexican anthropological context of working among indigenous people to make a single Mexican ethnicity. We have advanced to a dialogue among ethnics. Our approach is: "I belong to one ethnia, and I talk with someone from another ethnia. I try to understand his culture, and he tries to understand mine."

In the ecclesiastic context, we have advanced from a pastoral for the Indians to an Indian Pastoral—not a church for the Indians but an Indian Church. In the world of catechists, an Indian Church is being formed—a Church with Tzotzil face, a Tzeltal face or a Chol face, according to the community.

This is where we are at the moment—with a church that is not moved or conditioned by the good will of a missionary/priest. Most communities have sufficient deacons to live independently from the missionary, although there exists, of course, a link of respect and communion with him. We think this movement also has social repercussions. Our relation with God makes us question our relation to the world and with people. We recognize there is a God who loves us, who doesn't want our death but our life. This leads us to see there is a social structure that generates death and is against God's plan. It's interesting to listen to discussions about the kingdom of God. Suddenly the communities say what they need is a clinic or some other communal work. They begin to examine the lives of the first Christian communities. They read the Book of the Deeds of the Apostles or Paul's letters and they come to very practical conclusions, like having a common farm.

For example, in the Tojolabal zone, some farms are worked both individually and collectively, with the collective product divided according to the number of persons in a family, with one adult allowance for two children and an adult allowance for an old man even if he can't work. This is based on thinking about the Bible. When people begin to see that the poverty and exploitation in which they are living are not products of coincidence, nor are they God's plan but a product of an unjust social structure, they compare their communitarian life with the life offered by the government. They see a great difference. This generates a desire for change and justice, and, in many cases, the catechists become leaders in this movement for change and justice.

Another community effort is, as I have mentioned, the selection of ministers or catechists. On many occasions, a man or woman has had a dream that he or she considers a revelation. They ask to be a catechist and the community may agree. However, in most cases, when a community needs a catechist, it looks for a person with the proper qualifications. Or the community may be planning to name a deacon. They go according to tradition. The elders talk to a possible candidate; they talk to his wife; they talk with other members of the community and then, if everyone agrees, he is named and can receive instruction. This method lessens the power of the catechist. The force goes to the community, although the catechist is still the respected leader, able to direct and guide. Here, we see that a model of democracy and social and communitarian relations has emerged.

26
THE DIOCESE AND THE EZLN

In July 1974, Bishop Ruiz sponsored a three-day Indigenous Congress in which 587 Tzeltals, 330 Tzotzils, 161 Chols and 152 Tojolabals[1] were brought together to demand redress for centuries of oppression. Day laborers told of working from "sun to sun" for fewer than seven pesos a day, with children from the age of 10 beginning to work for one or two pesos a day. *Peons*, permanently attached to a ranch or plantation, were paid three or three and a half pesos a week, with workdays of 13 hours—this at a time when a 50-kilo bag of corn cost 70 pesos, rice cost seven pesos per kilo and chicken, as much as 28 pesos a kilo. "Paid" was a nominal term; they

---

1 Obregon (1997): 172

Bishop Samuel Ruiz

often received wages in merchandise or alcohol. If they needed money, they could borrow at 15 percent a month or 100 percent for seven months.

The delegates spoke in their own languages (with translators so they could understand what others were saying, although there were some who could speak four or five indigenous languages in addition to Spanish). They demanded land, instruction in farming skills, doctors, medicines, drinking water, schools (with teachers accountable to their communities), higher wages and arrangements for greater access to markets.

Although the Congress lasted only three days, its organizers, predominantly Jesuits, Dominicans, Marists and diocesan priests, maintained the Congress' name and network of catechists/translators. In January 1977, after Catholic priests formally separated from the Congress, its new secular leaders outlined long- and short-range plans. Both were unadulterated Marxism. For the long range, "The Indigenous Congress seeks to exchange the current socio-economic system for a society in which there is no private ownership of the means of production." The short-range aim was, "To awaken the consciousness of the proletariat in our communities, to form a truly independent organization and to continue organizing economic, ideological and political struggles with all the means at our disposal."[2] A few months later, the Congress formally dissolved.

The Congress had coincided with Bishop Ruiz's political challenge to the caciques of San Juan Chamula. To summarize: *Misión Chamula* was started in 1966 under Leopoldo Hernandez, known as Padre Polo. The training of catechists as social and political activists began in June 1969. The mission was officially ended the following October, but Padre Polo continued his activities and was able to manage the election of an opposition municipal president for the 1971-73 term and again for the 1974–1976 term. However, the caciques, with the help of the INI, arranged for a new election and imposed their own man. In 1977, the diocese withdrew all priests and catechists from Chamula. This proved fatal: families who hungered for spiritual sustenance could turn only to their evangelical relatives and neighbors.

The 1960s and '70s were decades of sweeping Mexican student dissent and the birth of a "New Left" ideology following the October 2, 1968, massacre of an estimated 200 student protesters at Tlatelolco Plaza in Mexico City. Activists concluded it was useless, if not suicidal, to mount a frontal attack against capitalism and a cacicazgo society. Instead, they decided to "Go to the People. Serve the people."

One was Adolfo Orive Berlinguer, an economics professor and son of a cabinet minister in the government of Miguel Aleman. At the Autonomous University of

2 Morales Bermudez (1991): 261.

Mexico (UAM) and later in Torreon, Monterrey and Durango in northern Mexico, he developed a philosophy called Popular Politics (*Política Popular; "Pepes"*), inspired by the Maoist belief in organization from below, with no leader dictating policy. One of Orive's first successes was the formation of a group called Coalition of Collective Ejidos among the Yaqui and Mayo indigenous people in the state of Sonora.

In October 1976, Bishop Ruiz went to Torreon to aid a priest, Jose Batarse, who had been arrested for taking part in a highway blockade as part of a demand for land. There, he marveled at, as he later said, "the discipline and organization of popular forces" organized by Orive[3] and invited him to Chiapas. He came in September 1977.

Many years later, in 1993, Mardonio Morales Lizalde, a Jesuit priest with 30 years of experience in the Lacandon region, quoted Orive as saying: "You have here work in the communities but are not prepared for political work . . . You take charge of pastoral matters and we will handle political organization. You have the communities in your hands. In this way we can complete our work."

Morales said the proposal was rejected but then more Ladinos arrived from the north. "They extended rapidly to all the jungle. If one Catholic community did not totally agree with them they were excluded and denied the sacraments of baptism and marriage. This divided the communities and many became Protestants. With this system of control of the assemblies they agreed on what would be sacrosanct and who would be followed. Soon, we who stood aside, were called dissidents because we did not subject ourselves to their commands."

An interviewer asked Morales: "Why did the Bishop not know anything of this?"

He replied: "My personal opinion is that Don Samuel saw this organization as a real advance toward improving the life of the people. He only saw the mask: he did not look behind it."[4]

There were two phases of northern influence. The first was Orive's "Pepes." They believed in working openly, in conjunction with government planning. They founded the Union of Unions (UU), which organized communities for credits and marketing arrangements. An expanded association, ARIC (Rural Association of Collective Interests)-UU, had similar interests. Two others were the Emiliano Zapata Peasant Organization (OCEZ), which organized a network of campesino groups for land reform and transport cooperatives, and the Independent Confederation of Agricultural Workers and Farmers (CIOAC), which fought for the legal rights of underpaid and maltreated tenant farmers and day laborers on big estates. They shouted, demonstrated, marched and organized land invasions, but they were not revolutionary. Their aim was "to help empower people to become the protagonists of their own destinies without directly challenging the government."[5] In short, they were seeking a clientelist niche within the Institutional Revolutionary Party. This was a Maoist mass line known as "fighting with two faces."[6]

Chiapas as a "foco" for a Mexican revolution

This was too mild for the diocese. The earlier arrivals were accused of being *gobiernistas* (government-men) and were encouraged to leave, opening the way for a second infiltration—this time of convinced revolutionaries who intended to manipulate the reformist zeal of Bishop Ruiz and many of his priests in order to

---

3 *Proceso*, Feb. 28, 1994. 4 Ibid. Sept. 13, 1994. 5 Collier (1994): 73. 6 Harvey (1990): 189.

establish a base to train indigenous cadres and recruits as soldiers in a war to replace the existing Mexican social and economic order with the verities of Marxism-Leninism. Their group was called the *Fuerza Nacional de Liberación* (FLN-National Liberation Force).

When the Zapatistas burst into the plaza of San Cristobal on January 1, 1994— bull-horning their grievances from a balcony of the municipal palace with the cry of "*Basta Ya*" (That's Enough)—they were hailed as leaders of an "Indian" revolt, but the fact that the incursion coincided with the day on which the North Atlantic Treaty Organization pact came into force should have been a seen as a red flag signaling that more was involved than the grievances of the neglected indigenous people.

Their leader, who called himself Marcos and modestly gave his rank as a *Subcomandante*, was completely unknown, but it was soon apparent that he was highly educated, and that the goals of the Zapatistas were long in the planning and ranged far beyond the fate of the "Indians." Marcos' first communiqué, on January 6, ran seven printed pages. The second, on January 11, ran two and a half pages. The next was on January 12. There were five dated January 13, one on January 17, two on January 18, one on January 19, four on January 20, one on January 26, one on January 29 and three on January 31. In length, they ranged from one to three printed pages. Then, when peace talks began in San Cristobal, Marcos presented 30 demands covering 22 closely printed pages. They called for a complete renovation of Mexico's politics and social practices.[7] Its name alone proclaimed the EZLN's goal: it was an army of "national" liberation.

In January 1995, in an effort to demystify Marcos, the government released his curriculum vitae. Rafael Sebastian Guillen Vicente was born in Tampico on June 19, 1957, to a family that owns a chain of furniture stores in the states of Veracruz and Tamaulipas. He has six brothers and a sister. His primary education was at Jesuit schools in Tampico and his secondary at the Higher Technical Institute in Guadalajara, also a Jesuit school. He did his obligatory social service among the Tarahumara indigenous people of Chihuahua as part of a Jesuit vicarate. From 1977 to 1980, he studied at the Faculty of Philosophy and Letters of the Autonomous University of Mexico and was awarded a degree with honorable mention for a thesis entitled *Philosophy of Education* (*Practical discourses and ideological practices*)—based largely on the writings of Louis Althusser and Michel Foucault. He took a master's degree from the Sorbonne in Paris and also received a degree for a translation from English. In May 1978, he presented seminar papers titled *Elements for an Analysis of Political Discourse* and *The Dominant Ideology* and presented a report, *Philosophy and the Production of Knowledge*, at a series of seminars titled *Critique of the Popular Movements in Mexico for the last decade.* In early 1979, at the Second National Meeting of Historians at UNAM, he gave an address, *The Struggle of the Masses and Ideological Struggle.*[8]

So much for the official record. Although he took no part in the raucous meetings and demonstrations that marked Mexican campus life, Guillen was, by then, a committed revolutionary. He had been recruited into the FLN, a group formed in 1969 that refused to accept Orive's Maoist line, insisting on pure Marxist-Leninism. Later, in a 42 page document, it described itself as a "political-military organization, whose aim is to seize power in Mexico City for workers and farmers

---

7 Bardacke (1995). **8** *La Republica* (Mexico City), Feb. 10, 1995.

and to install a popular socialist republic to integrate the battles of the urban pro-letariat with the battles of farmers and indigenous people in the most exploited region of our country and to form the *Ejército Zapatista de Liberación Nacional.*" That was 15 years before the EZLN surfaced in the plaza of San Cristobal.

(Except when otherwise noted, details of the antecedents and individuals involved in the EZLN are drawn from Carlos Tello Diaz, *La Rebelión de las cañadas.*)[9]

While still a student at the UNAM, Guillen spent one or two years training with the Sandinistas and later returned to northern Nicaragua for some months to help in the coffee harvest and for further training. In November 1983, he was appointed as an associate professor in the Autonomous University of Xochimilco, but he never showed up. Instead, on November 17th (they would later celebrate this as the anniversary of their arrival) he joined eleven men and women who were deter-mined to establish a base in the steep-sided las *Cañones* (Canyons), with walls 2,000 to 4,000 feet high, near the ejido of *Tierra y Libertad* (Land and Liberty) to the south of the Miramar Lagoon and near the virtually unpopulated 600,000 acres of tropical forest making up the Montes Azules Biosphere ecological zone.

They were all middle class. One was the son of the former rector of the University of Puebla. Another was a UNAM professor of ethics. Another—Silvia Fernandez, alias "Gloria"—had survived a police swoop in February 1974 on an FLN hideout in Nepantla in the state of Mexico (the area surrounding the capital, Mexico City) in which five men and women were killed. Fernandez had been a rev-olutionary since her teens. In the late 1970s, she took a course in communications at the Autonomous Metropolitan University (UAM), where Guillen was a part-time teacher, and recruited him into the FLN.

Even with the passage of years, the core FLN membership was surprisingly few. Marcos would later speak of "a group of fifteen or twenty guerrillas, at times as few as four."[10] Their leader was Fernando Yanez Munoz, alias "German." He had been the major organizer of FLN from its beginnings, preparing the pamphlets and maps and obtaining arms. Some years after the foco was established near Tierra y Libertad, he was captured by Federal police in Chihuahua, in a vehicle containing powerful weapons that he had just bought in the United States. The police tor-tured him for information about his accomplices, but he said nothing and was released on bail a few months later.

The second in command was Javier Ramirez, alias "Rodrigo." He was about 38 years old and had been a member of the FLN since the beginning of the 1970s.

Another member—Gloria Benavides or "Elisa"—was from Monterrey. She was then 26 and had been a militant for almost ten years. She had been arrested dur-ing the police raid of FLN hideouts in the mid-seventies, but was released under bail a few months later. She lived for some years in Veracruz and then in Tabasco as the companion of a comrade named Jorge Velasco. When he was killed in anoth-er police raid, she recruited and became the companion of a man who would become one of the most important of the conspirators.

He was Jorge Santiago, alias "Jacobo." After graduation from the seminary of San Cristobal, he was sent for advanced theological studies at the Gregorian University in Rome. On his return, he worked in Mexico City for the Episcopal

---

9 (1995). In an introductory note, Tello Diaz writes that his aim was to understand and not to judge, and that the book was based on documents and the testimonies of actual participants using, with a few exceptions, actual names.
10 Romero (1994): 57.

Commission for Indigenous Missions. He later moved to San Cristobal but then left the ministry to marry an American woman in Teopisca. In the autumn of 1983, he separated from his wife to establish a permanent relationship with Gloria Benavides.

The FLN's object, Tello Diaz writes, "was to create a rebel foco in Chiapas as the start of a revolution in Mexico," taking as their guide, "Marxism-Leninism that has demonstrated the validity of all the triumphant revolutions of this century."

The concept of a "foco," as a center in a remote area where cadres could be trained for a national uprising, was popularized by Che Guevara. He had tried to establish one in the Congo and then, when that failed, tried again in Bolivia, where he was killed in 1967.

In the early days, Santiago's role was critical. He belonged to a group known as the *Desarollo Económico Social de los Mexicanos Indigenas* (DESMI, Economic and Social Growth of Indigenous Mexicans). The incipient Zapatistas often traveled to the selva in a three-ton red truck bought with DESMI funds—ostensibly to carry supplies to a government CANASUPO general store. (A controversial program to distribute subsidized food to the poor). After discharging the goods, they would proceed to the guerrilla camp hidden in the canyons and there unload, among other things, guns and ammunition.

The camp was commanded by Silvia Fernandez—the woman who had recruited Marcos. "The Zapatistas were very content to live under her command. They said everyone loved her," Tello Diaz writes.

Initially, the camp operated under the cover of a DESMI health project. Tello Diaz writes that diocese "deliberately channeled government funds to finance projects in the region where they knew the authorities were Zapatistas." He specifically mentions Oxfam and Catholic Relief. With such help, the cadres added a tailor shop, a mule-transport business and several other projects.

Slowly, Santiago and Benavides began to make contact with the surrounding villages of the selva, administering vaccinations, teaching children and generally helping in whatever way needed in the fields. They and others also explored the deepest regions of the canyons. Whoever saw them in the mountains—tall, thin and fair skinned—might mistake them for tourists visiting the Miramar Lagoon.

Since "German" and "Rodrigo" traveled frequently dealing with organization's national planning, the entire Chiapas operation was often commanded by the next two ranking officers—Silvia Fernandez and Gloria Benavides. This participation of women in leadership positions sets off the FLN/EZLN from all other Latin American revolutionary movements. About a third of the core EZLN uniformed fighters were women, as well as the entire support staff.

The Violent Decades

The arrival of the FLN was preceded by—and later was simultaneous with—years of massive official repression. In 1978, the army and paramilitary troops evicted Tzeltals from the community of New Mount Lebanon, in the selva of Ocosingo. Two Tzeltals were killed, six tortured and 150 huts destroyed. The cause was the invasion of a finca owned by Hebert Stacpoole, who was said to control 250,000 acres divided among his family and *prestanombres* (borrowed

Zapatista woman millitia

names). Also in 1978, when the army attacked tenant farms in the municipality of Sabanilla, 16 Chols were tortured, houses were burned and crops destroyed. The attack was blamed on the *finquero* owner Wulfrano Constantino, said to control more than 10,000 acres.[11]

Alarm bells were also sounded in Mexico City by the revolutions of Central America. The village resettlement programs of General Efrain Rios Montt, in Guatemala in the early 1980s, sent 200,000 indigenous people fleeing into Mexico. The government reacted strongly. A former general—Absalon Castellanos—was appointed governor of Chiapas in 1982. When he completed his term in 1988, the CIOAC counted 102 killings, 327 "disappearances," 590 arrests, 427 kidnapings and tortures, 261 wounded and 12 women raped. The record of his successor, Patrocinio Gonzalez Garrido, was similarly blotted. In March 1989, Arturo Albores Velasco, the founder of OCEZ, was killed inside his paper store in Tuxtla Gutierrez. Later, *pistoleros* killed two OCEZ members in the municipality of Siltepec. Undaunted, 3,000 members of OCEZ staged a march and meeting on the Seventieth Anniversary of the assassination of Emiliano Zapata.[12]

This violence gave the FLN the cover needed to recruit and train their "militia" and to strengthen interaction with priests and catechists of the diocese. As Tello Diaz writes:

> The repression and assassination of cadres provoked the disgust of the [non-governmental] organizations, and the guerrillas began to penetrate the communities. They did not penetrate alone. The help of the diocese was fundamental. Afterward some recalled "They came with the Fathers." The campesinos did not have any way to fight for their rights. Thus, those who accompanied them (the Fathers) accepted the necessity of forming groups that, with arms, contributed to the defense of the communities. These groups, truthfully, at that time would have been unthinkable without the help of the Church.

In this instance, one of the key recruits to the FLN was Javier Vargas. He had been a member of the Congregation of Priests of Mary, but he married in the early '70s and became a catechist in Ocosingo parish with the rank of *tuhunel* (a traditional indigenous cargo. It is a Tzeltal word meaning "servant"). At the end of the '70s, he was appointed as tuhunel of tuhunels—the most prestigious of ranks.

"Vargas," Tello Diaz notes, "like everyone in the Diocese, was enthusiastic about the victory of the Sandinistas." To support this point, he quotes Bishop Ruiz as writing: "Christians must take part, without a troubled conscience, in the armed fight of the Sandinista Movement to achieve a new society."

Vargas lived in Nicaragua at the end of the '70s and returned in the beginning of the '80s. On his return, as a means of reinforcing his power in the Diocese, he formed an organization with the Tzeltal name of *Slop* (Race) made up of cate-

---

11 Barreda (1996): 200. 12 Ibid., pp. 199, 209, 210.

chists and tuhunels. Slop introduced them to the study of dialectal materialism, and they then spread the ideas among the dispersed settlements of the selva.

One member of Slop was Lazaro Hernandez, a Tzeltal who had studied with the Marists in San Cristobal and worked with other catechists in the Indigenous Congress. In the fall of 1985, as a member of Slop, he came to know Marcos, Silvia Fernandez and Fernando Yanez Munoz, the commander-in-chief.

Through persistent wooing and recruitment of catechists in leadership positions of ARIC-Union of Unions and, to a lesser extent OCEZ and CIOAC, the FLN spread its influence across the canyons and the selva: "All under the benign gaze of much of the Catholic establishment," Tello Diaz writes.

Tello Diaz is unequivocal about relations between the diocese and the guerrillas, writing: "The bishop of the Diocese in San Cristobal carried on talks, more or less regularly, with the leadership of the EZLN." He mentions Gloria Benavides and Javier Ramirez—the second in command—as the usual contacts. Many of their meetings took place in the Marist Seminary of San Cristobal.

He continues: "Many of the objectives of the Zapatistas were similar to those of a Diocesan Plan of 1986, which identified three forces to be opposed as part of the process of 'liberation:' the Federal government, the Chiapaneca oligarchy and North American imperialism, whose instruments were the sects and the cadres of the Summer Institute of Linguistics."

He writes of three nuclei of power in the diocese—the Jesuits of Bachajon, the Marists of Comitan and the Dominicans of Ocosingo. The Marists and Dominicans, he writes, were, "in general, in favor of the guerrillas." In addition to Ocosingo, they worked in Las Margaritas, where the EZLN grew strongest. Jesuits, on the other hand, ". . . were strongly against the guerrillas. They thought violence worsened the condition of the indigenous people and did not allow them to penetrate in the territory they controlled— the mountains of Chilon and Bachajon."

However, while avoiding revolutionary plotting, the Jesuits were neither passive nor quiet. The greatest public assertion of indigenous frustration was a demonstration, in March 1992, of men and women from 20 Chiapas municipalities. It was coordinated by the Jesuit Jeronimo Hernandez and led by Victor Guzman, a Chol from the town of New Bethany, in the municipality of Palenque. It was called *Xi'Nich* (The Ant) because it took 50 days, weaving back-and-forth for 1,106 kilometers through Palenque, Ocosingo and Oxchuc, then across the states of Tabasco, Oaxaca, Veracruz, Tlaxcala and Puebla, finally arriving in Mexico City on April 25. They called for new laws to recognize the languages and cultures of all the indigenous peoples of Mexico. They also demanded cancellation of an amendment to Article 127 of the Constitution that allowed for the sale or mortgage of ejido lands. On their final day, they went to the Basilica of Guadalupe to give thanks and held up a sign on which was written: "We want more bishops on the side of the poor."[13]

Beside the Jesuits, Tello Diaz writes of another major source of opposition to EZLN growth: "Protestants were opposed to violence as a matter of principle. The Catholic discourse was that of rebellion; that of the Protestants, in contrast, was of resignation. For the Catholics, they must create the Reign of God on earth; for the Protestants, on the contrary, they must seek Salvation in the Heavens . . . The

---

13 Rojas (1995): 207-215.

Protestants entered the communities to combat witchcraft, alcoholism, and extravagance, often with the help of the INI. This process gained strength in the 1980s, fomented by Governor Castellanos to weaken Samuel Ruiz."

The evangelical penetration of the selva was an outgrowth of the expulsions from Chamula and other Highland municipalities. By 1990, as Maria Concepcion Obregon writes, evangelicals comprised from 30 to 60 percent of the population of the Lacandon municipalities and their ever-growing presence, "provoked an enthusiastic reaction on the part of the Catholic Church, which decided . . . to intensify its pastoral labor. Priests and missionaries started to walk on foot to the most remote communities in their parishes in order to come to know the needs of their faithful and to develop a catechist community and with the help of these catechists translate parts of the Bible in the indigenuos languages."[14]

A major nexus of FLN strength was the eighteenth century Church of San Jacinto de Polonio in Ocosingo, where one of the pastors was the Dominican Pablo Iribarren who wrote the 1980 history of *Misión Chamula*. At least once a year, he staged a three-day ceremony presided over by catechists. All three of the leading catechists in his church were cadres. One—Pedro Lopez—would be killed in the attack on the market of Ocosingo. For a time, Marcos lived in the Ocosingo neighborhood of Barrio Norte.

Iribarren never masked his revolutionary leanings. He once wrote: "The social conscience and the demands and struggle have driven the people—searching for support—to the independent organizations that lack constitutional character and have socialist tendencies in varying degrees." On another occasion, he insisted the first priority must be to change, not individuals, but society as a whole: "In the process of the liberation of the people and our own process of solidarity there are different fronts of the same battle. There are the reactions of the powerful who are going to strike out with repression and defamation. There are also the reactions of the dominant groups within the church. These groups are not going to change without changing dominant groups within society, for there is no double analysis. The church cannot be purified without purifying the society."[15]

Growing Opposition and Growing Militancy

The EZLN never thought of itself as a Chiapas movement. Recruits were sent to study in a "School of Cadres," in Mexico City. When they returned to their communities, "they spoke of the contradictions of capitalism, scientific socialism and the value of the dictatorship of the proletariat." The most promising were then sent to the mountains of northern Chihuahua to work with the Tarhumara indigenous people in the Villista [from Pancho Villa] Front of National Liberacion.

Visits were reciprocal. Ladinos from other parts of the country might spend several months in the selva. One frequent visitor was Javier Elorriaga, alias "Vincente," from Guerrero. His parents were Spanish—a wealthy family who owned a hotel in Acapulco. Elorriaga had studied in Madrid and then in the Faculty of Arts and Letters at UNAM, where he was recruited by the FLN.

Cattle ranchers insisted that catechists instigated land invasions and the seizure of cattle from ranches with as few as 100 cattle—where owners would be destroyed if they lost even 10 animals. These small holders—and not the much

14 (1997):171.15 Floyd (1997): 76, 125.

publicized *tierratenientes*—were the principal supporters of municipal cattle owners associations.

These invasions were part of the violence that long preceded the arrival of the FLN. Always, Bishop Ruiz was blamed. After a particularly brutal army repression in November 1980, Manuel Mejia—a popular columnist for the Mexico City newspaper *El Universal*—under the headline "Subversive bishop preaches violence, already blood is running," accused the church of "organized fanaticism." He wrote: "Chiapas is being converted into an international subversive center led by the bishop of this diocese, Dr Samuel Ruiz Garcia, who . . . with the help of various priests (mainly foreigners) is the principal inventor of the climate of agitation, disorder and violence that prevails in our property."

He added that Ruiz's tactics had not always succeeded because ". . . groups of evangelicals also have worked many years in the sierra, converting the indigenous to their religion, which inculcates precepts of the Bible—first teaching them to read, eradicating alcoholism, teaching them to respect their neighbors and other moral precepts. This has been a barrier of protection when the foreign priests arrive, sent by the bishop not to catechize but to incite revolt."

Mejia described the foreign priests: "with long disheveled hair, long beards, dirty clothes and bad smelling—obviously without cassocks."[16]

More than a decade later, in September 1991, after the head of another cattle owners' association accused a priest, Joel Padron, who had worked in Simojovel for 11 years, of using his pulpit to incite violence in the guise of social justice, Governor Patrocinio Gonzalez Garrido had him arrested on charges of robbery, looting, carrying illegal arms, organizing gangs and inciting his parishioners to occupy land. He offered to release Padron if Bishop Ruiz would retract his denunciations of human rights violations. Ruiz called that blackmail and defiantly appointed Padron as director of the diocesan prison ministry. Three months later, the charges were dropped and Padron was released.[17]

Simultaneously, however, Ruiz began to distance himself from the Zapatistas. Tello Diaz writes: "Don Samuel privately lamented the help given to the FLN by the priests. Now they carry the Indians to the side of tragedy," he said. Marcos was at his side when he said this. "Here we do not have ARIC, we do not have the Word of God, we do not have the government of the republic. Here we have the *Ejército Zapatista de Liberación National.*"

When the priests began to pull back, indigenous members of the EZLN became upset. One told a priest: "You put us in the organization and now you leave."[18]

Jorge Santiago, "Jacabo," tried to mediate but Tello Diaz writes that it was too late: "The insurgents were very strong, too strong to be detained by the Church." In the summer of 1991, the Zapatistas took advantage of a rift in ARIC to lure dissenters into a new and more militant organization—the National Independent Emiliano Zapata Peasant Alliance (ANCIEZ). It was founded in July at a meeting in Coaxcatlan, Puebla. This was the zone of influence of "Frank," one of the oldest of the FLN cadres. He was an indigenous Mexican from Sabanilla in the selva. He was helped, Tello Diaz writes, "by the priests of San Juan Bautistas Coaxcatlan parish."

With ANCIEZ, the EZLN broke out of the selva to Tila, Yajalon, El Bosque, Larrainzar, Huixtan, Chanal and San Cristobal. Yet, because of the disagreement

16 Ibid., 172-73. 17 MacEoin (1996): 65-66. 18 *Proceso*, Sept. 13, 1993.

with priests, membership drifted away. Moreover, security was breaking down. In January 1991, a guerrilla camp was discovered in the Ejido Quintana Roo, with wooden rifles, uniforms, radios and documents incriminating Felipe de Jesus Toussaint, a priest of Sabanilla. Then there was a leak that the guerrillas were helped with arms by Heriberto Cruz, a priest of Las Margaritas.

Worst of all were the changes in the revolutionary world. Tello Diaz quotes Marcos as remarking ironically after the communist failure in the Soviet Union, "Socialism is dead. Long live conformism, modernity and capitalism."

The Sandinistas had also long-since been voted out of office. The final blow came in January 1992, when the guerrillas of El Salvador signed a peace accord at Chapultepec in Mexico City.

To raise morale, in April 1992 ANCIEZ staged an indigenous march in Ocosingo. They claimed more than 3,000 participated. Marcos was a spectator. He had just spent some weeks in Tampico, where he attended a conference against the North Atlantic Treaty Organization. He had occasionally visited his family in the previous nine years. This would be the last time.

In San Cristobal the following October 12, an estimated 9,000 paraded to mark the 500th anniversary of the discovery of America. There were participants from a dozen activist groups. The most numerous, and most noteworthy, were from ANCIEZ, with their discipline and the number of women taking part, some carrying bows and arrows. Marcos and Salvador Morales, "Daniel," filmed from the sidelines. Toward the end, ANCIEZ militants branched off to a nearby park and there tore down the bronze statue of Diego de Mazariegos—the *conquistador* of Chiapas. A speaker at the later closing ceremonies declared: "Today we end 500 years of the robbery, death and destruction of the indigenous people."

Despite such displays, the leaders knew the future was bleak. A meeting was called in January 1993, at an ejido named Prado, to discuss what Tello Diaz calls "the theme of the war of liberation in Mexico." Marcos, who commanded the "Front of Southeast" (Chiapas, Oaxaca and Tabasco), was chairman. With him were two men who had become his constant companions. One was Hector Ochoa, "Pedro," from Mexico City, who had been among the first arrivals. The other was Salvador Morales from Michoacan. He had lived with Marcos in the UAM of Xochimilco and was recruited at about the same time. He too was one of the first arrivals.

The debate was mostly between Marcos and Javier Ramirez, the second in command. Ramirez, who generally worked in Chihuahua, pointed out that the movement was weak in the northern and central states and maintained that, without their help, an attempted revolution would be confined to the southeast. Two women agreed—Gloria Benavides and Silvia Fernandez. Also a third, "Lucia," who was then the companion of the top commander, Fernando Yanez Munoz, "German." She said it would be better to wait another ten years so that the war could be finished in, at the most, one month.

Marcos, while acknowledging that many had abandoned the movement because of the quarrel with the church, estimated about 12,000 militants remained. He said they lived in communities that had been identified, and possibly targeted, by the Army and that it was necessary to take the initiative. He suggested it would be best to begin in 1994, the year of the next national elections. He

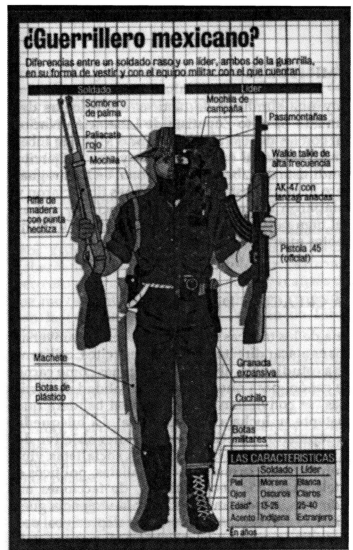

A illustration from Luis Pazos' book on Marcos and the EZLN, contrasting the equipment for officers with the wooden rifles and rubber boots of ordinary soldiers

was seconded by "Daniel," "Pedro" and "Vincente"—Javier Elorriaga. After some hours of debate, "German" agreed. With that, Rodrigo said he would leave. He got in his car and was seen no more.

The following fall, with planning well under way, there was news that made it more urgent than ever to begin without delay. Word leaked that Mexico had demanded, and the Vatican had accepted, that Bishop Ruiz be removed for using "a Marxist analysis of society." It was said he was "practicing a form of pastoral care that is reductionist and exclusive." Defiant as ever, Ruiz replied: "If I care for the 75 percent of the community without forgetting the 25 percent at the top, it does not appear to me to be reductionism but unification because now everyone is represented."[19]

Ruiz then went on the offensive. He flew to neighboring Yucatan, where Pope John Paul II was visiting, and handed the pope a 28 page document titled *In This Hour of Grace*, charging that indigenous people were oppressed and pushed to the margins of national life by deliberate choice; that the state attempted to maintain order without justice; that corruption reigned at all levels and that government officials were involved in the narcotics trade.[20]

Then, on January 1, 1994, came the brief Zapatista occupation of San Cristobal, Las Margaritas, Chanal, Altamirano and Ocosingo. Marcos' estimate of 12,000 militia proved wildly optimistic. Only about 900 men took part in this occupation: as few as one hundred entered Chanal. The only actions outside of Chiapas were attempts to blow up electric towers in Puebla and Michoacan. The retreat began on January 4 and Marcos on January 12 accepted a government-offered cease fire. The 12-day "war" left about 150 dead, half of them civilians. Those who were hurt the most were civilians. An estimated 20,000 indigenous people fled from soldiers, tanks and planes and suffered for months in refugee camps. When they returned to their lands, they found homes destroyed and property lost.

(Of the core EZLN leadership, only Marcos was in Chiapas for the uprising. In early 1995, when peace talks bogged down, Silvia Fernandez, Gloria Benavides and Javier Elorriaga—by then man and wife—were jailed and received long prison sentences. They were betrayed by Salvador Morales, the same "Daniel" who seconded Marcos' motion to begin the war. The following fall, Fernando Yanez, the commander-in-chief, fell into police hands when they stopped his car near Mexico City after seeing a driver with a rifle between his knees. He too received a long jail term, but all the sentences were commuted when the Zapatistas agreed to resume negotiations. Elorriaga then appeared as the EZLN media representative in Chiapas.)

The attempt to remove Diaz was put aside when he accepted the role of mediator. For middle-class Ladinos, who had long derided the "Red Bishop," this only seemed to confirm Ruiz's blessings for, if not actual involvement in, the uprising. In February, when the talks began at his cathedral, stones shattered the windows of his residence and "Wanted" posters were distributed of him wearing a Zapatista mask. He was denounced as a traitor, a promoter of violence and a corruptor of monks, seminarians and priests.

On February 13, 1995, he was brought before an extraordinary commission of 10 members of the federal legislature, the bishops of the other two dioceses of Chiapas (Felipe Aguirre Franco of Tuxtla Gutierrez and Felipe Arizmendi of

---

19 Reyes and Zebadua (1995): 23-24. 20 Ibid., 71-78.

Tapachula), Archbishop Adolfo Suarez Rivera (the president of the Mexican Episcopal Conference), the archbishop of Oaxaca and the bishop of Coatzacoalcos to answer the question that lay behind all the charges against him: Was he, in effect, teaching a Theology of Revolution?

A "synthesis" of the proceedings was published by *Proceso* on February 28. Ruiz conceded he had invited Orive to Chiapas but said he was tricked: "The left-wing political groups who came to Chiapas from Torreon took advantage of the religious infrastructure created by the diocese of San Cristobal de La Casas, and they carried on their activities in the Highlands and in the Lacandon jungle with a discourse that was not only Marxist but even atheistic." He quoted one of them as saying that the only use he had for the Bible was as toilet paper.

When pressed to say whether or not he knew a revolution was in preparation, he replied, "We detected certain lights, certain indications . . . We could not have anything more than a hypothesis that in some places or municipalities revolutionaries could be found. We thought it was confined to a rather limited zone . . . Not until almost the end of the year did we appreciate that it was much broader and more alarming."

To explore the role of catechists, three *Proceso* reporters interviewed Joel Padron, the priest who had been jailed at the end of 1991 on a charge of organizing a land invasion in Simojovel. He told them: "To be a priest or catechist in Chiapas never meant to carry the Bible in one hand and a rifle in the other...With or without religion, violence is produced by the desperation of the indigenous people in the face of their social needs." Still, he readily admitted that catechists were "conscienticized" about the shortcomings of Mexican society and revealed these questions in a catechist pamphlet:

> How can we defend our rights to a better life? Why is there poverty in our families and communities? What must we do so that our needs for education, health and other things are resolved? What problems do we have in the distribution and sale of our products? Why are those who announce the Good News persecuted? What is happening in these days in our diocese? Who is speaking ill of our diocese and Don Samuel? Why? What must we do so that God and His spirit is present in the elections?

What the catechists made of these teachings, he insisted, was their responsibility, not that church's. He cited the case of two priests, Camilio Torres and Gaspar Garcia, who took part in the guerrilla movements in Central and South America: "In these cases no one has said that it was the Church that took up arms but that it was a personal option . . . In this sense, it can be said that catechists in the EZLN were a personal decision."[21]

Unable to remove Ruiz, the government turned to more vulnerable targets. Between June and September 1995, Mexico expelled or denied reentry to, after brief visits abroad, seven priests and three nuns. One of the deported illustrates both the shortage of priests and the vulnerability of the diocese of San Cristobal. Loren Riebe of Los Angeles, California, had been a priest in the parish of St James the Apostle in Yajalon for 19 years—the only priest for 54 Tzeltal villages with a

21 March 7, 1994.

---

population of over 25,000 people. The government presented no evidence to support its charge that he and the others were somehow involved in the uprising. The losers were the Tzeltals of Yajalon. Riebe later described his mission in a speech in Las Cruces, New Mexico in July 1995:

> I have dedicated myself to pastoral sacramental work and to the preparation of Indian lay catechists...to teach scripture, church history and tradition. Through the course of the years, pastoral staff and I have been asked by the Indians to facilitate the formation of a cooperative food store, a small clinic, a public library, and a women's weaving cooperative. In 1990, the Indian catechists formed a non-profit organization to purchase a 15-acre ranch that could be developed as a residence for 45 Indian boys to attend high school. The next year, with the help of U.S. donations, they were able to obtain a house for the education of 25 Indian girls. There presently are over 100 high school boys and girls who receive scholarships from sponsors in the U.S. allowing them to attend high school, and 25 Indians are attending college. [Additional] projects . . . include a solar photovoltaic experiment to generate electricity, a new dormitory for 20 girls and a new dormitory for 50 more boys.

In August 1995, the Vatican named Raul Vera Lopez as coadjutor bishop. It was speculated that the appointment was designed to dilute Ruiz's authority and change the direction of the parish. However, it soon became obvious that Vera Lopez, a 50-year-old Dominican from Guerrero State, shared the options maintained by Ruiz.

The International Encounter

When the Zapatistas first occupied San Cristobal, thousands jammed the Zocalo, the central square of Mexico City, to chant approval. However, several leading Mexican commentators did not share the enthusiasm. Juan Miguel de Mora, the author of several works of social criticism, wrote a book accusing present and former governments of Mexico, and now the EZLN, of exploiting and manipulating indigenous peoples and of using them as "cannon fodder" to achieve their own ends: "It is evident that a person who has not the slightest political relevance, who is unknown to the entire nation and who controls hardly two or three hundred aborigines in the jungle, who tries to impose his criticism and his ideas and his form of government on the entire country, is someone with an inexact perception of the outside world." He also wrote of Marcos' "megalomania" and "messianic" declarations.[22]

Another—Cesar Romero Jacobo—described Marcos, who called himself "a professional of hope," as "a messianic type using his genius to fool and manipulate the people to satisfy his own ego and instability. Suppose that behind the mask there is a dull and ugly face?"[23]

But, among foreigners he was an instant icon. Dozens of books and articles, in English, French, German and other languages, hailed Marcos and the Zapatistas as harbingers of a new form of revolution. In late July and early August 1996, more

22 (1995): 155-191. **23** (1994): 17.

than 2,000 "hippies, punks, communists and middle-class leftists"[24] from 42 countries met at a remote community in Chiapas for the "First International Encounter Against Neoliberalism and for Humanity." (Neoliberalism is a neologism for capitalism. The criticism is that free market economics and the privatization of government monopolies are crushing the poor in the rush for profits.)

Delegates waded through ankle-deep mud, lined up for meals of scrambled eggs, rice, and beans, slept on hammocks, listened to speeches, shouted slogans and sat into the morning hours singing 1950's and 1960's lyrics against racism and in favor of international peace and harmony. They applauded when the masked

"A neologism for capitalism"

Subcommander Marcos appeared on a white horse and rushed to take his picture. That's about all most saw of him. Only a favored few were invited to a four-hour round-table discussion of the evils of Neoliberalism and the promises of Zapatismo and heard Marcos give a long talk about his struggle and his visions.

One foreign guest described the International Encounter as a junction "between utopia and nostalgia." A French newspaper called it "surrealist." Pavel Lungin, a Russian movie maker, called it a "carnival," adding: "We are being used as human shields"—a thought that would be elaborated in the years to come.

(A week after the Encounter, when 1,200 delegates from 88 Mexican leftist organizations gathered in Guadalajara, a reporter noted there were "no French philosophers, or international authors," and that delegates ate regional specialties and rice and beans for 60 cents a meal, in contrast to the 100 dollars-a-week food charge for invitees to the Encounter.)[25]

The Marcos Enigma

Marcos is unique in many ways—including his humor and literacy. While revolutionaries usually hunger for attention, Marcos has shunned the press and has granted interviews to a select few. When the government issued an order (soon rescinded) for his arrest, he moved deeper into the Canyons to a community called La Realidad, then a five-hour drive from San Cristobal—the last few hours over a dirt road. He joked, "It's a little difficult to arrive at reality."

Regis Debray, the French author whose ties with erstwhile Latin American revolutionaries date from the time he was with Che Guevara in his fatal attempt to establish a revolutionary foco in Bolivia, spent two days with Marcos in his jungle sanctuary. In an article for *Proceso*,[26] he described Marcos as "The man in the ski mask ... with a sense of practical detail to moderate the indispensable megalomania ... that has allowed him to live for 11 [sic] years on beans and live clandestinely ... without chocolate or press conferences."

24 *Mexico City Times* Aug. 5, 1996. 25 Ibid., Aug. 19, 1996. 26 May 30, 1996.

Rafael Sebastian Guillen Vicente,
alias Marcos

He asked about Marcos' costume, which gives him the appearance of a guerrilla *manqué*—bandoliers across his chest, like Emiliano Zapata, but the cartridges do not match his weapon; old shoes and a frayed cap atop his mask.

"A Zorro with a black ski mask, cap with three stars, crossed bands for bullets, pipe the style of Che," Debray noted.

"Why the broken boots and hat not repaired," I asked.

"It's more scenic," he replied with a grin.

"How long will it be before you lay down your arms and take off the ski mask?" Debray asked. "When do you think your method of fighting the war will be ended?"

"The day when every indigenous person enjoys the same rights as a White in every part of the Republic; the day when the system of party rule has ended and when elections are no longer a synonym of fraud. Now an opponent is bought or killed. This must change. I'm fed up," Marcos replied.

"Will you hold out until then?" Debray asked.

"In the worst of cases we . . . can return to the catacombs another 10 years or more . . . Time is on our side. The economic situation will not get better. There is no doubt that we will win."

A War of Low Intensity

The peace negotiations that began in February 1994 were broken off in September 1996 after President Zedillo ruled that draft proposals on indigenous autonomy—the key Zapatista demand—had to be debated and modified, if thought necessary, by the legislature in Mexico City. Marcos took this as a rejection and ended the dialogues, telling his representatives to "return to the jungle."

It then became evident that the peace talks were one arm of a two-pronged "War of Low Intensity" to contain and eventually eliminate the Zapatistas. On one hand, the national and state governments built roads, opened schools, distributed thousands of books in the indigenous languages, provided piped drinking water and implemented social assistance programs, health clinics and marketing cooperatives to, in the familiar phrase of the American war in Viet Nam, "win the hearts and minds of the people."

At the same time, the army extended its presence in the conflict area, establishing bases and building access roads deep within the previously trackless Zapatista zone of control. The government knew it would raise a storm of international criticism if it directly assaulted the Zapatistas and, instead, employed the classic counter-guerrilla tactic of paramilitary groups.

A document leaked to *Proceso* revealed that, in October 1994, the general commanding the Seventh Military Region, with headquarters in Tuxtla Gutierrez, had drafted a plan "to break the support relationship that exists between the population and the transgressors of the law." Military intelligence services were to "secretly organize certain sectors of the civilian population, including ranchers, small business owners and individuals characterized by a high sense of patriotic duty, who will be employed in support of our operations." About a half-dozen of such groups were formed—one with the innocuous name of "Peace and Justice" but another with the more ominous name of *Mascara Roja* (Red Mask) because of the red bandanas they used to cover their faces.[27]

From the earliest days of the Catholic church's role as mediator, the *Centro de Derechos Humanos Fray Bartolomé de Las Casas* (Friar Bartolome Human Rights Center, named after the *Conquistador* priest who ruled that Indians were not animals, but human beings with souls), which is an adjunct of the San Cristobal diocese, was the information source and coordinator for foreign groups determined to come to the rescue of the Zapatistas. It's estimated that, in the four years following the uprising, between 2,000 and 3,000 Americans participated in these "solidarity" trips.[28] In May 1998, the four leading groups formed a "Mexico Solidarity Network."

They are: the National Commission for Democracy in Mexico (NCDM), based in Los Angeles and El Paso; *Servicio Internacional para la Paz* (SIPAZ, International Peace Service), based in Santa Cruz, California; Global Exchange, with offices in San Francisco and San Cristobal and Pastors for Peace (IFCO), based in New York and Chicago. In addition, there are two major Mexican groups: the "Center for Indigenous Rights" and the "Coordinating Agency of Non-Governmental Organizations for Peace" (CONPAZ).

For years, backpackers gathered at the Friar Bartolome doorstep in San Cristobal to volunteer, often after reading of the Zapatistas on 50 or so World Wide Web sites (see Appendix II). A dispatch by ABC New reporter Deborah Amos, titled "Internet Zapatista Chic" and speaking of "spring-break revolutionaries," quoted the reason one volunteer gave for making the long trip: "When the foreigners are here, the army doesn't come in."[29]

The intricacies of politics and religion in Chiapas are far beyond all but a handful of visitors. Marcos always insisted he wanted to establish a neutral, nonpolitical consensus on liberty, equality and justice, yet his supporters are identified with the center-left PRD—the major challenger to the ruling PRI in central and southern Mexico. While evangelicals shun secular affairs and seldom express interest in day-to-day political events, their conservative philosophy makes them a natural ally of the PRI.

The Friar Bartolome center gave a brief report on the division that is tearing communities apart in a 1997 publication titled "*Ni Paz ni Justicia*" (Neither Peace nor Justice—a play on the name of the paramilitary group Peace and Justice):

> Although the roots of the problem in the northern region are essentially political, the conflict has been presented by some as a religious issue. There are obvious parallels between the ideological differences of the PRI and the PRD and the religious polarization that has emerged

27 *Processo*, Jan. 4, 1998. **28** *La Jornada*, Aug. 3, 1998. **29** May 8, 1998.

between the conservative teachings of the evangelical churches and the Liberation Theology movement within the Catholic Church. There is also a strong relationship between the leadership of "Peace and Justice" and some evangelical pastors. In fact the roles have sometimes overlapped ... Because of the growing religious intolerance, in which both the Catholic and the evangelical churches have been participants, religious leaders, in particular from the Presbyterian Church and from the diocese of the Catholic Church in San Cristobal, have promoted new ecumenical initiatives aimed at nurturing a process of reconciliation in the communities. This task is as difficult as it is necessary in order to revitalize the weakened peace process.[30]

The ecumenical initiative cited in the publication was a two-day meeting in San Cristobal in April 1997 of 35 pastors and lay leaders from Catholic, Presbyterian, Baptist, Pentecostal, Adventist, Mennonite and Nazarene congregations. Lazaro Gonzalez, a Baptist professor and director of the *Consejo Indígena Campesino Evangélico de México* (CICEM, the Council of Indigenous Campesino Evangelical Churches, an association of 40 Baptist, Methodist, Presbyterian and Pentecostal congregations) conceded that evangelicals and Catholics had a long history of antagonism in Mexico as a whole and especially in Chiapas.

He was joined in organizing the event by Abdias Tovilla and Msgr Felipe Toussaint Loera. The meeting was primarily devoted to personal stories of discrimination and biblical reflection in light of these testimonies, with small groups worshiping, praying and singing together. During the closing session, participants were asked to undertake specific acts of reconciliation between evangelicals and Catholics in Chiapas. The conference ended with a joint communion service presided over by Tovilla and assisted by Catholic, Presbyterian, Baptist and Pentecostal leaders.

The following September, the CICEM coordinated a second, three-day, round of meetings in San Cristobal. Other conveners included Msgr Toussaint, Abdias Tovilla and Esdras Alonso Gonzalez. It included 70 Chol, Tzotzil, Tzeltal and Spanish-speaking representatives of Catholic, Baptist, Church of God, Full Gospel, Presbyterian and Seventh-Day Adventist congregations. As with the April meetings, the Baptist Peace Fellowship of North America (BPFNA) was the financial sponsor, with contributions from the Presbyterian Church in the United States, the Mennonite Central Committee and the Board of International Ministries of the American Baptist Churches USA.

The indigenous representatives told of expulsions, murders and thefts and charged that the other side, whoever that might be, supported either the PRI and paramilitary groups or the PRD and the EZLN. On reflection, they concluded the conflict was political and that the urgent need was for religious leaders to serve as mediators for peace and reconciliation in the communities.

Since both the pro-Zapatistas and the paramilitary groups were indigenous, the Revolt of the Indians had obviously deteriorated into a war of Indians against Indians. According to a SIPAZ estimate, in the previous two years, more than 300 had been killed and 4,000 displaced from their homes (although half were able to

---

30 The report is reproduced under the title "The Tragedy of the Chols: A people torn apart by violence," in *SIPAZ Report*, Vol. 2/2, April 1997.

return)—most of them in the northern Chol region.

The most extensive and active paramilitary group in the Chol areas and the central Highlands was Peace and Justice. According to the publication "Neither Peace Nor Justice," this group was organized in the city of Tila in early 1995 and "began its . . .attacks on the population in March. The first victims were catechists, school teachers and community leaders."

The publication identified the founder of Peace and Justice as Samuel Sanchez Sanchez, an evangelical Chol schoolteacher from Tila, who was elected to the state legislature in October 1995, when a Zapatista election boycott resulted in large-scale abstention. Members of Peace and Justice were accused of responsibility for an attempt, in November 1997, to ambush bishops Ruiz and Vera Lopez near Tila.

In the summer of 1997, the Zapatistas again urged supporters to boycott the forthcoming national elections, and, on election day, July 6, scattered bands stormed polling stations in the Highlands, ripping up and burning ballots. They left a statement reading: "We need a new society and a new Constitution and we won't get those by voting for some political party." As it turned out, an opposition coalition won control of the lower house of the Mexican Congress, giving the ruling party its worst defeat in history.

The destruction of ballot boxes was most widespread in the Tzotzil municipality of San Pedro Chenalho, where Zapatistas had proclaimed the autonomous community of "San Pedro Emiliano Zapata." Fatal clashes between PRI supporters and the Zapatistas became endemic, and refugees from both sides fled the most dangerous zones. PRI supporters and evangelicals say 18 of their followers were killed over a period of six months, including four Presbyterians—three teenagers and a middle-aged woman—murdered in November 1997 by hooded men using high-powered weapons. They were shot in the back and "finished off with machete blows, causing the separation of their arms and legs."[31]

Then, just before Christmas, men wearing the red face coverings of Red Masks massacred 45 villagers—seven men, 20 women, 17 children and a one-month-old baby—in the Chenalho subdivision of Acteal. Most of the victims were gunned down by high-powered weapons aimed at their backs. In February 1998, Abdias Tovilla issued a statement on behalf of CEDECH:

> The motive for this multiple murder was an act of hatred and revenge for the harassment and other murders that had taken place beforehand at the expense of the families of those who attacked on this occasion. The attack was encouraged by violent groups who are interested in destabilizing the region, who are ambitious for economic, political and social power and who want to divide the inhabitants of the indigenous communities, setting them against each other in order to achieve their own ends. Instead of struggling for legitimate rights and noble causes in their region, they have brought misery and poverty, leaving many widows and orphans to fend for themselves in very sorry conditions.

---

31 *Novedades* (Mexico City), Nov, 16, 1997.

The mayor of Chenalho was fired for trying to cover-up the massacre, and a soldier was arrested and later sentenced to prison on charges of supplying an AK-47 assault rifle and helping to train the assailants. President Zedillo dismissed Governor Cesar Ruiz and ordered a statewide search for hidden arms. But, simultaneously, the government expelled a Jesuit priest—Michel Henri Jean Chanteau—a Frenchman who had served in Chenalho for 32 years. Rev Chanteau was candid about his sympathies for the Zapatistas but denied he was a supporter of Marcos.

Less than a decade earlier, events in the mountains of Chiapas would hardly have rated more than a few paragraphs in the most international of newspapers. Now, with cyberspace, a call went out after the Acteal massacre for support of the Zapatistas. In just 20 days, according to a compilation prepared by Stefan Wray, of the Department of Culture and Communication of New York University, there were more than 122 actions involving "tens of thousands" of people in 61 cities and towns in 15 countries on four continents. These ranged from protests and vigils at Mexican consulates, the inking of graffiti in Oslo, a "legislative initiative" in Switzerland, the occupation of the Mexican consulate in Ancona, Italy, a blockade of the Mexico City stock exchange, a teach-in at the University of Hamburg in Germany and the leafleting of the marketplace in Melbourne, Australia.

The message was heard by those who mattered. Among others, Mary Robinson, the former President of Ireland and now the United Nations High Commissioner for Human Rights, called for a resumption of peace talks. And, although the United States has rarely commented on Chiapas affairs, Secretary of State Madeleine Albright told a Senate hearing that the United States was "pressing" Mexico to resolve the situation.

Simultaneously, American and European Zapatista supporters descended on Chiapas to act as shields and to protest. By then, the government had set up checkpoints on roads leading to "autonomous" settlements and turned away all visitors. The most persistent were deported, including an American woman who tried twice to get to La Realidad, the entrance to Marcos' jungle lair. On the third try, she was seized and put on an airplane without even being allowed to retrieve her car.

In April, 134 Italians arrived by bus and headed directly to the village of Taniperla. They brushed aside police and stormed into the village cradling purple hyacinths in their arms, only to be assaulted by several hundred men and women waving clubs and machetes. "Peace, peace," they shouted. Then a group of Zapatista women ran up and there was hair pulling and scratching. The police put the Italians back on their bus and sent them to Tuxtla Gutierrez to be deported.

A few weeks later, a "Pastors for Peace" delegation led by Lucius Walker, a Methodist minister from New York, arrived in Taniperlas on the last stop of a 10-day mission to carry food, blankets and other supplies to indigenous communities. By then, Taniperlas was fully occupied by the police and pro-Zapatistas had fled. About 30 men blocked the bus and hammered it with clubs, breaking the windows. Walker tried to hold a prayer meeting but soon left, vowing to return.

In April, Mexican immigration officials tried to end the problem by raising the barrier for foreign "observers." To give time for processing, thirty days before their planned arrival they would have to submit a detailed plan, with the group to be limited to no more than ten persons and a limitation that the sponsoring organization had to be in existence for ten years or be recognized by the United Nations.

But then, in September, a Federal Court judge in Mexico City—ruling on an appeal by an American, Tom Hansen—overturned his deportation the previous February. She ruled that Hansen's activities could not "in any way be considered illegal or dishonest," in that he was an observer and not a participant, and so did not violate the prohibition against foreign meddling in Mexico's internal affairs.

The flood of foreigners had touched a raw nerve. *New York Times* reporter Julia Preston wrote: "The deepening polarization in Chiapas has brought out a zealous nationalism sometimes bordering on xenophobia in pro-government political forces both humble and mighty...A prominent Chiapas journalist has devoted his newspaper columns to decrying the 'satanic intervention' of unnamed foreigners [and] a local labor federation called for foreign residents to be rounded up and expelled from the Indian highlands."[32]

Contributing to the debate, Lolita de la Vega, an anchorwoman for the TV Azteca network, reported on a helicopter trip she made to La Realidad. Her footage showed she and her crew were greeted by several people who appeared to be non-Mexican and who demanded to see their press credentials, photographed them, took one of their videotapes and eventually asked them to leave. In an interview, Ms de la Vega said she felt she had been kidnaped by strangers who, she concluded, were foreign members of the Zapatista army. "We saw that it wasn't an Indian movement. Foreigners were in command of our Indians. It brought back memories of the Spanish conquest," she said.

In March 1998, about 18 months after the breakdown of peace negotiations, the Zedillo administration sent a bill to Congress with proposals to modify the Constitution to grant additional rights to indigenous Mexicans, saying it wished "to put the negotiating process back on track." Since the proposal first went to the Senate, where the PRI still had a comfortable majority, opponents charged that Zedillo was trying to by-pass the Zapatistas. Bishop Ruiz dismissed it as "mock legal initiative."

President Zedillo then began a campaign to gather support for his iniatitive. In April, in a speech in Santiago, Chile, Zedillo charged that the EZLN was the primary paramilitary force in Chipas and accused Zapatistas of waging a propaganda war. "I am not going to sign a blank sheet of paper," he declared. "We are all subjected to this slanderous . . . Internet war in which the figure of Señor Rafael Sebastian, better known as Marcos, has aroused among intellectuals in Europe and North America, but I obviously can't make decisions based on that kind of propaganda," he added.[33]

In a speech Tuxtla Gutierrez in late May, he spoke of "theologians of violence" who "shield themselves in their hierarchy and defend humanistic and religious motivations and who, for many years, have contributred to the conditions of confrontation and division in the State of Chapas."

Almost simultaneously, Ruiz was criticized by leading members of the Catholic hierarchy, including Cardinal Norberto Rivera. Echoing this, *Nuevo Criterio*, Mexico City's Catholic newspaper, said it was wrong for Ruiz to "criticize a positive initiative and to clearly take one side when his position should be the one of mediation."[34]

---

32 Feb. 14, 1998. 33 *La Jornada*, April 18, 1998. 34 *Reuters*, April 2, 1998.

Then on June 7, Ruiz resigned from his four-year role as the chief mediator, citing what he descried as the government's "constant and growing aggression" against his diocese.

Still Zedillo continued his anti-Ruiz barrage. In a speech in Simojovel in early July—on his fifth visit to the state within two months—he said "the government does not want there to be victors or vanquished, the government only wants the triumph of Mexico . . . and in order to achieve it we can no longer accept grand-standing, messianic leaders, nor apostles of hypocrisy."

Marcos who had previously been described as messianic by both Juan Miguel de Mora and Cesar Romero Jacobo, remained hidden in his "catacombs," but not out of touch. He sent a long communique in January 1998 and another a month later. Then months went by with no word. Even his supporters, when questioned, said they did not know where he was. Finally, in July, two faxes arrived "From the mountains of southeast Mexico"—his customary vague location. One read: "Yepa, yepa yepa! *Ándale, ándale, ándale! Arriba, arriba!* (Go on! Get up!) Yepa, yepa!" It carried his distinctive signature and "Speedy Gonzalez," the Warner Brothers cartoon character who always outruns more powerful opponents. Marcos had often used this as a cognomen. The other message was in Nahuatl, the language of the Aztecs, which is still used in parts of central Mexico, including the birthplace of Emiliano Zapata. This read: "Zapata lives. Your father is here. He is not dead yet."

With that, the stream of long essays resumed, dealing with everything from the government's failure to deal with the miseries of widespread floods to a story about a Tojolabal boy who had to learn to button his shirt.

One ended on a note few would understand: "Tan, tan. A gift of memories. Today, the 8th of September, is the birthday of Deni Prieto Stock (assassinated by the government on February 14, 1974, in San Miguel Nepantla, Mexico State). We all celebrate her."

After the January 1994 uprising, the EZLN attempted to create an image of itself as a post-modern champion of "Indians" and grass roots democracy. This recollection of Nepantla was a rare admission that its FLN roots were nourished by Marxism-Leninism, the Sandinista revolution in Nicaragua and the struggle for a "dictatorship of the proletariat."

27
AUTONOMY

Briefly stated, the proposals for autonomy that were put aside by the Zedillo government called for granting new Constitutional rights to indigenous people. Each ethnic group would have an executive committee and judicial mechanisms to administer traditional "usages and customs." Furthermore, to guarantee their economic future, the autonomous units would be granted a proportional share of national, state and local revenues and the right to the revenues from natural resources within their borders. Zedillo was supported in newspaper opinion columns and in interviews with leading Mexican jurists and legislators, who argued that to legislate autonomy would be to Balkanize Mexico and deepen racial division by legalizing two classes of citizens. Ignacio Burgoa Orihuela, a judge and respected constitutional expert, said: "There is no Army of National Liberation in our country. There is only the Mexican Army. The EZLN is only a rebel group that has committed crimes since January 1, 1994. The proposed reforms are unconstitutional because they would put the indigenous people above the authority of the constitution."[1]

There were also practical objections. Since "usages and customs" are part of an oral culture, it was asked how could anyone be sure what was rightful tradition? Some pointed to Oaxaca, with more than 20 different linguistic groups, often living in the same municipality. How would such jigsaw puzzles be sorted out? Similarly, what about the Lacandon region of Chiapas, where a single community of immigrants from the Highlands might have Tzotzils, Tzeltals and Tojolabals speaking their mother tongue at home but Spanish as a lingua franca? How could each have autonomy?

The Zapatistas and their supporters brushed aside objections and went about forming their version of an autonomous indigenous society. In May 1998, a group calling itself *Centro de Investigaciónes Ecónomicas y Políticas de Acción Comunitaria*, (CIEPA, Center for the Economic and Political Investigation of Communitarian Action), published a paper titled "The Future of Profound Mexico (Reflections on Autonomy)," describing this new way of doing politics. It said the EZLN had established some 30 municipalities, all of which declared themselves in rebellion and that ...

> This meant a new way of living and of relating to the different indigenous communities. . . In other words, community autonomy has begun to be exercised along with a refusal to receive governmental help while peace, justice and dignity do not exist . . . Property taxes will not be paid, electrical energy fees will not be paid (in those few places where this service exists), official institutions will not be permitted to enter. Everything will be done to resist all that can divide, coopt, corrupt, etc. The indigenous people also have named their own authorities and commissions: Education, Health, Honor and Justice, Human Rights, Women, Ecotourism, Language, etc., with representatives chosen from the local indigenous communities, which have worked out their own laws in their own language. It is rightly the beginning of an alternative, which, while facing a series of challenges and obstacles, has challenged the local political bosses by constructing a power base from below. Their motto is "Power is not taken. It is constructed."

Another article, written in April 1998 by a woman identified as Mariana Mora, was posted on the Internet under the title: "The EZLN and Indigenous Autonomous Municipalities." It showed the actual workings of a Zapatista autonomous community. She wrote, in part:

> In the autonomous municipality *17 de Noviembre*, located in the region of Altamirano, educational promoters from the region's 75 communities meet regularly through workshops and meetings in

1 *Cuarto Poder* San Cristobal Jan. 14, 1997.

order to create the municipality's new educational system. Those responsible for carrying out this monumental task, firmly rooted in Tzeltal history, attempt to write the municipality's own educational materials, create a bilingual teaching system, train local teachers, and eventually provide nongovernmental schools for the region's 20,000 inhabitants ... The fact that the rebel municipalities define their own educational system, along with all other social, political, and economic aspects of the indigenous autonomous regions, does not remove the state from its responsibilities. If and when the Mexican government complies with the peace accords, it would still be required to channel funds, as it is obligated to do so under the Constitution. However, the communities forming the municipalities would have the right to choose how these funds would be administered.

The reference to "75 communities" should be underlined. The Zapatista concept of autonomy is not the traditional concept of self-rule based on a single group's language and culture but rather on a politicized mixture of ethnicities. This overcomes the handicap of different linguistic groups occupying the same region and often intermarrying, but what if some objected to the books published by these new autonomous communities, perhaps on the grounds that they brainwashed students and distorted Mexican history? What would prevent "postmodern" Zapatista caciques and their World Wide Web of supporters from using the same excuses to expel them as the caciques of Chamula did in the name of preserving communal *costumbres?*

This is not a rhetorical question: it is exactly what happened in Nicolas Ruiz, a community with a population of 8,000 about 25 miles south of San Cristobal. A tightly-knit group of Zapatistas declared the town to be an autonomous municipality and then, in May 1997, evicted some 30 families, or more than 200 individuals, because "they did not respect traditions and customs." It was an updated Orwellian concept that some are more autonomous than others.

The following June, Governor Roberto Albores Guillen, declaring that the town was being held as hostage, sent in several hundred police who spread tear gas and kicked in doors to arrest about 140 of the autonomous leaders. He said: "We don't care if they're sympathizers of the Zapatista National Liberation Army or if they're Muslims. All we care about is that they respect the law."

Albores, who took office in January after the previous governor was dismissed following the Acteal massacre, said the arrested men, all identified with the PDR, did not allow others to choose their political parties, denied them religious freedom, made unilateral decisions and would not allow the government into the town to build a road and a health clinic. Hopefully, he said, "We won't have to conduct any more raids as long as these groups understand that we're in a new Chiapas."

What is Autonomy?

Is autonomy a political function or does it consist of an individual's right to choose? In this sense, indigenous evangelicals, who are a major part of the population of the Highlands and the selva, have achieved autonomy in their families, churches, communities and seminaries. They have created spiritual and social spaces where they speak their mother tongues and follow traditional communitarian patterns of social organization. In addition, with men such as Abdias Tovilla, Esdras Alonso and Domingo Lopez Angel, they have their autonomous social and human rights organizations. The fact that Abdias and Esdras are non-indigenous demonstrates that autonomy does not have to be based on genetics or linguistics.

Moreover, an evangelical group that objects to the existing leadership is free to form its own churches, an option often exercised, as demonstrated by the existence of clone churches almost side by side, differing only in their ministers and deacons. Also, if they don't like what is taught in government schools, they can form their own. However, outside their churches and community organizations, obeying the biblical injunction to give Caesar his due, indigenous evangelicals are content to follow the same laws and election results as other Mexicans.

The man most qualified to speak on the subject of indigenous identity is Jacinto Arias Perez, the Harvard-educated former Chiapas Secretary for Indigenous Affairs. His book, *El Mundo Numinoso de los Mayas* (*The Numinous World of the Mayas*), was quoted extensively in Chapter 2.

✵ ✵ ✵ ✵ ✵

Some have said that our communities are closed, that we do not except change, but that is not true. There are many indications, many currents, that clearly show we do not live in closed communities. Those who have known us for the past 40 or 50 years, especially for the past 20 years, can make comparisons showing all kinds of changes. Even a small thing. If you travel on the back roads of Chamula you can still see the thatched roofs of houses. They stand out because they are rare. Almost every house now has a tile roof. There are roads, schools, teachers, and other professionals who are fully accepted in their communities. I respect and welcome these and other changes, but, in so doing, I am not rejecting my community. I was a member of my municipal council, and, despite all the ideas and thoughts that I developed during a long career, I have not lost the respect of my people. If I return as a former member of the municipal government, I use their manners and language because my community requires it, but our respect is mutual. I am not rejected as a modern man, and, as a modern indigenous person, I do not reject them.

I know the indigenous people must change. We cannot say that the cargo system and fiestas of the saints are the only religion of indigenous peoples. This is an error of historical perception. We must review the history of the indigenous people as people shaped by historical facts—what some call the encounter of two worlds—and, from this point of view, think of their future.

There are traditionalists who defend the past. They say we are Catholics and must worship San Pedro, or San Pablo, or other saints, or the gods of the mountains or the moon. This is false. To be indigenous does not necessarily mean that someone must think only in a certain way. What is happening now is a search for a new identity. The indigenous man or woman does not know exactly what the future will bring, because they are beset by many confusing forces. Mexico has many political currents. One of them is *Indigenismo*—that is, the integration of indigenous people. Many indigenous people are against this. They say, "We have to defend ourselves. If we integrate we will become Mestizos." However, they also say, "We need sufficient resources to develop and grow. If we are to have an historic future, we must also have a positive attitude toward the future. We have to conserve what we have not just by ourselves but within the structure and laws of the Mexican national state. We cannot withdraw within our shells, only defending ourselves against attacks. We must be more open. We must surely learn from history."

Indigenous people assimilated the Catholic religion so that it became part of their identity, while they retained their indigenous consciousness. In the same way, the evangelical religions can be assimilated and become part of their identity without losing their indigenous consciousness. They can assimilate new forms of modern Catholicism or Protestant evangelicalism and create a new indigenous identity. I think that is the point where we now are.

There were expulsions and everyone was talking about Article 24 of the Constitution and the freedom of religion. There are some who believe traditions must be maintained and others who say many of these traditions cannot be sustained. There is a new generation speaking Spanish and dressing differently. So we have people who want to maintain our customs but at the same time people who want to adopt new forms of living. Friction is part of the process of modernity. There is friction not only between Catholics and Protestants but also among evangelicals.

We have indigenous people who have been converted. They have been changed. They say, "I have left one kind of way for another. What I was, I no longer want to be because it was of no use to me. I want to embrace a new life, a new road." This is normal. To reject the past is to arrive at the future. However, the indigenous people also say that many things in our lives have value and that it is not necessary to reject or destroy everything. We can embrace new ways and form new indigenous cultures. We can integrate the evangelical religion in the same way we integrated with the Catholic religion.

Most of the expulsions have taken place among the Chamulans. We must remember that the Chamulans are the most compact community. They have a special historical position. Of all the people of Chiapas, it was the Chamulans who put up the greatest resistance to the Spanish conquest. Among other peoples there was almost no resistance. Thus, according to their history, there is strong resistance to change. Even the expelled Chamulans continue to speak their own language. They want to return to their own communities.

Here we see another change. What was once seen as a religious problem has been transformed into a problem of land and of politics. To my way of thinking, this is positive. People no longer want to fight about religion. If you can no longer attack someone as a religious insurgent you can attack him as a political dissident, so the struggle is seen as a contest between the PRI and the PRD.

Domingo Angel Lopez is a good example. He has been elected to the state legislature, so that when he revisits Chamula it will not be as an evangelical but as a member of a party in opposition. He has been rejected and has suffered in his own body, but he does not want his people to keep living with those prejudices. He wants to change them. He wants to do this through politics. I think that is very positive.

Many things are changing. In the indigenous municipalities we are seeing lawyers, engineers, economists and sociologists as community presidents or members of community councils. One reason why there have been so many evangelical conversions is the uneasiness of young people. There is great dynamism among them. They have gone to school. They have courage, spirit, and brazenness. Now a new religion comes that offers something to them. There are also changing political organizations. Both offer messages that touch their lives.

We recognize that Mexico is a multi-cultural society. We say indigenous people have to read and write in their own languages but Spanish as well. We must welcome all cultures, all the contributions of humanity. The values of the world will be part of our culture. We have to assimilate everything. The evangelical religions, as well as Catholicism, are part of our cultures.

There is also a struggle for autonomy, but we don't know exactly what that means. There are many bad interpretations of autonomy. Does it mean that each community rules itself, so someone can say: "I am going to establish a law and whoever does not obey it will go the jail?" I am against this, but we can still have a form of autonomy that allows different discourses. As Secretary for Indigenous Affairs in Chiapas, I defended the diversity of ideas and the diversity of religions.

When I was young, I attended a theological school and studied to be a priest. I know what religion is. I have read comparative religion. I respect all religions. Equally, as a former member of government, I am of the PRI, but I also say I am not a militant or a proselyte. It is the same with religion. I am not a militant. I can understand an evangelical religion and an evangelical church. I occasionally go to the Catholic church. I believe I must more or less go that way, but I have always rejected religion where it exhibits fanaticism.

We can hope that rationality and intelligence will create unity among indigenous peoples. We can be sure that, in 20 or 30 years, we will see different forms of indigenous beliefs. Indigenous people are going to school. The government of Chiapas is developing a system of scholarships for indigenous peoples so they can study whatever and wherever they want. We do not have an indigenous university nor do we have the resources to create one, but we have the human resources. We now have a State center for indigenous languages, arts, and literature. The Tzotzils, Tzeltals, and others have their own writers, poets, and artists. We are rediscovering and developing ourselves anew.

An evangelical rally, 1986

Appendix I

This table of expulsions from Chamula appeared in a 1995 report of the Mexican National Commission on Human Rights. Less extensive expulsions from other municipalities are omitted. Chamula is divided into communities (*parajes*) based mainly extended kin ties. The fact that conversions follow kin lines, explains why there are repeated expulsions from a single community. The numbers listed here are far below the estimate accepted by the Human Rights Commission of about 15,000 expelled because this list is mainly compiled from newspaper reports and statements of individuals to evangelical organizations, not taking into account those who might be called self-expelled. As noted in Chapter 9, there are houses in Nueva Esperanza occupied by from five to ten families. Arable land is in short supply in Chamula. If a branch of an extended family had a base in a refugee colony in San Cristobal or elsewhere, and if the family wished to become evangelical, it would be logical to leave Chamula voluntarily and let relatives take over their property rather than allowing it to be confiscated by others.

Jan. 21, 1966 . . . . . . Two evangelicals are shot in Yaavalcash.
Mar. 5, 1966 . . . . Two cousins are jailed in Chamula.
Feb. 8, 1967 . . . . Three children killed and a house in burned in Zactz.
Jan. 4, 1968 . . . . Three evangelicals shot and wounded.
Nov. 1 1974 . . . . Catholics and evangelicals expelled from 26 communities.
Oct. 20, 1974 . . . . . . Twenty-nine Seventh-Day Adventists expelled.
Jan. 20, 1975 . . . . . . House of evangelical burned.
Aug. 15, 1976 . . . . . . Six hundred evangelicals expelled from Chamula.
Aug. 22, 1976 . . . . . . Twenty-six beaten and expelled from Joltzemen.
Aug. 23, 1976 . . . . . . Evangelicals jailed and expelled from Zactz.
Sept. 12, 1976 . . . . . A house burned and evangelicals expelled.
Nov. 18, 1976 . . . . . . Eighteen persons beaten and expelled.
Nov. 30, 1976 . . . . . . Evangelical killed in Chiotic.
Nov. 9, 1977 . . . . Twenty-nine families expelled from Nichén and Milpoleta.
Oct. 25, 1978 . . . . . . Eighty evangelicals expelled from different communities.
Feb. 16, 1978 . . . . . . Seventy-five evangelicals expelled from different communities.
March 4, 1980 . . . . . Thirty-four families beaten and expelled from Muquem.
July 14, 1981 . . . . . . Miguel Gomez Kashlan killed.
Sept. 9, 1982 . . . . . . Thirteen families expelled from Chlimjoveltic and El Romerillo.
Sept. 23, 1982 . . . . . Various families expelled from seven communities.
May 26, 1983 . . . . . . Three families expelled form El Romerillo.
Sept. ?, 1983 . . . . . . Eleven expelled from Cocolté.
Feb. 16, 1984 . . . . . . Twenty-five expelled from Chicuntaltic.
Oct. 24, 1984 . . . . . . Thirty persons expelled from various communities.
Nov. ? 1984. . . . . Twenty-three expelled from Botamesté.
Nov. 4, 1985 . . . . Five jailed and expelled from Cruxtón.
Dec. 11, 1986 . . . . . . Four families expelled from Zeteltón.
Jan. ? 1987. . . . . One family expelled from Yolbacox.
Aug. ? 1987 . . . . Six families expelled from Nichén Majomut.
April 7, 1988 . . . . . . Four families expelled from El Pinar and Yaalboc.
April 14, 1988 . . . . . Eight families from three communities jailed and expelled.
April 19, 1988 . . . . . A family beaten and expelled from Tentic.

April 21, 1988 . . . . . One man beaten and expelled from Tentic.
May 8, 1988 . . . . Seventy persons expelled from Yalhichin.
May 10, 1988 . . . . . . Four families expelled from Majomut.
Aug. 15, 1988 . . . . . . One family expelled from Bapot.
Sept. 21, 1988 . . . . . Forty-eight families expelled from El Romerillo.
Oct. ? 1988 . . . . Sixty-eight persons expelled from EL Romerillo.
Mar. 15, 1989 . . . . . . Three families expelled from La Ollas.
Mar. 15, 1989 . . . . . . Two families expelled from Bachen and Bautista Chico.
April 10, 1989 . . . . . Four families expelled from Chilimjovelti.
April 26, 1989 . . . . . Five families expelled from Bachen.
April 18, 1989 . . . . . One family expelled form Chilhó.
April ? 1989 . . . . One family expelled from Pachil.
May ? 1989 . . . . Ten families expelled from Chamula ceremonial center.
June ? 1989 . . . . Three families expelled from Icalumtic.
Aug. 16, 1989 . . . . . . Four families expelled from Bautista Grande.
Aug. 16, 1989 . . . . . . Three families expelled from Custán.
Aug. 17, 1898 . . . . . . Four families expelled from Rancho Narváez and Santa Ana.
Nov. 8, 1989 . . . . Two families expelled from Zeteltón.
Dec. 22, 1989 . . . . . . Two families expelled from Maojomut.
Aug. 26 1990 . . . . . . Twenty-three families (50 persons) expelled from Yaalchin.
Oct. 23, 1990 . . . . . . Fifty persons expelled from Yaalchin, three women raped.
Nov. 16, 1990 . . . . . . Eleven families expelled from Callejón.
Jan. 24, 1991 . . . . . . Five persons jailed and expelled from Chilinjoveltic.
Mar. 31, 1992 . . . . . . Sixty-two evangelicals jailed in Chamula community center.
Jan. 9, 1993 . . . . Expel two families (17 persons) from Icalumtic.
Feb. 9, 1993 . . . . A man in Yolonjonchuntic given four days to leave or "we will burn
your house and kill you."
April 9, 1993 . . . . . . One family (eight persons) expelled from Joltzemen.
June 6, 1993 . . . . . . One hundred and one persons expelled from Cuchulumntic.
Sept. 5, 1993 . . . . . . House of a family in Cuchulumntic burned after family ordered to
leave on threat of death.
Sept. 5, 1993 . . . . . . Two hundred and ten persons begin leaving Yaltén after warning to
evacuate by October 10 or they would be killed.
Sept. 6, 1993 . . . . . . Jail and expel two families (11 persons) from Arvenza I.
Sept. 7, 1993 . . . . . . Two persons beaten, jailed and told to leave Cuchilumntic.
Sept. 8, 1993 . . . . . . Twenty-nine families (150–200 persons) expelled from El Pozo.
Sept. 10, 1993 . . . . . Three families (seven persons) expelled from Yabante.
Sept. 19, 1993 . . . . . Expel one family (17 persons) from Bapot.
Sept. 19, 1993 . . . . . Jail and expel one family (four persons) from Arvenza II.
Sept. 23, 1993 . . . . . Expel three families (17 persons) from Bapot.
Sept. ? 1993 . . . . Expel two families (eight persons) from Milpoleta.
Sept. 26, 1993 . . . . . Two persons expelled from Hucuntic.
Oct. 7, 1993 . . . . Four families (24 persons) expelled from Tzontehuitz.
Oct. 13, 1993 . . . . . . One family (four persons) expelled from Yaaltzunin.
Oct. 15, 1993 . . . . . . Ten families (50 persons) expelled from Yaltén.
Oct. 17, 1993 . . . . . . Two families (four persons) expelled from Tentic.
Oct. 17, 1993 . . . . . . Eighteen families (83 persons) expelled from Botamesté.
Oct. 19, 1993 . . . . . . About fifty persons expelled from Yaltén.
Oct. 22, 1993 . . . . . . Two families (nine persons) expelled from Pilalchén.
Oct. 26, 1993 . . . . . . Four families (15 persons) expelled from El Pozo.

Jan. 30, 1994.. . . . . . Beat, jail and expel man who returned to Chumulmuntic several months after being expelled.

Mar. 29, 1994. . . . . . Expel 228 Jehovah's Witnesses from Pugchen Mumuntic.

Aug. 6, 1995. . . . . . . Eleven men and women expelled from Arvenza I.

Aug. 9, 1995. . . . . . . Four men expelled from Arvenza II.

APPENDIX II

Zapatismo came at the nadir of hopes for world revolution. The fall of the Berlin Wall appeared to be the final defeat of Marxism while the Sandinista disgrace in Nicaragua seemed to signal victory for American-led neoliberalism. Che Guevara was nothing more than a picture on a dorm wall. Then the masked, pipe-smoking *Subcomandante* Marcos emerged from the jungle: articulate, joking and leading a tattered band of the romanticized Mayan living fossils. Aging veterans of demonstrations and picket lines and college students still searching for something to shout and march for were overjoyed.

The students had something no earlier would-be revolutionaries possessed, the World Wide Web. With the click of a mouse, Marcos' communiques and other writings, as well as the comments and articles that appeared in magazine or newspapers anywhere in the world, could be sent from site to site, bypassing the traditional media that is invariably considered a tool of repression and capitalism. The first Web site appeared in March 1994, a bit more than two months after the incursion into San Cristobal. It was established by Justin Paulson, a recent graduate in English from the University of Pennsylvania, who said he got his information from newspapers and magazines, including German, Italian and Portuguese publications translated and passed on by members of voluntary organizations. As others became involved, their computer and artistic skills led to an explosion of Web sites and elaborate discussion lists and conferences. In the summer of 1996, these "cyberspacial" circuits made it possible to organize the Chiapas International Encounter. (Paulson showed up for this meeting and requested an interview with Marcos. It was refused.)

A Second Intercontinental Encounter to combat, as its sponsors proclaimed, international capitalism disguised as neoliberalism was held in Spain in late July 1997. Web sites were organized in Spain and other countries to exchange dozens of papers, not only for the loosely estimated 3,000 who showed up but for the thousands who could not attend. During the Encounter, distant participants were briefed on the daily discussions; however, they missed the fun, games and singing *A Las Barricadas*, the song of the July 1936 Barcelona anarchists.

Harry Cleaver, an associate professor in the Department of Economics of the University of Texas at Austin, writes:

> In the last few years, concern with the ability of such non-governmental networks to undercut national governments and international agreements has grown. This concern has arisen, in part, from the growing strength such networks have derived from the use of international computer communications ... Surprisingly, no catalyst of that

growth has been more important than the indigenous Zapatista rebellion in the southern Mexican state of Chiapas and the widespread political mobilization to which it has contributed. The computer networks supporting the rebellion have evolved from providing vehicles for the familiar, traditional work of solidarity (e.g., material aid and the defense of human rights against the policies of the Salinas and Zedillo administrations) into a kind of electronic fabric of opposition to much wider policies. Today those networks are providing the nerve system of increasingly global challenges to the dominant economic policies of this period and, in the process, are undermining the distinction between domestic and foreign policy and even the present constitution of the nation-state.[1]

Clever created and maintains the Chiapas 95 Internet lists and web pages. The sites listed below are from his "Zapatistas in Cyberspace, A Guide to Analysis and Resources" (http://www.eco.untex.Edu/faculty/Cleaver/zapincyber.html).

What has yet to be proved is the critical and intellectual worth of the information transmitted via the World Wide Web. However, the Internet is not solely to be blamed, since this shortcoming applies as well to the printed page.

Barry Carr,[2] in a review of 20 of what he describes as the "avalanche" of Zapatista-related books, concludes by quoting Yvon Le Bot's introduction to his *Subcomandante Marcos, El sueño zapatista* (The Zapatista Dream).[3] Le Bot claims the Zapatistas represent "one of the most significant and powerful attempts to combine identity," modernity and democracy in a world where struggles against globalization and neoliberalism have often taken authoritarian paths predicated on a narrow, exclusionary vision of identity.

Still, Carr writes, "the books reviewed here tell us pitifully little about the political, cultural or social processes engaged in by neozapatista communities. There is much assertion about the communitarian, horizontal and democratic character of decisionmaking, about break throughs in gender relations, etc., but they are mostly assertions based on an uncritical reading of the prescriptive content of Zapatista declarations and on the aspirations of EZLN cadres revealed in interviews with sympathetic outsiders."

World Wide Web Sites

Acción Zapatista (USA)
Against Neoliberalism & For Humanity (Australia)
Chiapas95 (USA)
Chiapas Menu (USA)
Chiapas Para el Mundo (USA)
Clandestine Home Page (USA)
Comitato Chiapas Torino (Italy)
Coordinamento Zapatista per l'Italia (Italy)
C.s.o.a. La Strada (Italy)
Ejército Zapatista de Liberación Nacional (USA)
EZLN:Tierra y Libertad (Japan)
Frente Zapatista de Liberación National (USA)

1 Cleaver (1997). 2 (1997). 3 (1995).

IAN: Initiatives Against Neoliberalism (USA)
Life Among the Maya (USA)
Mark's [Irish] Solidarity Page (Ireland)
Movimiento Civil Zapatista de Yucatan (Mexico)
Mujeres Zapatistas Zapatista Women (Mexico)
NCDM: National Commission for Democracy in Mexico (USA)
RSM: Le Reseau de solidarite avec le Mexique (Canada)
SIPAZ International Service for Peace (USA)
Softbomb (USA)
Solidaridad Directa con Chiapas (European)
Tatanka Group Homepage (Italian)
VIVA ZAPATA! (French)
Zapata Mexico Solidarity Committee of Amsterdam, Holland
Zapatista! (USA)
Zapatista Cooperatives' Homepage (Mexico)
ZAPNET: Zapatista Net of Autonomy & Liberation (USA)

Selected Bibliography

Ahlstrom, Sidney. 1972. *A Religious History of the American People.* New Haven: Yale University Press.

Alonso Gonzalez, Esdras. 1995. *San Juan Chamula: Persecución de Indigenas y Evangélicos.* Bogotá, Colombia: *Editorial Alfa y Omega.*

Arias, Jacinto. 1991. *El Mundo Numinoso de los Mayas, estrutuara y cambios contemporáneos.* Government of the State of Chiapas: *Instituto Chiapaneco de Cultura.*

Baldwin, Deborah J. 1990. *Protestants and the Mexican Revolution: Missionaries, Ministers, and Social Change. Chicago:* University of Illinois Press.

Bardacke, Frank and others. 1995. *Shadows of Tender Fury: the letters and communiqués of Subcommander Marcos and the Zapatista Army of National Liberation.* New York: Monthly Review Press.

Barreda, Andres and all. 1996. *Chiapas.* Mexico City: *Instituto de Investigaciónes Económicas.*

Bastian, Jean Pierre. 1996. *"Violencia, etnicidad y religión entre los mayas del estado de Chiapas en México." Mexican Studies/Estudios Mexicanos:* 12/2: 301–313.

Carr, Barry. 1997. "From the Mountains of the Southeast: A Review of Recent Writings on the Zapatistas of Chiapas." *Journal of Iberian and Latin American Studies* (Australia): 3:2.

Cleaver, Harry. 1997. "The Zapatista Effect: The Internet and the Rise of an Alternative Political Fabric." *Journal of International Affairs* 51/2 (Spring): 621–640

Collier, George. 1994. *Basta: Land and the Zapatista Rebellion in Chiapas.* Oakland, California: A Food First Book.

Cowan, Marion. 1962. "A Christian Movement in Mexico." *Practical Anthropology (Sept.–Oct.)*: 193–204.

de Mora, Juan Miguel. 1995. Yo Acuso: *A Los Gobiernos de Mexico y al EZLN!* Mexico City: Edamex.

Dyrness, William A. 1996. "Vernacular Theology." In, George R. Hunsberger and Craig Van Gelder. *The Church Between Gospel & Culture: The Emerging Mission in North America.* Grand Rapids, Mi: Eerdmans.

Escobar, Samuel. 1998. "A Missiological Approach to Latin American Protestantism." *International Review of Missions* 87:345: 161–73.

Esponda, Hugo. 1986. *History of the Presbyterian Church of Chiapas.* Coyoacan, D.F.: *Publicaciónes El Faro.*

Fernandez Liria, Carlos. 1992. "*Enfermedad, familia y costumbre en el Periférico de San Cristóbal de Las Casas." Instituto Chiapaneco de Cultura Anuario 1992.* Tuxtla Gutierrez: Government of the State of Chiapas: 11–57.

Floyd, Charlene. 1997. *The Government Shall Be Upon Their Shoulders: The Catholic Church and Democratization in Chiapas, Mexico.* Unpublished Ph. D. diss., City University of New York.

Gimenez, Gilberto. 1988. *Sectas religiosas en el sureste: aspectos sociográficos y estadisticos.* Mexico City: *Cuadernos de la casa chata.*

Gluckman, Max. 1965. *Politics, Law and Ritual in Tribal Society.* Oxford: Basil Blackwell.

Gossen, Gary. 1989. "Life, Death, and Apotheosis of a Chamula Protestant Leader: Biography as Social History." In, Victoria Bricker and Gary Gossen. *Ethnographic Encounters in Southern Mesoamerica: Essays in Honor of Evon Zartman Vogt, Jr.* Austin: University of Texas Press: 217–229.

Gutierrez, Gustavo. 1973. *A Theology of Liberation: History, Politics and Salvation* (Originally published 1971. Translated and edited by Sister Caridad Inda and John Eagleson). New York: Orbis Books.

Harvey, Neil. 1990. "Peasant Struggles and Corporatism in Chiapas." In, Joe Foweraker and Ann C. Craig, *Popular Movements and Political Change in Mexico.* Boulder: Lynne Rienner Publishers: 183–198.

Hefley, James and Marti. 1974. *Uncle Cam: The Story of William Cameron Townsend.* Waco, Texas: Word Books.

Hernández Castillo, Rosalva Aída 1992. *Entre la victimization y la resistencia étnica: revision critica de la bibliografia sobre Protestantism en Chiapas.* Government of the State of Chiapas: *Anuario 1992, Instituto Chiapaneco de Cultura:* 165–186.

Iribarren, Pablo.1980. *Misión Chamula: Experiencia de trabajo pastoral de los años 1966–1977 en Chamula.* (Typed manuscript, San Cristobal de las Casas, April 22, 1980).

Jeffrey, Paul. "Evangelicals and Catholics in Chiapas, Conflict and Reconciliation." *Christian Century,* Feb. 19, 1997.

Katzenberger, Elaine, ed. 1995. *First World, Ha Ha Ha: The Zapatista Challenge.* San Francisco: City Lights.

King, Linda. 1994. *Roots of Identity: Language and Literacy in Mexico.* Stanford: Stanford University Press.

Knight, Alan. 1990. "Revolution and Indigenismo: Mexico, 1910–1940." In, Richard Graham, ed. *The Idea of Race in Latin America 1870–1940.* Austin: University of Texas Press.

Le Bot, Yvon. 1995. *Subcomandante Marcos: El sueño zapatista.* Mexico City: Plaza and Janes.

Lopez Meza, Antonio. 1992. *Sistema ReligiosoPolitico y las Expulsiónes en Chamula, Chiapas, Mexico.* Master's thesis, *Universidad Autonoma de Chiapas, Escuela de Ciencias Sociales, Campus III.*

MacEoin, Gary. 1996. *The People's Church: Bishop Samuel Ruiz of Mexico and Why He Matters.* New York: Crossroads Publishing.

Marcus, Joyce and Judith Francis Zeitlin. 1994. *Caciques and their People: A volume in honor of Ronald Spores.* Ann Arbor: Museum of Anthropology, University of Michigan.

Medina Hernandez, Andres. 1991. *Tenejapa: familia y tradición en un pueblo tzeltal.* Tuxtla Gutierrez: Instituto Chiapaneco de Cultura.

Mexican National Commission of Human Rights. 1995. *El Problema de las Expulsions en los Comunidades Indigenes de Los Altos de Chiapas: Segundo Informe.* Mexico D.F.

Morales Bermudez, Jesús. 1991. *El Congreso Indígena de Chiapas: Un Testimonio.* Tuxtla Gutierrez: *Anuario 1991 Instituto Chiapaneco de Cultura.*

Morquecho Escamilla, Gaspar. 1992. *Los Indios en un proceso de organización. La organización indigena de los altos de Chiapas ORIACH.* Master's thesis, *Universidad Autónoma de Chiapas, Escuela de Ciencias Sociales, Campus III.*

Obregón R., Maria Concepción. 1997. "La rebelión zapatista en Chiapas, antecedentes, causes y desarrollo de su primara fase." *Mexican Studies/Estudios Mexicanos.* 13/1: 149–200.

Orta, Andrew. 1995. "From Theologies of Liberation to Theologies of Inculturation: Aymara Catechists and the Second Evangelization in Highlands Bolivia." In, Satya R. Pattnayak, ed. *Organized Religion in the Political Transformation of Latin America.* New York: University Press of America.

Pazos, Luis. 1994. *Porque Chapas?* Mexico City: *Editorial Diana.*

Rasgado Cruz, Abel and Orlando Diaz Solis. 1992. *Formas de Expansión y Penetración de las Religiosas No Catolicas en Los Altos de Chiapas.* Master's thesis, *Universidad Autonoma de Chiapas, Escuela de Ciencias Sociales, Campus III.*

Reyes F., Arturo and Miguel Angel Zebadua Carboney. 1995. Samuel Ruiz: *Su lucha por la Paz en Chiapas.* Mexico City: *Ediciónes del Milenio.*

Rojas, Rosa. 1995. *Chiapas, La Paz Violenta.* Mexico City: *La Jornada.*

Romero Jacobo, Cesar. 1994. *Marcos: Un professional de la esperanza?* Mexico City: *Grupo Editorial Planeta.*

Rus, Jan. 1994. "The Subversion of Native Government in Highland Chiapas 1936–1968." In, Joseph Gilbert and Daniel Nugent, eds. *Everyday Forms of State Formation: Revolution and Negotiation of Rule in Modern Mexico.* Durham: Duke University Press.

Sanchez Franco, Irene. 1995. *"Los Presbiterianos Tzeltales de Yajalon, Chiapas."* Master's thesis, *Universidad Autonoma de Chiapas, Escuela de Ciencias Sociales, Campus III.*

Santiago Garcia, Rosana. 1993. *"El analfabetismo en la colonia Nueva Esperanza."* Master's thesis, *Universidad Autonoma de Chiapas, Escuela de Ciencias Sociales, Campus III.*

Slocum, Marianna C. 1956. *"Cultural Changes Among the Oxchuc Tzeltals." In, Estudios Antropológicos publicados en homenaje al Doctor Manuel Gamio. Mexico, D.F.: Direción General de Publicaciónes:* 491–495.

Slocum, Marianna with Grace Watkins. 1988. *The Good Seed.* Orange, CA: Promise Publishing Co.

Stephen, Lynn. 1997. "ProZapatista and ProPRI: Resolving the Contradiction of Zapatismo in Rural Oaxaca." Latin American Research Review 32/2.

Sterk, Vernon Jay. 1992. *The Dynamics of Persecution.* Unpublished Ph. D. diss., Fuller Theological Seminary.

Tello Diaz, Carlos. 1995. *La rebelión de las Cañadas.* Mexico City: *Cal y Arena.*

Thompson, Phyllis. 1978. *Count It All Joy!* Los Angeles: Gospel Recordings.

Vogt, Evon Z. 1969. *Zinacantan, a Maya Community in the Highlands of Chiapas.* Cambridge: Harvard University Press.

Wallis, Ethel Emily and Mary Angela Bennett. 1959. *Two Thousand Tongues to Go: The Story of the Wycliffe Bible Translators. New York:* Harper and Brothers.

Wasserstrom, Robert. 1983. *Class and Society in Central Chiapas.* Berkeley: University of California Press.

INDEX-NAMES

Aguilar Ochoa, Daniel, IV, 30, 41
Aguirre Franco, Bishop Felipe 55, 152
Ahlstrom, Sidney, 74, 103-104
Albores Guillen, Governor Roberto, 163
Albright, Secretary of State Madeleine, 159
Aleman, President Miguel 140
Alonso Gonzalez, Esdras, 88-91, 114, 157, 164
Amos, Deborah, 156
Arias, Jacinto:
    Indigenous autonomy, 164-166;
    Indigenous beliefs, 14-15
Arizmendi, Bishop Felipe 152
Aubrey, Andre, 1-2
Aulie, Wilbur and Evelyn (Woodward), 21-22

Baldwin, Deborah J., 19
Bastian, Jean-Pierre, 2
Batarse, Rev Jose, 141
Beekman, John and Elaine, 21
Benavides, Gloria, "Elisa," 144, 149
Bentley, William, 22, 35
Burgoa Orihuela, Justice Ignacio, 162

Camacho Solis, Manuel, 114
Cardenas, President Lazaro, 19, 47
Carr, Barry, 170
Caso, Alfonso, 47
Castelazo Sanchez, Jesus, 129-132
Castellanos, Governor Absalon, 111
Castellanos Cancino, Manuel, 24, 31, 41-42, 101
Cleaver, Harry, 169-70
Cho, Paul Yonggi, 91
Cowan, Marion, 42-71
Cruz, Rev Heriberto, 149
Cruz Patishtan, Ciriolo, 118-119

de Jesus Toussaint, Rev Felipe, 149
de la Madrid, President Miguel, 111
de la Vega, Lolita, 160

de Mora, Juan Miguel, 153, 161
Dryness, William, 135

Elorriaga, Javier, "Vincente," 147-48, 151-52
Escobar, Samuel, 25
Esponda, Hugo, 39

Fabregas Puig, Dr Andres, 6-7, 113
Fernandez, Elmer, 125
Fernandez Liria, Carlos, 17-18
Fernandez, Silvia, "Gabriela," 143-44, 146, 149

Gerdel, Florence, 26-36
Gimenez, Gilberto, 3
Gomez Bautisa, Santos, 102-103
Gomez Hernandez, Miguel "Kashlan," 8, 56-60, 70
Gomez Sanchez, Francisco, 29-30, 39
Gomez Santis, Roberto and Micael, 101-102
Gonzalez Garrido, Governor Patrocinio, 85, 101-102, 112, 148
Gonzalez, Lazaro, 157
Gossen, Gary, 56-57
Grajales, Governor Victorico, 48
Gramsci, Antonio, 49
Guevara, Che, 144
Gutierrez, Gustavo, 48
Guzman, Victor, 146

Hansen, Tom, 160
Heneveld, Tim and Sharon, 36
Hernandez Castillo, Rosalva Aida, 1, 3
Hernandez, Rev Jeronimo, 146
Hernandez, Rev Leopoldo, "Padre Polo," 50-53
Hernandez Lopez, Pastor Gaspar, 92-94
Hernandez Perez, Pastor Pedro, 38-39
Hofman, Samuel and Helen, 36

Iribarren, Rev Pablo: Links with EZLN, 147; *Misión* Chamula, 50, 54; On "purifying" society, 147

Jacobs, Kenneth, 57-58
Jarvis, David, 31
Jimenez Guzman, Pastor Rene, 133-135
John Paul II, Pope 18-19, 151
Juarez, President Benito, 19

Katzenberger, Elaine, 92
King, Linda, 12
Knight, Alan, 13
Komer, Richard, 123

Le Bot, Yvon, 170
Lopez Angel, Domingo, 84-88, 113-114, 164
Lopez Gomez, Pastor Juan, 104-106, 110-11
Lopez Hernandez, Pascuala, 60-65
Lopez Lopez, Salvador, 68-72
Lopez Moreno, Governor Javier, 116
Lopez Mucha, Juan and Domingo, 26-29
Lopez Vasquez, Felipe, 99-101

Marcos, Subcomandante:
Communiques, 142, 161; Curriculum vitae as Rafael Sebastian Guillen, 142; "Megalomania" and "Messianic," 153, 161; Reclusive, 154; Recruitment into FLN, 142-153; Regis Debray interview, 154-155; Training in Nicaragua, 143; Vote to begin uprising, 149-151. *Also see* EZLN
Medina Hernandez, Andres 15-17
Mendez Juarez, Juan, 108-109
Meyerink, Paul and Dorothy, 36
Mora, Mariana, 162-63
Morales Lizalde, Rev Mardonio, 141
Morales, Salvador, "Daniel," 149, 151
Morquecho Escamilla, Gaspar, 54-55

Ochoa, Hector, "Pedro," 149, 151
Orive Berlinguer, Adolfo, 140-42

Padron, Rev Joel, 148, 152

Pasciencia clan, 39-42
Patishtan Diaz, Pastor Salvador, 65-67
Perez Hernandez, Pastor Mario, 120-21
Perez Perez, Cusberto, 123-25
Paulson, Justin, 169
Preston, Julia, 160

Ramirez, Javier, "Rodrigo," 143-44, 149
Ridderhoff, Joy, 7, 25
Riebe, Rev Loren, 152-53
Rios Montt, Gen Efraim, 145
Robinson, UN Human Rights Commissioner, Mary, 159
Romero Jacobo, Cesar, 150, 153, 161
Rossi, Cardinal Angelo, 52
Ruiz Garcia, Bishop Samuel:
Brought before inquest commission, 152; Criticized as "Red Bishop," 148, 152; Diocesan Plan of 1986, 146; Distances from EZLN, 148; Early History 8, 48; Goals, 10; Invitation to "Northerners," 141; Links with EZLN uprising, 11, 146; Named peace mediator, 151; Option for the poor, 49; Presents petition to Pope John Paul II, 151; Promotes autochthonous church 135-36; Resigns as mediator, 161; Rumored removal as Bishop, 151; Withdrawal from Chamula, 55
Ruiz Jimenez, Pastor Rafael, 76-78
Rus, Jan, 47, 49

Sabines, Governor Juan, 54, 111
Saenz, Moises, 19, 47
Salinas de Gortari, President Carlos, 68, 92, 113
San Juan, Manuel, 119-20
Sanchez Franco, Irene, 37-38
Sanchez Rodriguez, Pastor Luis, 95-96
Sanchez Sanchez, Samuel, 158
Santiago, Jorge, "Jacobo," 144, 148
Sherwood, Ann, 25
Slocum, Mariana, 22-26
Sozaya, Guillermo, 29
Stephen, Lynn, 92-93

Sterk, Vernon Jay, 121-22
Stoll, David, 20-21
Suarez Rivera, Archbishop Adolfo, 152
Suenens, Cardinal Leo Jozef, 135-36

Tello Diaz, Carlos, 143-151
Toussaint Loera, Msgr Felipe, 136-39, 157
Testa, Aaron, 104, 110
Tovilla Jaime, Abdias, 78-81, 88, 90-91, 105, 118, 120, 157-59, 164
Townsend, William Cameron, 19, 22, 47
Trujillo Velasco, Juan, 21
Tsima, Martin Gomez, 24-27

Valente, Flaviano Amatulli, 19
Vargas, Javier, 145-46
Vasquez Alegria, Villaney, 127-29
Vazquez Mendez, Jesus, 106-108
Vera Cortez, Teodoro, 125-27
Vera Lopez, Bishop Raul, 153-54
Villa Rojas, Alonso, 22-23
Vogt, Evon Z., 13
Von Bronkhorst, Steve and Susan, 101-102

Wasserstrom, Robert, 13
Walker, Rev Lucius, 159-60
Wallis, Ethel, 22-23
Weathers, Kenneth, 39, 41-42
Wray, Stefan, 159
Woodward, Evelyn, 22

Yanez Munoz, Fernando, "German," 143-44, 146, 149, 151

Zedillo, President Ernesto, 155, 159-161

INDEX-SUBJECTS

Acteal massacre, 158-59
American Bible Society, 31
Arvenza I and II, 117-121
Autonomy, autonomous:
    As "post-modern" cacicazgo, 163;
    Indigenous limiting factors, 162;
    Negotiations, 155, 160-64; Within
    evangelical society, 1-2, 122; Zapa-
    tista autonomous communities,
    158-64
Aymaras, 135

Baptist Biblical Institute, Monterrey, 126
Baptist Churches, 4, 125-127
Baptist Peace Fellowship of North
    America (BPFNA), 157
Bible Translations:
    Chol versions, 21; Volumes pub-
    lished, 31, 36-37; Tzeltal versions,
    36, 94; Tzotzil versions, 42, 45-46
Brothers of the Divine Shepherd, 48, 52, 54

Caciques, cacicazgo, 3, 6, 16-17
Catechists:
    as modernizing process, 2;
    Recruitment and training, 50-53,
    135-139
Catholic Church:
    Competition with evangelicals, 17;
    Creating autochthonous church, 2;
    Handicaps to growth, 4-5; Mexican
    Episcopal Conference (CEM), 19;
    Medellin Conference (CELEM II),
    49; Neglect of parishioners leaving
    field for conversion, 17; Our Lady of
    Guadalupe seen as idol, 5; Priests
    expelled, 152-53, 159; Repression
    during Mexican revolution, 48;
    Vatican II, 48-49. *Also see* Bishop
    Ruiz; Theology of Liberation;
    Catechists

Catholic Charities (Relief Services), 52, 144
Center for Anthropological Investigation of the Southeast (CIESAS), 3
Center for Indigenous Rights, 156
Chiapas:
Evangelical growth, 3; Population, health, literacy, 12
Chols:
Bible translations, 21; Separate presbytery, 21, 36

Christian Solidarity International, 105

Coordinating Agency of Non-Governmental Organizations for Peace (CONPAZ), 156
Council of Indigenous Campesino Evangelical Churches (CICEM), 157

Democratic Revolutionary Party (PDR), 1, 157
Dominican Order, 48, 52, 54, 140, 146

Ecumenical peace meetings, 157
Evangelical (s):
Accepting "God's will," 19-20; Analogies with Methodists, Baptists, Puritans and African-Americans, 68, 74, 103-104; Bible warnings and promises, 6; Churches and communities as sharing social spaces, 5, 18; Conversion seen as anti-shaman movement, 13; Curing, 17-18, 74, 76, 121, 131-32, Emphasis on family life, 8, 124-25, 134-35; Emphasis on salvation, 75; Error of functionalist reasons for growth, 1, 124; Farmer-preachers, 103-04; Growth, 3-4, 33-35, 120, 133-34; Inculcating autonomy and modernity 2, 7, 95, 164-66; Injunctions against idol worship, 5-6, 25, 39-41; Internal democracy, 71-72; Internal discipline, 31-33; "Made in USA," 19; Mexican government support, 19; as multicultural-impetus, 7; Prayer and fasting, 61, 70, 89, 121, 123, 132-33; Proselytizing through families, 46-48; Reliving Christian history, 5-6; Role of evangelical churches in preserving ethnicity, 2, 37-38, 130; Schools, 72, 124; Seeding new churches, 70, 93-94, 124, 128, 130-31; Seen as sects, 2, 18-19, 90; Selection of elders, deacons and pastors, 5, 70-71, 93-94, 134; Similarities with traditional practices, 2, 5; Views on EZLN ideology, 91, 94, 96, 128-29
Evangelical Seminaries, 66, 80, 94
Expulsions (see Persecution)
EZLN formation and revolt:
Aid from diocese, 144-47; as appeal to national conscience, 92; Cadres school, 147; Internal debate on start of uprising, 149, 151; First International Encounter, 153-54; Leaders arrested, 151; Leadership, 143-144; Metamorphosis from ANCIEZ, 148-49; Nepantla killing of FLN cadres, 143, 161; Occupation of San Cristobal and other cities, 92, 113, 142, 151, 169; Opposition to NAFTA, 92; Origin within National Liberation Force (FLN), 143; Peace negotiations, 113-14; Plan for revolutionary foco, 144; as "Revolt of the Indians," 78, 113, 158; Second International Encounter, 169; Small size of assault forces, 151; Web site support groups, 169-71; "Zapatista chic," 156. *Also see* Marcos

Flannelgraph, 24, fn 8
Foreign observers: 156, 159-60
Friar Bartolome Human Rights Center, 156

Global Exchange, 156
Gospel Recordings, 25, 42
Helping Hands, 105

Indigenous Congress, 139-40
Indigenous society:
Beliefs, 14-18, 100; Cargos, 2, 5, 9,
13; Curanderos, "witch doctors," 2,
13-14; Disappearing, 12; Faulty education, 99; Languages and subdi-
alects, 2, 38, 96; Traditional
concepts and practices, 13-18; Use
of alcohol, "posh," "chicha," 15-16,
90, 100
Institutional Revolutionary Party
(PRI), 2, 47
Inter-American Indian Institute, 20
International Peace Service (SIPAZ), 156
Internet (cyberspace):
Call for international anti-Mexican
protests, 159; Early publicity for
EZLN, 169; Zapatista Web Sites,
169-70; Zedillo denounces, 160-61

Jehovah's Witnesses, 114
Jesuits, 48, 139, 141-42, 46, 159

Ladino churches, 21-22, 37
Ladinos, 11, 16-17, 48

Maoist, Maoism, 141, 143
Marists:
Seminary, 50; Links with EZLN, 146;
Indigenous Congress, 140
Marxist, Marxism-Leninism, 22, 41, 91,
151-52
Mayas as academic "Living fossils," 13
Ministerial Alliance of the Highlands
of Chiapas, 90
Mennonite Central Committee, 157
Mexican National Commission of
Human Rights, 6, 78
Mexican Episcopal Conference (CEM),
19
Mexico [pro-Zapatista] Solidarity
Network, 156

Misión Chamula, 50-52
Mission Aviation Fellowship, 41, 45

National Action Party (PAN), 52-53
National Liberation Force (FLN), see
EZLN,
North American Free Trade Association
(NAFTA), 92
Nazarene(s), 89, 133-35

Open Doors–Human Rights NGO, 2, 8,
82, 105
Orthodox Church of San Pascualito,
55, 112
Oxfam, 52, 144

Pastors for Peace (IFCO), 81, 156,
159-60
Paramilitary groups, 156-58
Pentecostal(s):
Churches, 67-78, 89; Disciplined
and ascetic, 73-74; Percentage of
evangelical population, 73;
Resemblance to Separate Baptists,
Puritans, Quakers, 74-75
Persecution:
Appeals for justice unanswered, 54-
55, 68, 83-85, 111; Amatenango, 102-
103; Aquacatenango, 104-111;
Estimated expelled, 6; Finding
employment for expelled, 69, 84-87;
Government punishment for perse-
cution, 101-103, 105-111; Is it reli-
gious? 6; Linked with politics, 86;
Mitontic, 10, 96-101; Sit-in at
Bureau of Indigenous Affairs, 83,
112-117; Reciprocal kidnapings and
fatal encounters, 85-86, 88, 115-16,
119-20; Reconciliation and end of
persecution, 102, 116, 120-21;
Refugee colonies, 4, 6, 65, 67-68, 72,
81, 85, 124; Returned refugees
attacked, 83
Presbyterian (s):
Canadian Presbyterian aid, 61;
Churches, 4-5, 14, 21-22, 30, 37, 40-

41, 57, 68, 73, 79, 93-95, 99-100, 102;
Division of Chiapas churches into
three parts, 36; Early history in
Chiapas, 21, 123; Mexican church
separate from Presbyterian Church
of USA, 21; Theological Seminary
(Coyacan), 19
Popular Politics, (Pepes), 140-41
Protestants:
Early missionaries, 19; Term not
used, 20. *Also see* Evangelicals

Reformed Church of America, 22, 36,
101, 122
Regional Council of Indigenous
Peoples of Highland of Chiapas
(CRIACH), 83, 87-88, 115
Regional Organization of Indian
Peoples of Highlands of Chiapas
(ORIACH), 83-84

San Juan Chamula:
Cacique links with PRI, 8, 47, 50,
90, 112, 153; Cacique use of UN and
government supplies, 53-54, 82;
Catholics replaced by Orthodox
church, 55; Defense of traditions, 7,
47-49, 51; Instances of expulsions,
167-169; *Misión* Chamula, 50-53
Separatists (Puritan, Baptist), 68, 71
Seventh-Day Adventists, 54, 85-86,
127-29
State Committee for Evangelical
Defense in Chiapas (CEDECH),
79-83, 158
Summer Institute of Linguistics:
Diocesan program against, 146;
History, 16-17, 19, 39, 48, 135, 146;
INI protection for early translators,
24, 31, 41-42, 102, 147; Polemics, 22-
21. *Also see* Marianna Slocum,
Marion Cowan

Theology of Liberation, 48-49, 75, 157
Tlatelolco Massacre, 140
Tzeltal Church, 22-37. *Also see*

Marianna Slocum
Tzeltal Cultural Center, Buenos Aires
Ranch, 36-37, 37 fn 11, 102
Tzotzil Church, 38-47. *Also see* Marion
Cowan

Victrolas, "Talking Boxes," 25-27, 29,
43, 136

War of Low Intensity 155-56
Women (role of), 122-23
Wycliffe Bible Translators
(see Summer Institute of
Linguistics)

ABOUT THE AUTHOR

I came to realize the power of the Bible to transform lives when I researched a book about Jerry McAuley who, alone in a prison cell, read the Bible for the first time in his life and had a vision of God. He was released and began rebuilding his life. In 1871, he founded the first Christian rescue mission for drunks and others deemed beyond redemption. Through apostleship, missions spread across the United States and the world and countless of thousands of men were fed, given a place to sleep and taught the Bible. The Spirit does not come easily to those in utter despair, but it does, and to this day the chain of transformation and apostleship that began with a single man and a single Bible in a bleak prison cell is unbroken.

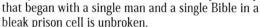

This book is about evangelism, but I write as a journalist. From 1953 to 1963, after ten years as a budding newspaper journalist and radio news writer in New York, I was a CBS foreign correspondent and free lance magazine writer in India and Southeast Asia, Africa and Latin America.

When I resettled in New York (with my wife and three children), I saw the city through the eyes of a newcomer, including homeless men made dysfunctional by drugs and alcohol. I asked myself a question that would be obvious to any foreign correspondent: not why were they there, but what was being done to help them. After research, I wrote *Jerry McAuley and His Mission*, published in 1967 by Loizeaux Brothers of Neptune, New Jersey. A revised edition was published in 1990.

By profession, I was a news writer and producer of television documentaries for CBS and later NBC. Among other programs, I was associate producer for "A Tour of the White House with Mrs John F. Kennedy." In 1985, I took early retirement from NBC and became a special correspondent for the New York Times in Afghanistan. I then wrote *Among the Afghans*, published by Duke University in 1987. After extended journeys to India, I wrote *Averting the Apocalypse: Social Movements in India Today*, published by Duke University in 1990. With further research, I was the lead writer of *Democracy in India: A Hollow Shell*, published by The American University Press in 1994.

All the while, curiosity led me to the origins of Chinese life in New York. I amassed eight, thick, single-spaced typed volumes containing more than three thousand newspaper articles and reports, which became *Alas! What Brought Thee Hither? The Chinese in New York 1800-1950*, published by Fairleigh Dickenson University in 1997.

On and off before I became a journalist, I lived for two years in many parts of Mexico. In the early 1990's, several books and many magazine articles were written about Protestantism in Latin America, but little about Mexico. I wondered what was happening in a country I had once thought of as a second home. When the Chinese book was in its final stages, I made a preliminary survey. I read in a Spanish journal that Protestants formed 40 percent of the population of Chiapas, but foreign interest fixated on the Zapatistas. There was talk of an "Indian" revolt but the indigenous people seemed more concerned with God than revolution. People were talking about the indigenous people but not to them. I decided to go to Chiapas to find out what they were doing and why.

Printed in the United States
214737BV00001B/25/A